ABOUT THE AUTHORS

LAURA SJOBERG is Assistant Professor at Virginia Tech in Blacksburg, Virginia. Her first book, *Gender, Justice and the Wars in Iraq*, was published in 2006. She has published articles on just war theory in the *International Journal of Feminist Politics*, *International Politics* and *International Studies Quarterly*. Her research focuses on gender, just war theory, international security and international ethics.

CARON E. GENTRY is Assistant Professor of Political Science at Abilene Christian University, Texas. Her previous work has been published in the journal *Terrorism and Political Violence*. Her research interests are gender, terrorism and political violence.

MOTHERS, MONSTERS, WHORES

WOMEN'S VIOLENCE IN GLOBAL POLITICS

LAURA SJOBERG & CARON E. GENTRY

ZED BOOKS
London & New York

Mothers, Monsters, Whores: Women's Violence in Global Politics was first published in 2007 by Zed Books Ltd, 7 Cynthia Street, London N1 9JF, UK and Room 400, 175 Fifth Avenue, New York, NY 10010, USA

www.zedbooks.co.uk

Copyright © Laura Sjoberg and Caron E. Gentry 2007

The rights of Laura Sjoberg and Caron E. Gentry to be identified as the authors of this work have been asserted by them in accordance with the Copyright, Designs and Patents Act, 1988

Designed and typeset in Monotype Garamond
by illuminati, Grosmont, www.illuminatibooks.co.uk
Cover designed by Andrew Corbett
Printed and bound by Edwards Brothers Inc., Ann Arber, MI USA

Distributed in the USA exclusively by Palgrave Macmillan, 175 Fifth Avenue, New York, 10010, USA

All rights reserved. No part of this publication may be reproduced, stored in a retrieval system or transmitted in any form or by any means, electronic, mechanical, photocopying or otherwise, without the prior permission of Zed Books Ltd.

A catalogue record for this book is available from the British Library
Library of Congress Cataloguing in Publication Data available

ISBN 978 1 84277 865 4 hb
ISBN 978 1 84277 866 1 pb

CONTENTS

	ACKNOWLEDGEMENTS	vii
ONE	INTRODUCTION: A WOMAN DID THAT?	1
TWO	NARRATIVES OF MOTHERS, MONSTERS AND WHORES	27
THREE	TRIPLE TRANSGRESSIONS AT ABU GHRAIB	58
FOUR	BLACK WIDOWS IN CHECHNYA	88
FIVE	DYING FOR SEX AND LOVE IN THE MIDDLE EAST	112
SIX	GENDERED PERPETRATORS OF GENOCIDE	141
SEVEN	GENDERING PEOPLE'S VIOLENCE	174
EIGHT	CONCLUSION: LET US NOW SEE 'BAD' WOMEN	199
	NOTES	226
	REFERENCES	243
	INDEX	271

ACKNOWLEDGEMENTS

Laura and Caron would like to thank readers of various versions of this project, including Christine Sylvester, Francine D'Amico, Sita Rancho-Nillson, Marilyn McMorrow, Fran Pilch, Cynthia Enloe, Susan Northcutt, Melissa Brown, Sandra McEvoy, Christopher Marcoux, David Winter, Jindy Pettman and Louise Knight.

We are also grateful for the comments of audiences at the 2006 and 2007 International Studies Association Conferences, at the 2006 ISA-West Conference, and at Duke University when we presented earlier versions of this material. We are also indebted to productive comments from our editor, Ellen McKinlay, and anonymous reviewers at Zed Books. Additionally, many thanks to Dr John Harrison and the Institute of Defence and Strategic Studies at Nanyang Technological University, Singapore, for providing us with valuable information.

We owe debt, individually and collectively, to the community that is the Feminist Theory and Gender Studies Section of the International Studies Association, not least for the 'title lottery' which finally seems to have netted one for this book.

Caron would like to thank Laura for this amazing working experience. What began as a small conversation in Waikiki has led to a very rewarding project. As a brilliant, gracious and incredibly kind person,

Laura expressed a belief in my work that came not a moment too soon. Thank you for working with me to give a voice to women who have been overlooked and marginalized.

Caron could not have completed this project without the support of the University of St Andrews, which provided her with monetary and research support. Additionally, Caron wishes to thank Abilene Christian University for nurturing a professionally supportive environment. The administration and faculty has proven itself to be dedicated to professional development through the provision of monetary support and personal encouragement.

Many people have helped Caron with her professional accomplishments. The incredible teachers in her life include, but are not limited to, Professors Khavita Khory, Joan Cox, Vincent Ferraro and Penny Gill at Mount Holyoke College, and Professors Paul Wilkinson, Nicolas Rengger, Rick Fawn and John Anderson at the University of St Andrews. Caron's life as a feminist in a cold town in Scotland would not have been possible without the support and encouragement of Cynthia Enloe, who graciously answered and began a correspondence with a stranger, and Christine Laennec, a fellow knitter and feminist conversation partner. ISA 2004 was an eventful experience that led to excellent conversations with Sandra McEvoy and Francine D'Amico.

I always promised that my first book would include mention of time spent studying and carousing in Broon's and North Point Café. I owe an immense debt to the people who supported and heard my criticisms of the representations of female terrorists (birds with bombs) as we spent hours in both places. Thank you for some amazing times Suchitra Dutta, Maria Siemer, Anders Strindberg, Anthony Richards, Ian Hall and John Harrison. The encouragement and friendship extended by Kristen and Trygve Johnson, Steven and Gina Prokopchuk (and children), Mary Abbott and Sybil Davis have made a significant impact on my life. My life in Abilene would be unimaginable without the music and friendship of JamisonPriest, the mentoring and friendship of Brenda Bender, and the friendships found on Sunday mornings. Last to be mentioned but by no means least are the lifelong friendships I found at Mount Holyoke. To those who have put up with my workaholic silences and my quirks for over ten years (Mar, Hummel, Silver, Em, Ericsking, Jeanne and Kelsey), thank you.

My students at Abilene Christian University have provided me with endless amazement as they have challenged me to think about my discipline in a different light. A few who must be thanked personally for their involvement as my research and teaching assistants: Erin Baldwin Day, Lizz Alvarez, Melissa Joy Landry, Melanie Booker Fry, Alaina Bearden and Matthew Greenberg.

Finally, none of this would have been possible without the love and support of my parents and family.

Laura wishes to thank, first and foremost, Caron Gentry, who introduced her to new ideas and new literatures as she struggled to make sense of her nascent fascination with violent women in feminism specifically and International Relations generally.

I am indebted to the institutional support of the Women and Public Policy Program and the Belfer Center for Science and International Affairs at the Kennedy School of Government, the Women's Studies Department at Merrimack College, the Political Science Department and the Kenan Institute for Ethics at Duke University, Boston College Law School, the University of North Carolina Law School, and, last but not least, the Political Science Department at Virginia Tech.

With mentors as wonderful as Ann Tickner and a rock-solid support system including the likes of Hayward Alker, Carol Cohn and Nick Onuf, it would be hard to do anything but succeed; I owe them my career. Conversations with many feminist colleagues have been essential to the ideas in this book, among them Cynthia Enloe, Susan Northcutt, Carol Cohn, Lauren Wilcox, Jenny Lobasz, Jen Heeg, Sandy Whitworth, Anne Runyan, Susan Wright, Suzanne Bergeron, Theresa Lund, Francine D'Amico, Rose Shinko, Sally Ruddick, Catharine MacKinnon, and others that I am certain to have missed out. Other colleagues have also contributed to the breadth and depth of this project through their editorial insights and substantive questions. Debt is owed to Amy Eckert, Mia Bloom and Charli Carpenter for conversations that made certain that I was questioning my assumptions and supporting my contentions.

I owe a personal debt to a number of the people (and chihuahuas) in my life who made this work possible. They include alternative sources of income and office space from Morgan Dodge (Durham, NC) and Rudman & Winchell (a law firm in Bangor, Maine). The Boston Debate League helps me remain committed to critical activism. April, my older chihuahua, reminds me that there's no writer's block a good puppy kiss cannot cure; Gizmo, my younger one, disciplines my work by whining every time I get up and take a break. Chris Marcoux, with whom I parent my puppies, is a source of smiles and laughs when the work gets hard.

Finally, though I did not intend to make a tradition of ending acknowledgements in my books with a negative inspiration, this one was, well, too precious to exclude. While it would be in poor taste to list the speaker by name, the gentleman who introduced me at a book signing in September 2006 said that 'gender is to war like horseradish is to dessert'. As a lifetime enemy of all things vegetable, I am inspired by that comment every day to work harder, faster and better. Mr Horseradish: you'll see.

TO OUR PARENTS

ONE

INTRODUCTION: A WOMAN DID THAT?

> A female suicide bomber dressed like a man detonated an explosive belt outside a U.S. military facility in the northern Iraqi city of Tall Afar on Wednesday, killing at least five civilians and injuring more than 30, the military said. The unidentified woman was the first known female suicide bomber in the insurgency that began after the U.S.-led invasion of Iraq in 2003. (Spinner 2005)

> Her face is familiar to millions of people around the world as one of two smiling American soldiers seen in a picture standing behind a group of naked, hooded Iraqis stacked in a pyramid. ... Harman is accused by the Army of taking photographs of that pyramid and ... of Iraqis who were told to strip and masturbate in front of other prisoners and guards. (CBS News 2004)

Women are capturing hostages, engaging in suicide bombings, hijacking airplanes, and abusing prisoners. Moreover, they are doing so on the front page of the *New York Times* (2004) and other major international newspaper. This image of women runs counter to inherited perceptions of women as maternal, emotional, and peace-loving (Kaufman-Osborn 2005: 597; Eisenstein 2004; Ehrenreich 2005). It has also been said that violent women disrupt feminist images of liberated women as capable and equal, but not prone to men's mistakes, excesses or violence (Ehrenreich 2005; Mason 2005; Cohler

2006). The salience of the women's identity as *women* is rising, as women's violence receives more attention, proportionally, then men's (Enloe 1990). Women's violence is often discussed in terms of violent women's gender: *women* are not supposed to be violent. This is one tenet on which various understandings of gender seem to converge. A conservative interpretation of gender sees women as peaceful and apolitical, a liberal view understands women as a pacifying influence on politics, and feminists who study global politics often critique the masculine violence of interstate relations.[1] Women's violence falls outside of these ideal-typical understandings of what it means to be a woman.[2] These women fall into the historical categorization of 'bad' women (Summers 1975).

This increasing attention to women's violence comes at a time when gender-sensitive policies are at an all-time high in global politics. The combination of the rising popularity of gender mainstreaming policies, the continued salience of the Beijing Platform for Action, and increased international attention to the gendered impacts of war, including wartime rape, make it appear as if gender subordination is on its way out in global politics. Many have declared the twenty-first century the Century of the Woman (Jacobs 2002; Constable 2006; Clinton 2000). The United Nations Security Council passed a resolution adopting gender mainstreaming as official policy, the 1995 Fourth World Conference on Women received unprecedented attention, and women's issues have increasing prominence on the agendas of international organizations. In addition to the gender mainstreaming policies of the United Nations (Hafner-Burton and Pollack 2002), the Security Council (True 2003), the European Union (Bretherton 2001), and many international organizations, including the International Labor Organization (Razavi and Miller 1995), the International Monetary Fund (Kabeer 2003), and the World Bank (Pyle and Ward 2003), have gender equality mandates built into their legal structures which have been enforced to varying degrees. In this gender-emancipatory international atmosphere, reactions to and stories around women's violence betray lingering stereotypes about what women are and what they should be. Scholars, activists and citizens alike have broadened their understandings of what a woman is. Now, in many places around the world, women work outside of the home, participate in governance, and are largely recognized as deserving social equality with men. Where women's roles have expanded, a broadened understanding of what it means to be a woman creates the appearance that gender subordination is being deconstructed. Richter-Montpetit asks for whom gender inequality is deconstructed, and at whose cost that deconstruction is achieved (2007: 51). This study of women's violence explores those questions by demonstrating that gender stereotypes and subordinations have changed shape and become less visible, but still very much exist.

Does women's violence expose feminism's weaknesses? Or does it provide another area for the application of feminism's strengths? We study women's violence in global politics with the aim of determining what their actions mean both for global political perceptions of women's characteristics and for feminist theories of women's roles in international relations. Feminists who study war (ourselves included) often talk about how 'masculine violence' in international politics devastates women's lives.[3] Political dialogue often expresses concern to protect 'womenandchildren' from wartime violence and women from wartime rape (Enloe 1990, 1993).[4] The disproportionate impact of war on civilian women has become an issue of great importance in global politics.[5] Certainly one can say accurately that these concerns cover many women's experience in international relations – from Africa to Alabama. Still, women all over the world are engaging in political violence – in increasing numbers, some argue (Bourke 1999; Moser and Clark 2001; Alison 2004).

What does it mean for the stereotype of 'peaceful woman' that a woman was on the front page of the *New York Times* sexually molesting an (apparently dead) Iraqi prisoner? What does it mean for women's maternity that a suicide bomber pretended to be pregnant to hide explosives? Though they are a minority, many women of diverse sociocultural backgrounds express their personal and political dissatisfaction by violent means (Alison 2007; Bloom 2007). A female terrorist or war criminal is incompatible with traditional explanations of all women as the 'peaceful people' whom 'war protects' and who 'should be protected from war' (Elshtain 1987; Young 2003; Goldstein 2001). Elshtain argues that women are characterized in narratives justifying the making and fighting of wars as 'Beautiful Souls', innocent of the war but the thing that warriors are responsible for defending (1987a, 1987b). Women, in these discourses, become at once the victims and the causes of the war (Elshtain 1992a). Elshtain borrows the concept of Beautiful Souls from Hegel (Elshtain 1987a; Hegel 1977). They are 'frugal, self-sacrificing, and, at times delicate' and work to 'preserve the purity of heart' by fleeing 'from contact with the actual world' when violence erupts (Elshtain 1992a; Peach 1994). A Beautiful Soul is fragile, removed from reality, and in need of protection in a way that the protector receives substantial honour for success (Sjoberg 2006; Elshtain 1992a, 1992b). The Beautiful Soul/woman is expected to be against war and violence, but to cooperate with wars fought to protect her innocence and virginity. In this way, states perpetuate a gendered 'protection racket' which marginalizes women while appearing to foreground their interests (Peterson 1977; Stiehm 1982; Blanchard 2003). The stereotype of women's victimization holds fast largely because it is not entirely untrue; the impacts of war are often gender-oppressive. Violent women may even be among the women who are oppressed by the war. Still, in the traditional sense, a female suicide bomber or war criminal is not a 'woman whose common experience gives concern for human security' (Tickner 1991) – even though many women use their common experiences to begin human security dialogues (Hoogenson and Rottem 2004; Hoogenson and Stuvoy 2006; Hudson 2005).

The 'answer' to this problem appears to be very simple. Women have been subordinated in global politics, which impacts their social and political options and frames of reference. Still women, like men, are capable of violence. As women's freedoms increase, so will their violence. Women, like men, commit violence for a variety of reasons, some rational and some irrational. Women, like men, sometimes see violence as the best means to their political ends. Women, like men, sometimes commit senseless and heinous acts out of depravation or some other socio-economic motivation.[6]

Yet this apparently simple solution to the problem of female violence has not been the prevailing reaction to either individual incidents or the general phenomenon of women's violence. Instead, women who commit violence have been characterized as anything but regular criminals or regular soldiers or regular terrorists;[7] they are captured in storeyed fantasies which deny women's agency and reify gender stereotypes and subordination.

IDEAL TYPES OF WOMEN IN GLOBAL POLITICS

In order to understand gendered stories about women who perpetrate violence, an understanding of gender and its meanings is important. Though the word 'gender' is commonly used, the underlying meaning is not easy to read or decode. Instead, gender is an intersubjective social construction that constantly evolves with changing societal perceptions and intentional manipulation. Feminist scholars contend that the social division between male and female is unnatural and reifies *gendered* power disparities (Peterson 1999: 38). In common parlance, the term 'sex' identifies biological differences between people understood as men and people understood as women (Youdell 2006; Haraway 1988). Usually, gender describes socially constituted difference between the same groups (Childs 2006).

While the distinction between biological sex and social difference seems clear enough, some scholars question the ease of making the distinction between biological sex and social gender (Butler 1990; Fausto-Sterling, 2005; 2000). Some feminists investigate whether social or biological differences came first (MacKinnon 2001), while others see the sexed body and social gender as constructions reliant on each other for existence (Butler 1990; Fausto-Sterling 2005). Ann Fausto-Sterling sees an overlap between the sexed body and social gender in many areas, including professional success and sexual promiscuity (2005: 1448). Still, Fausto-Sterling's analysis preserves the notion that sex is limited to male and female. A closer look reveals that even the biological dichotomy between male and female is the product of the social construction of simplicity where complexity exists (Sjoberg 2007; Youdell 2006; Hester 2004).

There are, in fact, biological sexes that cannot be understood as either male or female (Braendle and Felix 2006). There are persons who fall into the biological categories asexual, intersexual (formerly and now controversially known as hermaphroditic), and transsexual.[8] While these categories and their members will not be the main focus of this book, their existence and the neglect that they face in everyday sex and gender discourses demonstrates both the depth and the complexity of gender construction, which is a key point in this book (Butler 2004).

Sex/gender categories, whatever their genesis, are often divided into masculinities and femininities (Paecheter 2003). Masculinities and femininities are made up of behaviour expectations, stereotypes, and rules which apply to persons because they are understood to be members of particular sex categories (Enloe 2004). The exact content of genders changes with various and shifting socio-political contexts, but gender subordination (defined as the subordination of femininities to masculinities) remains a constant feature of social and political life across time and space (Rissman 2005; Hey 2006). Social classification and treatment based on perceived gender is called *gendering* (Hartmann 2006; Tickner 2001). In global politics, gendering is not always consistent in content or specific result, but always involves assumptions based not on an individual's characteristics but on assumed group characteristics (Skapoulli 2004).

The fact that gender is socially constructed should not be taken to mean that gender and gender subordination are somehow less real – that social construction, when discussing gender, is a synonym for fake or non-existent. Instead, social constructions such as gender *construct* social life (Prugl 1999). People live gender and genderings across time, space and culture (Stoller and Nielsen 2005; Dimen and Goldner 2002). Given the diversity of masculinities and femininities, men and women, it would be unrepresentative to characterize a *gendered experience* as if there was something that all people perceived to be men or all people perceived to be women shared – it is false to assume that gender commonality makes life experiences similar. Instead, each perceived member of a gender group differs, and these different people live gender differently. The genderings that they experience are diverse; as are the processes by which they operate (Hooper 2001). Perhaps the common thread between genderings in global politics, if there is one, is the near-universality of gender-subordinating discourses, like the narratives included in the pages of this book.

For the purpose of the analyses in this book, 'gender is a set of discourses which can set, change, enforce, and represent meaning on the basis of perceived membership in or relation to sex categories' (Sjoberg 2007; Connell 1995; Gibson-Graham 1994). Gender discourses, so defined, are everywhere in global politics: in interstate relations, international development and international security (Tickner 2001). This book argues that gender discourses dominate today's increasing recognition of and concern for women's violence.

In these gendered discourses, deviant women are set up in opposition to idealized gender stereotypes. They are characterized as the exception to clearly understood gender norms. Established gender norms portray women as naturally nurturing, emotionally sensitive and domesticated. These qualities associated with women and femininity have been traditionally characterized as inferior to those associated with men and masculinity (Stone 1996; Demichele 2004; Banerjee 2005). These gender norms have been sustained throughout the ages and across cultures to stabilize social relationships and uphold traditional values. This book argues that the treatment of women's violence in global politics demonstrates that traditional gender norms remain intact and thriving. Gender norms serve as an evaluative framework for people trying to make sense of the world. People weigh individuals' actions through expectations of gendered behaviour, consciously or unconsciously (Butler 2004; Childs and Krook 2006).

In today's world, once a person acts outside of the ideal-typical gender role assigned to them, that person is open to criticism not only for their behaviour but for the gender transgression involved in its perpetration (Sirin et al. 2004). Men who are not perceived as masculine enough suffer merciless teasing, and are sometimes the victims of open hostility and violence (McCreary 1994).[9] Women in military and paramilitary forces face the threat of criticism for their behaviour outside of their gender roles. In military organizations, women often have two choices: to sleep with men and be identified as sluts, or to refuse and be labelled as lesbians. As one 'administratively dismissed' accused-lesbian WRAC said in an interview with Enloe: 'Men soldiers don't respect WRACs [Women's Royal Army Corps (UK)] at all. If you're in it, you're a lesbian or a slut. And there's a real pressure to sleep with men' (Enloe 1983: 141–2). Women are also criticized for falling outside of gender ideal types in paramilitary organizations. For example, when women in Northern Ireland 'abandon' their 'primary role as mother' by becoming involved in paramilitary operations, they 'forfeit' a sense of 'innocence or purity' (Dowler 1998: 164). These women are 'often seen as tainted' because they have 'plunged into the unnatural' (Dowler 1998: 166–7).

Gender stereotypes exist and persist in a world where women are often invisible and frequently ignored, both in international relations specifically and in global politics more generally. If 'international relations' is the study of political relations between the governments of nation-states, women are often left out of state leadership positions and important roles in interstate negotiations. On the other hand, 'global politics' refers 'not simply to the actions of states or between states but to how these actions are embedded in a global context marked by international but also sub-, trans-, and supranational process' but 'does include more than interstate actions' (Peterson and Runyan 1999: 5). If, 'as current events suggest, it is not only state power but also transnational political, military, economic and social processes that are the "what" of today's "real world",' women's roles in these processes are often downplayed, ignored, or understudied (Peterson and Runyan 1999: 5).

While women remain seriously under-represented in positions of power all over the world, a sense that exclusion based on gender is coming to an end permeates the discourse of many governments and the feminist advocates that push them to be more inclusive. Across states and cultures, women are visible in many new places filling roles traditionally reserved for men. Though women remain a stark minority in positions of political leadership across the world and gender integration is geographically and culturally uneven, women's representation in parliaments has increased fourfold in the last fifty years (onlinewomeninpolitics.org 2007). Women are occupying with increasing frequency positions as soldiers, political leaders and military strategists (Tickner 2001). At the same time that women become visible in politics, they are also included in the ranks of war criminals, terrorists, suicide bombers and perpetrators of genocide. Seeing women in roles, both good and bad, traditionally reserved for men often creates the perception that women are achieving equality in global politics when, in actuality, public discourses communicate another message when we read between the lines.

An example is the celebration that accompanied the 'watershed moment for gender equality when the United States deployed female soldiers to a war zone for the first time in the 1991 Gulf War' (Curphy 2003). While many feminists celebrated, Cynthia Enloe noted that the media coverage that the women soldiers received, which was disproportionate to their representation as soldiers, might not be all good news for those interested in gender equality (Enloe 1993). Instead of a victory for gender equality, Enloe argued that the disproportionate coverage of women soldiers *as women* showed the rising salience of traditional gender expectations (Enloe 1993: 202–3). These stories, then, were not of gender equality but of ideal-typical militarized femininities, which captured women's roles as soldiers within the traditional boundaries of femininity. As the salience of women's rights increases, so does the salience of women's gender (Enloe 2000). Women soldiers were 'not *soldiers* but *women soldiers*; their gender marked their identity in militaries' (Sjoberg 2007: 83). Likewise, women who commit acts of violence in defiance of national or international law are not seen as criminals, warriors or terrorists, but as *women criminals, women warriors*, or *women terrorists*. The operative element of this characterization is that these narratives include a group that is 'suicide bombers' or 'war criminals' or 'perpetrators of genocide' *and* a separate group that is women who would otherwise be members of those groups but for their femininity. Because women who commit these violences have acted outside of a prescribed gender role, they have to be separated from the main/malestream discourse of their particular behaviour. These additional categories do not exist in behavioural choices where women's participation is expected or accepted (women mothers, women ballerinas, women housekeepers, or women flight attendants). The politics of gender, especially gender in military situations, have garnered increasing attention in domestic, regional and international politics over the last two decades; womanhood is more recognized rather than more integrated in these situations.

Even though women's integration into global politics where previously only men were allowed is a victory for those who oppose gender subordination, it should be treated cautiously and is by no means the last step. Women's integration is a highly controlled process that places women in positions of power and gives them opportunities to engage in violence. Though women are technically included, the inclusion process has paid little attention to the discursive and performative elements of gender subordination (Butler 1993, 2004; Hey 2006). As a result, the discursive structures of gender subordination are preserved even in an increasingly gender-integrated international political arena (McNay 2004).

Gender equality is more than women having the same jobs as men or even doing the same things for the same money and recognition. Women who have 'men's jobs' do not enter them on a gender-equal or gender-neutral playing field. A woman in a man's job is a 'woman who can make it as a man' not because the masculine values required to do that job have been questioned or changed, but because she adopts those values, qualifying as masculine despite her womanhood (Sjoberg 2007: 93). In this context, masculinity is a complex construct, not strictly descriptive of men individually or collectively but based on a set of accepted values associated with masculinity and therefore merit (Connell 1995, 1990). Women have been 'added' as capable members of institutions, but the institutions have not changed.

In fact, even when women are allowed into men's roles, more is required of them than is required of the men that usually fulfil those roles. (Sjoberg 2007; D'Amico and Beckman 1995). While it is assumed that men are qualified and legitimate political actors until their masculinity is questioned (United States citizens, for example, would never ask whether or not a man was capable of being president) women are assumed to be excludable until they prove that they belong in the masculine public sphere (Elshtain 1981). D'Amico and Beckman contend that women can only succeed in politics through hypermasculinity, by *emphasizing* masculine traits more vigorously than their male colleagues, since they are assumed unqualified until they can battle their way in (1995: 8). In this way, discourses that expect women to serve in particular roles exclude both women's agency and feminine values from the political arena (Sjoberg 2006). Similarly, discourses of gender subordination related to women's violence in global politics exclude women's agency in that violence. Women who participate in violence that is not endorsed by state governments are not described as women with particular characteristics, but as less than women and as less than human. Women's violence must be specially accounted for, and is often explained as a flaw in women's femininity and a flaw in their humanity.

THE STUDY OF WOMEN'S PROSCRIBED VIOLENCE IN GLOBAL POLITICS

Through several empirical studies of women's violence in global politics, this book interrogates both global political understandings of gender and conventional feminist analyses of those understandings. It focuses on women's *proscribed* violence. Proscribed violence is that violence which is denounced, condemned or prohibited by the laws of states or the laws between states. We recognize that the proscription of violence does not make it necessarily morally unacceptable (sometimes the laws of states or between states prohibit the just actions of revolutionaries and freedom fighters), but contend that proscription affects the discourses used both by political officials and by media outlets about women's violence. Likewise, while there is a substantial amount of women's violence covered by and endorsed by state justifications (for example, women who fight wars as a part of state militaries) *and* that violence is certainly the subject of gender-subordinating discourses, those discourses differ substantially from the ones examined in this book about women who commit violence in defiance of their governments and international law.

We approach the issue of the narratives of women's proscribed violence in global politics through an explicitly feminist outlook, using gendered lenses. Jill Steans explains gendered lenses as a method for the study of international politics, instructing:

> To look at the world through gender lenses is to focus on gender as a particular kind of power relation, or to trace out the ways in which gender is central to understanding international processes. Gender lenses also focus on the everyday experiences of women as *women* and highlight the consequences of their unequal social position. (Steans 1998: 5)

Spike Peterson and Anne Sisson Runyan describe lenses as 'filters' which organize, prioritize and categorize knowledge (1999: 1). These filters, consciously or unconsciously, 'foreground some things, and background others' in all research and knowledge formulation (Peterson and Runyan 1999: 21). This book is written through the lenses of international relations (IR) feminism, which takes the observation of gender subordination as a starting point for analysis. Feminists in international relations have 'challenged the discipline to think about how its theories might be reformulated and how its understandings of global politics might be improved if gender were a category of analysis' (Tickner and Sjoberg 2006: 186). As a part of this mission, feminists have 'critically re-examined key concepts in the field' in order to 'draw attention to women's invisibility and gender subordination in the theory and practice of global politics' (186).

This project challenges inherited notions of femininity and popular characterizations of women's violence, arguing that using gender as a category of analysis would improve these understandings. It critically re-examines narratives of women's violence which deny violent women both agency and womanhood. It tries to draw attention to the invisibility and subordination of women's violence. As feminism tries to *find* women and amplify their overlooked and silenced voices, this project tries to find the voices of violent women and understand what they mean for the theory and practice of feminism and of global politics more generally. This book focuses on women's violence outside of the legitimation of state sponsorship. The violence in this book is for whatever reason a departure from what is considered justified violence in global politics, outside the justificatory narrative of the state system.[10] The book explores the stories about and experiences of women war criminals, women suicide bombers, women terrorists, and women perpetrators of genocide, asking where and what women are, and how they are portrayed. Our concern is not only to include women, or to identify the masculinities which perpetuate women's exclusion, but also to demonstrate that gender fuels global politics, and global politics is one of the many sites that reproduce gender.

Women engaged in proscribed violence are often portrayed either as 'mothers', women who are fulfilling their biological destinies; as 'monsters', women who are pathologically damaged and are therefore drawn to violence (Gentry 2006); or as 'whores', women whose violence is inspired by sexual dependence and depravity. Each narrative carries with it the weight of gendered assumptions about what is appropriate female behaviour. The mother narratives describe women's violence as a need to belong, a need to nurture, and a way of taking care of and being loyal to men; motherhood gone awry. The monster narratives eliminate rational behaviour, ideological motivation, and culpability from women engaged in political violence. Instead, they describe violent women as insane, in denial of their femininity, no longer women or human. The whore narratives blame women's violence on the evils of female sexuality at its most intense or its most vulnerable. The whore narratives focused on women's erotomania describe violent women's sexuality as both extreme and brutal; while the whore narratives that focus on women's erotic dysfunction emphasize either desperation wrought from the inability to please men or women as men's sexual pawns and possessions.

The narratives of monster, mother and whore have fully othered violent women. Their behaviour, their wilful participation in political violence, has transgressed the norms of typical female behaviour. By biologically determining what acceptable female behaviour is, neither storyteller nor story consumer must hold women accountable for their actions or understand the complex schemas of relational autonomy constructing and reifying gender roles. These narratives instead portray violent women as a product of faulty biology or faulty construction. Violent women are not women at all, but singular mistakes and freak accidents. If violent women are a product of faulty biology, our image of real women as peaceful remains intact, and violent women cannot be held accountable for their actions. If the women who commit violent crimes and political violence (those who frequent the pages of this book) can be discredited *as women* and seen as 'bad women' or 'femininity taken to an irrational extreme', then they can exist in a world that holds intact the stereotype of women's fragility and purity. Even in narratives which seek to make violent women singular and uphold the image of *the rest of women*, though, it is possible to blame femininity for women's transgressions. While the mother, monster and whore narratives other and isolate violent women, they do so on gendered terms, which characterize the women perpetrators as not only aberrant, but aberrant because of their flawed femininity. Very few researchers actually depict violent women as rational actors, even though scholars often characterize violent men as rationally or logically motivated.[11] This book confronts this problem head-on by pointing out stereotyped, stylized narratives about violent women's actions and providing alternatives which at once recognize the gendered nature of violence and women's agency in committing it.

WHERE ARE THE WOMEN?

Feminist scholars focus on finding women in global politics and interrogating gender subordination. Given this, one would expect feminist scholarship about violent women to find violent women's voices and explain both their complexities and their rationale. While this complexity is not universally absent from feminist scholarship, it is absent frequently enough to demonstrate cause for concern. While there has been a recent proliferation of scholarship interested in violent women,[12] even scholarship from a feminist perspective often fails to interrogate narratives about violent women as mothers, monsters and whores. Some feminist work entrenches these narratives, directly or indirectly (Bloom 2007, 2005; Victor 2003; Morgan 1989). In reading the current canon on violent women, one discovers that biological determinism still exists and actually has expanded. Most of the work on violent women attributes their motivation to a problem with a woman's biological make-up and rarely deals with a woman's intellectual capability to make deliberate choices, or the socio-political context in which those decisions are made. Even when women's agency is recognized as possible, often the bulk of the analysis is focused on women's participation as a personal, rather than political, choice (Bloom 2007). This ability to make deliberate choices is a question of agency and autonomy; the ability to make deliberate political choices is a question of which 'sphere' (public or private) women's lives are lived within. Violent women, whether terrorists, suicide bombers, war criminals or perpetrators of genocide, interrupt gender stereotypes about women, their role in war, and their role in society more generally: women who commit proscribed violence are not the peaceful, war-resistant, conservative, virtuous and restrained women that just warriors protect from enemies (Elshtain 1987; Ruddick 1983; De Groot 2001). Instead, these women are a security threat themselves.

The field of law has been addressing the problem of women's violence systematically for more than a decade, addressing women's participation in violent crime at the intrastate level. Scholars working in a field called feminist criminology have analysed the role of gender in women's crimes, the stories told about them in the courtroom and the court of public opinion, and the judges and juries which convict and sentence them. Laureen Snider describes contradictions in public presentations of the relationship between gender, agency and women's violence. Because of the salience of idealized notions of gender and women's identity, assigning agency in a crime situation to a woman corrupts a widely held image of women as both generally and specifically innocent (Snider 2003: 351). Feminist criminology was developed to critique the lack of space for violent women in criminology's gendered constructions of violent offenders. Feminist criminologists recognize that, even where laws assign women culpability for violent crimes, sex-role stereotyping is prevalent both in perceptions of agency and in the punishment structure for crimes committed by women (Keitner 2002; Lloyd 1995). These stereotypes reveal the continued salience of traditional gender norms and remind both the female criminals and the consumers of their tales that a woman who commits proscribed violence, in her home or in global politics, has committed 'a double transgression: the crime for which she is being tried and her disregard of a gender stereotype which denies her mental capacity to commit such a crime' (Keitner 2002: 40; Sjoberg 2007).

In other words, a woman willingly engaged in a violent crime ignores the expectation that women should be pure, innocent and non-violent (Keitner 2002: 69). Given the entrenched nature of the expectation that women are non-violent, when women commit violent crimes most accounts of these crimes fail to expose the falseness of the underlying gender ideal-types. Instead, they look elsewhere to explain women's violence. Many stories emphasize the singularity and corruption of violent women, who are set up as a foil to normal women, who remain pure and in conformity with gender norms (Sjoberg 2007; Shapiro 2002). According to feminist criminologists, 'since Lizzie Borden, public accounts of women's violence at once deny women's capacity to commit crimes and demonize them for having done so' (Sjoberg 2007: 96; Keitner 2002: 54).[13] This framework for analysing women's violence is internally contradictory, gender-subordinating, and inadequate for attempts to understand women's violence or individual violence in global politics more generally.

Instead, the gendered lenses of feminist research suggest a relational autonomy approach that reformulates the concepts of choice and obligation (Sjoberg 2006). In this project, gendered lenses consciously foreground gender, because 'the questions we can ask about the world are enabled, and other questions disabled, by the frame that orders the questioning' (Ferguson 1993: 7). Gender lenses show gender bias in theories of individual choice and individual violence. Most theories of individual obligation assume that behaviour limitations have been agreed on, either explicitly or implicitly, by words or social contract (Hirschmann 2004, 1989). The story of fully independent choice is oversimplified as it applies both in macro- and in micro-politics. Many behavioural constraints (such as obligations, laws and proscriptions) are not selected, either in negotiation or in social contracts. Seeing gender bias in global politics points out 'the bias of the very structure of obligation (its being defined solely in voluntaristic terms, and the fact that *nonvoluntary obligation* is an oxymoron) toward a masculinist perspective which automatically excludes women from obligation on an epistemological level' (Hirschmann 1989: 1229).

This book is not arguing that women who commit proscribed violence *by choice* are fully responsible for their behaviour in each instance, or that men are, or even that each choice to engage in violence is made with equal knowledge or freedom of action. Instead it argues that gender lenses help to point out the gendered inadequacy *both* of current conceptions of women's violence in global politics *and* of individual violence in global politics more generally.

Instead of delineating agent and structure and fully assigning 'the blame' to one or another, this book looks at the complex construction of choice, both at the time of the violence and in public narratives about women's violence after the fact. A feminist understanding of the function of consent 'interrogates the assumption that all responsibilities are assumed freely' (Hirschmann 1989: 1241). Instead, a feminist conception of responsibility acknowledges that a part of behaviour is response, often complex or involuntary, and frequently not chosen. According to Hirschmann, 'choices and the selves that made them are constructed by context, discourse, and language; such contexts make meaning, self-hood, and choices possible' (2004: xi). In such a framework, 'a fully consistent consent theory would have to include (perhaps paradoxically) the recognition that not all obligations are self-assumed' (Hirschmann 1989: 1239).

This relational autonomy framework does not deny the fact that people make choices. Instead, it sees that every choice is not completely free in a world of intersubjective construction and power disparity (McKenzie and Stolgar 2000). As opposed to the gendered frameworks of many of the narratives presented in this book, which describe men as choosers and women as without the agency to choose, relational autonomy takes the interdependence of all choice as a starting point. While women's violence takes place in a global political context dominated by masculinities with gendered expectations and gendered emotional and social pressures, the tendency to deny women any agency in their decisions to commit violence is one that is also fraught with gender subordination. This tendency to deny women's agency stems from discomfort with the idea that women can chose to commit (sometimes heinous) violence. Discomfort with women's violence reflects the continued salience of the stereotype of women as innocent and incapable of violence. The women studied in this book are not only capable of violence, but decided to engage in acts of violence that would 'normally' (i.e., if committed by a man) be characterized as rape, murder, terrorism and genocide. While their choices are not independent of the gendered social and political contexts of their local and global worlds, women's actions also cannot be seen as entirely outside of the realm of their choice and their agency (Keitner 2002; Sjoberg 2007).

A feminist relational autonomy framework can accommodate this complexity. The current political culture of storytelling about women's violence excludes the possibility that a violent woman rationally chose her violent actions. By contrast, a relational autonomy framework takes gender considerations into account (by acknowledging contingency and interdependence) without entrenching gender subordination (by failing to recognize women's agency) (Snider 2003: 357). The traditional female offender is pictured as either innocent or irrational because of her gender, much like the traditional image of a woman portrays her as unable to think, reason, or work like a man (Snider 2003: 356). Feminist criminology has 'contributed to the constitution of a self-aware, robust female offender, equipped with languages and concepts of resistance, on an individual if not collective level' (Snider 2003: 356). A relational autonomy framework can apply these insights to women's proscribed violence in global politics. After the application of such a framework, the female offender is no longer necessarily innocent or biologically flawed, but a complicated construct (Snider 2003: 356).

WHERE ARE THE FEMINISTS?

If feminist theory often asks where the women are, it seems only appropriate to ask where feminist theory is in finding and understanding women's proscribed violence in global politics. Linda Kelly argues that 'female violence presents … a threat to feminist theory' (Kelly 2003: 756). She contends that feminist theory provides a means and method for discrediting female violence and denying female agency (Kelly 2003: 819). Critics contend that feminists have thus far only been willing to accept very specific and simplified characterizations of women and the forces that drive them to kill (Morrissey 2003). Referring to common defences in women's trials for violent crimes, Morrissey explains that 'the legal strategies and media portrayals involved in these cases deny women's agency rationality by depicting their actions as determined by their victimization' (Morrissey 2003: 23). In feminism, Morrissey argues that violent women are either portrayed as irrational or pathological, much like the portrayals of mainstream media accounts (102). She claims that women who do not fit the feminist constructions of the violent female subjects are ignored in feminist scholarship (156). Morrissey's point is that, while feminism claims to advocate for women's *equality*, feminists really harbour a belief in women's superiority by denying the shortcomings in women's socio-political behaviour.

While there is some truth to this claim, we do not mean to overemphasize it. It is not feminists specifically who came up with or operationalized the idea of women as above men's sins – this is part of the (subordinated) image of women which has been salient throughout modern history. It is not that women in gender ideal-types have *no* advantages over men; it is that men's advantages are valued more in the political sphere. It is completely consistent, then, to call a belief that women are better than men when it comes to controlling violent behaviour an inherited image of a misogynistic culture which 'prizes' women for their virtues while subordinating them for the femininity of those perceived virtues. This inherited image has not entirely disappeared from societal discourse generally, or feminist discourse specifically.

While both Kelly and Morrissey make valid points about previous feminist work on women's violence, we argue that a feminist analysis of women's violence is both natural and essential. It has been alleged that feminists benefit by maintaining that violence is a result of patriarchal society (Gentry 2006: 8; Ehrenreich 2004). This removes women who participate in violence from responsibility, and maintains an image of women as 'above' masculine violence.[14] War, acts of terrorism, and violence may be related to patriarchy, but all people, women included, have choices about their participation. The degree of this choice is an interesting question, which will be explored later in the book, but the existence of a choice should be universally recognized. A woman's involvement in political or criminal violence is not necessarily *men's fault*; nor does it make her less of a human being or less of a woman.

Many have been quick to declare the death of feminism for one reason or another. Charli Carpenter encourages us to study gender without feminism (i.e. without an interest in gender emancipation?) (2002), while others argue that feminism is too narrow, too broad, too focused or too disorganized. Morrissey argues that feminism does the very thing that it critiques: represents women inaccurately. This may be true of some feminist work on violent women, but is not *necessarily* true. International relations feminists have, at various points, resurrected the image of violent women to analyse the (positive and negative) gender implications of their stories and obtain a more holistic understanding of women's roles as victims and agents in global politics (e.g. Moser and Clark 2001). Still, *feminist* cross-cultural study of the narratives women's violence in global politics remains a relatively new area for international relations scholars. Violent women's increasing visibility in war (as soldiers, as sex abusers, and as suicide bombers) demands that they receive attention. Many feminists' first reaction to stories about violent women have been about gender: *a woman did that?* Still, claims that violent women confound or are antithetical to feminist scholarship are overstated.

The military, media and public reactions to violent women in international relations, in fact, demonstrate the need for feminist scholarship rather than making it obsolete. In global politics, it often appears as if problems of gender subordination are being solved. Many have used the recent proliferation of women's violence to argue that if women can commit violent crimes, there is nothing left that women are incapable of (Ehrenreich 2004). The appearance that women's violence is a sign of increasing equality is supported by important actual changes in women's lives like improved literacy rates, access to job markets, income equality and health care. We are not arguing that these are not real improvements in women's lives, only that they are used as proxy for the end of gender subordination when they really serve the accidental and indirect purpose of perpetuating it.

From the beginning of feminist thought, concern for gender subordination has always been (at least in part) about agency. Women's suffrage in the United States was dependent upon people's belief about women's ability to vote intelligently. Opponents of women's vote in the United States claimed that women were not biologically able to think critically enough to worry about politics. The analogy is imperfect, granted, because voting is desirable for women to do, while violent crime is something undesirable. But the moral of the story is similar: society still denies women's agency. The spectrum of women's capacity has expanded, but a spectrum still exists, and it is narrower than the spectrum we use to visualize men's capacities. Public stories about women's violence betray a collective incapacity to deal with these women's *choice* to commit heinous violence. This collective incapacity reflects and demonstrates the fact that gender subordination has changed in form, but not in substance or pervasiveness.

Feminism at its best is not about claiming that women's judgement is better than men's. It is not about claiming that the world would be different if women ran it. It is instead about analysing the manifestations of gender in global politics. Feminists do not claim that all women are innocent, or that women's violence should be blamed on men's oppression. Instead, feminist scholarship uses gender as a category of analysis to complicate ideas of agency, interdependence and criminality. Violent women have agency in their violence. They also make their decisions in a world of relational autonomy where no choice is completely independent. This is not unique to violent women, however; feminists in international relations and elsewhere show that violent men live in a world of relational autonomy as well.

We intend to demonstrate that the lesson to be taken for feminist international relations is twofold: first, international attitudes about women still tend to stereotype them as incapable of entering certain arenas of social and political life (here, violence); second, violent women's motives and means in global politics provide a fruitful area for further study. A feminist criminologist argues that battered women's violence towards their husbands is often a statement against the specific oppressor (the husband) as well as against the general oppressor (men) (Morrissey 2003). Studying women's violent (and non-violent) reactions to oppressive international situations should tell us something about the sociology of women's relationships with the global political order. Studying women's violence in the absence of any obvious oppression should lead us to a more progressive understanding of women as subjects and femininity as a construct. Like all violence, women's violence is an unfortunate presence in global politics. The recent visibility of violent women, however, provides a feminist international relations a pathway to demonstrate women's continued subordination in global politics and to study it from a unique perspective.

Even though men and women have both biological and socially constructed differences, we argue that the theories of political and extrajudicial violence that apply to men can both apply to women and be made gender-sensitive. Interrogating the narratives of violent women as mothers, monsters and whores occurs in three phases. First, it requires critiquing the content of the narratives. Second, it requires asking why narratives with inaccurate content remain dominant. Who benefits from the false and fantastic portrayal of violent women? In criminal law, this question is called *cui bono?* (who stands to gain?), a Latin adage that means the person or people guilty of committing a crime may be found among those who have something to gain from its commission. Certainly, as our research shows, the women themselves are not the beneficiaries of these narratives. We argue that the tellers and consumers of these gendered narratives are, consciously or unconsciously, invested in a certain image of what women are. Third, it requires reformulative narratives of women's violence specifically and individual violence generally to achieve gender sensitivity and refrain from perpetuating gender subordination.

A STUDY OF WOMEN'S PROSCRIBED VIOLENCE IN GLOBAL POLITICS

The following chapters provide a theoretical and empirical basis for the argument that there is ongoing bias in gender discourses in global politics which resist recognizing women's agency, and for the construction of a more complex approach to women's violence. This book attempts to recognize women's capacity to engage in violence, to point out places where other analyses refuse to recognize this capacity, and to explore the implications of gendered narratives about women's violence for the study of gender, violence and global politics. The narratives of mother, monster and whore reveal the gendering of current understandings of women's violence in global politics across space and culture. A relational autonomy framework provides a more nuanced understanding of women's participation in proscribed violence, with a gender-cognizant discourse of motivation and action.

In Chapter 2, we introduce the mother, monster and whore narratives which marginalize violent women and deny their agency in global political discourses. We explain that the employment of these narratives is discursively and materially significant in the perpetuation of gender subordination in global politics. These narratives not only subordinate violent women, we demonstrate, but betray the continued salience of gender norms in global politics which subordinate women and femininities generally. The chapter concludes by articulating a framework for understanding these narratives as systems of signification both within and across the cases studies contained in the following empirical chapters.

The next four chapters contain the book's four empirical case studies. The book looks at United States military women's violence at Abu Ghraib, at women's involvement in suicide bombings in Iraq and Palestine, at women's roles in the Chechen 'black widow' attacks, and then at women who participated in or led campaigns of genocide. These cases were chosen because they show the mother, monster and whore narratives crossing religious, ethnic, cultural and national boundaries as a part of a global trend of denying women's agency in violence. From Pennsylvania Avenue to Palestine and the Smoky Mountains to Serbia, the form of the mother, monster and whore narratives shifts, but their basic content is recognizable: real women, white or black; African, European, Asian or American; Christian or Muslim, do not commit heinous violence against the wishes of their men or their states.

Chapter 3 contains the first of these four empirical case studies. Entitled 'Triple Transgressions at Abu Ghraib', this chapter opens with an introduction to women's proscribed violence within military structures. It shows the continuity of the mother, monster and whore narratives of women's war crimes within military structures, using examples from stories of women who were members of the Nazi German SA and SS. It moves on to discuss the United States military's characterization of women soldiers' deviant violence in other cases. The next section recounts the stories of (and the stories told of) soldiers Lynndie England, Sabrina Harman and Megan Ambuhl, who were implicated in the prisoner abuse at Abu Ghraib, as well as the narratives surrounding the role of Janis Karpinski, their commanding general. Then the chapter details the elements of the mother, monster and whore narratives in the characterizations of the women involved with the abuse at Abu Ghraib. It concludes by framing these narratives in terms of Americans' idealized militarized femininity. It explains that American women soldiers involved in war crimes have committed a triple transgression: against the laws of war, against their femininity, and against the military's prescribed roles for *military* women.

Chapter 4, entitled 'Black Widows in Chechnya', continues the book's case studies with a look at the narratives surrounding Chechen *shakhidki*, or female holy warriors, dubbed by the Russian government and international media 'black widows'. After giving a brief introduction to the wars in Chechnya between 1994 and 1996 and 1999 to the present, this chapter describes the conflict's gendered dimensions and gendered actors. A second section situates these gendered actors and their conflict in the history of the rhetorical construction of the Russian–Chechen conflict. Next, we introduce Russian government, as well as national and international media, accounts of the Chechen *shakhidki*. This introduction details the narratives which present these women as monstrous and vengeful but helpless and controlled, all the while using a comparison with Palestinians to further distance them from their actual political purposes. This analysis locates the mother, monster and whore narratives in these accounts. The chapter concludes by demonstrating how the labels assigned to Chechen women insurgents serve many masters: denying women agency in their choices but blaming femininity for their actions and the war more generally, justifying the conflict generally and attacks on women specifically, and revitalizing Russian militarized masculinities.

Chapter 5, entitled 'Dying for Sex and Love in the Middle East', explores the topic of suicide bombing in more depth as it examines the cases of female suicide bombers in Palestine and Iraq. The chapter begins by situating this book's analysis within the academic literature on suicide bombing, which treats women's participation in the Palestinian liberation movement and al-Qaeda substantially different than men's. It relates the stories of female suicide bombers as told in the media and in governmental reactions to their attacks. We then point out the presence of the mother, monster and whore narratives in the stylized stories of female suicide bombers. Specifically, we relate the mother narrative as a linchpin for understanding Middle Eastern women who participate in or initiate suicide attacks. The chapter concludes with a gender analysis of the stories around women's suicide bombing, contending that gendered stories of the conflicts in the Middle East spill over into gendered stories about the women who participate in them.

The final case study in the book, Chapter 6, entitled 'Gendered Perpetrators of Genocide', analyses women's perpetration of genocide and the gendered narratives which surround that participation. It opens with a brief introduction to the concept of genocide and the ways in which that concept and its perpetration have been gendered in global politics. A second section introduces narratives told of women participants in genocide and genocidal rape, generally and specifically, in the media and academia. It relates those narratives to gendered tropes about genocide perpetrators and their victims. The chapter continues by examining the first of two case studies of particular women accused of taking leading roles in perpetrating genocide: Biljana Plavsic (in the ethnic cleansing of Bosnian Muslims and Croats in the 1990s). This case study includes background information about the Bosnian break from Yugoslavia, the corresponding Serbian break from Bosnia, and the war which resulted. It then relates the narratives surrounding Plavsic, who served as the president and vice-president of the Bosnian Serb republic during the ethnic cleansing. After generally relating the gendered stories about Plavsic, we identify the mother, monster and whore narratives in the characterization of her actions. The second study on an individual provides similar information concerning the case of Pauline Nyiramasuhuko in the Rwandan genocide in the summer of 1994. Nyiramasuhuko, a minister in the Rwandan government at the time, stands trial for both genocide and genocidal rape. The chapter concludes by discussing the lessons to be learned for the analysis of women's participation in genocide specifically and analysis of genocide more generally.

Chapter 7, entitled 'Gendering People's Violence', brings together the theoretical framework for synthesizing experiences of women's violence and the narratives told about them. It evaluates purportedly gender-neutral theories of individual violence in global politics, exposing both the tendency only to apply those theories to men and the masculinized assumptions about individuals and about the global political arena they contain. We argue that men's political violence has been accepted and normalized: global political actors try to curtail or minimize it, but are not shocked by its existence or befuddled by its implications. We contend that we will not understand women's violence until we understand it *as violence*, and that this observation helps us see genderings not only in understandings of women's violence, but of individual violence in global politics more generally. As a way forward, this chapter proposes the adoption of a relational autonomy framework for understanding individuals and their violent choices in global politics. A relational autonomy framework recognizes gendered subjects who engage in political violence as actors with agency in a relationally autonomous world; parts of a gendered social system but able to make choices in it. This framework begins the process of degendering women's violence in global politics, as well as the global political arena more generally.

Chapter 8, entitled 'Let Us Now See "Bad" Women', offers some insights for international relations theory, by way of concluding the book. It observes that, even as theories of international relations have begun to recognize and incorporate 'the individual' as an actor in global politics, that individual actor has almost always been gendered male, reactively autonomous, and occupying a traditionally understood place of power. Expanding on Cynthia Enloe's understanding that the personal is international, this chapter examines how international relations constitutes violent women's lives, and violent women's lives constitute international relations. It discusses the ways in which the women in each of our four empirical chapters *are* international relations, and presents some insights about how international relations theory could change as a result of the serious study of the women in this book and the stories told about them. The chapter concludes by suggesting the contributions of this work on women's violence for the field of feminist international relations, and for the study of global politics more generally. It makes three main theoretical contributions. First, it demonstrates that the radical denial of women's agency in public discourses about women's violence betrays latent gender subordination in our understandings of human identity. Second, it shows that these stereotypes also betray the gendered understandings that we hold of both violence and non-violence; those gendered understandings reverberate in the practice of global politics. Finally, it reveals that these observations about gender and violence suggest the evolution of a new, under-the-radar sort of gender subordination evolving in global politics: one that *tells stories about* gender liberation while maintaining the discursive and material structures of gender subordination. Women's violence, intentionally or not, disrupts that quiet but disturbing trend of subtle subordination.

TWO

NARRATIVES OF MOTHERS, MONSTERS AND WHORES

A narrative is a story about an event or set of events recounted for an audience or readership. A dominant narrative is one spoken by a voice or voices which receive substantial audience, such that the dominant narrative becomes *the account* (though there may have been many) of women's violence. The audience then internalizes the narrative as their own intellectual, emotional or even sensory understanding of that event or set of events (Huston 1983: 271). Narratives, often in the form of stories or metaphors, 'frame' complicated events to fit into discrete categories, allowing people to process large amounts of information with limited cognitive capacity (Tannen 1993; Croft and Cruse 2004). As Tannen explains, 'no communicative move, verbal or non verbal, could be understood without reference to a metacommunicative message, or metamessage, about what is going on – that is, what frame of interpretation applies to the move' (1993: 3). That is to say, no communication is independent of the frames it is spoken and heard through. For example, though most people do not understand the diversity of species of snakes, most people can describe what they mean by the word 'snake', and know one when they see it. People, narrative theorists argue, use these shortcut categories to understand every facet of their lives, from personal relationships to global politics (Khong 1992; Lakoff and Johnson 1980).

Metaphorical or associative categories serve a dual function in our memory capacities: they organize events which people see and digest, and they serve as predictions and instructions for new situations that people face (Lakoff 1993). For example, when confronted with a new task at work, many people categorize that task as 'like' a similar task that they do know how to do, and extrapolate how to accomplish the new task from the knowledge of the similar one (Lakoff and Johnson 1999, 1980). Discourses explaining violence in global politics play a similar role. Huston explains that 'war imitates war narrative imitates war' (Huston 1983: 273). In a war narrative, 'two figures are of capital importance: the protagonist and the antagonist' (Huston 1983, 273). The protagonist is the hero of the war story. As Nancy Huston explains, 'it is no accident that whereas there are reams and reams of "heroic" verse, there is no such thing as "enemic" verse', because the tellers of war stories cast themselves as the victors (1983: 273). In this way, war narratives are the foundation which create the possibility for war and direct war-fighting. Wars perpetuate empirical bases for the continuation and enrichment of war stories. Together, war and war stories weave a cycle which can be referred to as the war system (Reardon 1985; Cuomo 1996; Goldstein 2001).

These stories both justify violence and marginalize the content of agency and victimization. In these triumphal narratives, 'the actual number of victims – *a fortiori* their innocence and guilt, are secondary considerations; what counts is the capacity to kill the triumphal narrative of the enemy' (Huston 1983: 273). The best war story not only wins the war, it *is* the war. In this way, wars and war narratives are not discrete phenomena, but parts of the same whole. Huston confirms that 'it is crucial to conceive of these physical violences as being *linguistic as well*' and linguistic violence as physical as well (1983: 278).

Each instance of violence or war in global politics can be described by more than one narrative in international political discourse. There is not one story which is objectively true or universally accepted, but several stories which could be 'the story' of a given war or conflict. Indeed, narratives compete for dominance in the press, during political campaigns, and in the work of non-profits, volunteers and activists. In these competitions, dominance comes in the form of attention and salience. Baudrillard argues that 'we live in a world of *referendum* where all signs and messages present themselves in question/answer format' (1979: 124).[1] Because aspiring truths compete, political and social 'research cannot be carried out wholly within the unalloyed logic of a single, 'pure' formative discourse' (Hall 1999: 2). On the contrary, actual inquiries depend on hybrid practices that involve extra-logical mediations among *different* formative discourses employed *in relation to* one another' (Hall 1999: 3).

By 'extra-logical', Hall is implying that there is some involvement of emotion or instinct in the competition of discourses. This is an important point, but only part of the story. There is also a politics in the competition of discourses. Here, Robert Cox (1986) is informative. According to Cox, problem-solving theory is an attempt to explain international interaction in the context of and within the acceptable limits of the current framework of the international system. On the other hand, critical theory is theory which is capable of envisioning both realities that fall outside of the domains of analysis of the current framework and a world in which an alternate framework could replace the current framework (Cox 1986). Critical theory, then, engages in political protest against the dominance of (apparently) value-neutral approaches. Feminist theory is a critical approach, bound up in *contending* that the dominant discourses should include women and other marginalized voices.[2] This study points out the places where the (apparently) value-neutral dominant discourses of women's violence in global politics, as represented by the mother, monster and whore narratives, exclude women's agency and other marginalized perspectives.

GENDERED NARRATIVES OF WOMEN'S VIOLENCE IN GLOBAL POLITICS

Women's violence in global politics is often described in terms other than and separate from those used to describe men's violence. As Wight and Myers recognize, 'when a woman commits an act of criminal violence, her sex is the lens through which all of her actions are seen and understood' (1996: xi). A violent woman's womanhood is 'the primary explanation or mitigating factor offered up in any attempt to understand her crime' (xii). Susan Gubar hypothesized that the gendering of stories about violent women is a 'representation of male dread of women and more specifically of male anxiety over female control' (1977: 380). The gendered characterizations of women's violence found across time, religion, culture and state are the mother, monster and whore narratives. These narratives offer different 'explanations' for women's violence, but share the dual move of denying women's agency in their violence and condemning women's femininity. Throughout this chapter and the book, we distinguish these narratives both conceptually and empirically. Still, it is important to note that many stories of women's violence include more than one of these gender tropes, hybridizing the mother, monster and whore narratives.

MOTHER

> I saved you. Every man in Greece knows that.
> The bulls, the dragon-men, the serpent warder of the Fleece,
> I conquered them. I made you victor.
> I held the light that saved you. (Hamilton 1940: 129)

These are the words the great sorceress Medea says to Jason as she learns of his betrayal. In many ways a woman engaged in proscribed violence is depicted as the modern Medea – as a violent, evil woman who commits treacherous acts for her man or as a woman whose love has forsaken her; much like Jason forsakes Medea, driving her to revenge. Throughout her story, Medea's motherhood successes and failures dictate her violent actions. Medea sacrifices all classically female (private) goals for her love of Jason. She betrays her father (by supporting Jason's tasks) and kills her brother (in order to help Jason escape). In murdering her brother and then King Phineas, she commits evil to demonstrate her love for a man and for the promise of marriage.

Even one of history's most famous villainesses is not credited with her own violent choices. Instead, her violence is characterized as reliant on her role as a wife and mother, and thus not of her own doing. In order for Medea to help Jason on his quest for the Golden Fleece, which would restore his kingdom to him, Aphrodite asks Cupid to make Medea fall in love with Jason. In response to this manipulation, Medea, feeling the first flush of love, cries out, 'wits are futile/ Against this heat. Some god's bewitched my senses,/ Charmed my will. Is this called love?' (Ovid 1958: 187). Throughout Ovid's account, Medea regrets her actions against her father ('Shall I betray my father's kingdom, crown ...?'), and does not completely comprehend her love for Jason (188–9). Furthermore, her most horrific act, even her most infamous act, is her murder of their two sons, 'her blood-red steel had pierced the bodies/ Of their two sons', in order to hurt Jason as much as he had hurt her (199). To realize the goal of marriage, the story explains that Medea betrayed and murdered family, and to revenge Jason's betrayal of love she struck out at another feminine virtue, her children.

The stories of Medea[3] depict her violence as the after-effects of Aphrodite's manipulation in order for Jason to achieve political power. She is used, like many women are, as a sacrifice for the greatness of the men in her life. Ovid makes Medea 'far more bloody, more savage in her behaviour than the heroine conceived by Euripides' (1958: 186). Additionally, Ovid 'invests' in his Medea the 'trappings of superstitious horror': '[Medea] belongs to Ovid's world of night, a figure of *nightmare* in its original meaning' (emphasis true to text) (1958: 186). Thus Medea commits ruthless violence, arguably political violence, for the sake of love. While there are traces of the monster narrative, especially in Ovid's account, the violence for which Medea is known is the murder of her sons to avenge her husband's actions.

Blaming women's intense and desperate link to motherhood for their violence is not limited to the Greeks, but is a persistent narrative across time, place and culture in history. For example, millennia and continents away, in Rudyard Kipling's poem, 'The Female of the Species', women 'are more deadly than the male' because they are 'launched for one sole issue', and driven by mothering instinct (Kipling 1923). Mothering instinct, as described by Kipling, is a stronger motive for violence than 'male diversions', because women's 'honour dwells' in 'death by torture for each life beneath her breast' (1923).

Even today, in media accounts of women engaged in political violence, the women's violence is often attributed to vengeance driven by maternal and domestic disappointments (Dickey 2005; Ragavan et al. 2003a). As 'femme fatales' (Ragavan et al. 2003a: 33) women's political violence is not seen as driven by ideology and belief in a cause, but instead as a perversion of the private realm. Just as Medea's violence was directed towards (either to achieve or destroy) the feminine 'virtues' of marriage and children, today's women's violence is characterized in similar terms. Women who engage in proscribed violence are placed into biologically determined categorizations, depicted in maternal or domestic language. They are 'told' as women who are fulfilling or avenging what is supposed to be women's biological destinies of wife and mother, elements which also define the private sphere. Violent women are often depicted as avenging lost love and/or a destroyed happy home.

For example, one article consistently places emphasis on Palestinian women's loss: 'My heart aches … for my dead husband', another woman's older brother was killed by Israeli soldiers, or an Israeli researcher's interpretation that women acted because 'they had been disappointed in love' (Jaber 2003: 2). The women are described as so stricken by grief and fear due to the loss of their men that they have no control over their actions. If women have any decision-making power in their actions, it is limited to decisions about their femininity and maternity – taking care of or avenging their men. The political reasoning the women give is presented as secondary (if at all), even though it is powerful:

> [W]e have waited long, heard a lot of poetic words, make-believe, promises and talk of peaceful solutions, justice and fairness for the Palestinians, but look around you, tell me what you see.
> We have nothing – nothing. Just empty, meaningless words that have brought us nothing. So it is time we abandon the talk and take our destiny into our own hands. Dramatic maybe, violent maybe, but there is no other way. Our acts are cries of desperation in the hope that someone will eventually heed us. (Jabar 2003: 2)

Another article that examines female Palestinian suicide bombers criticizes the mainly Western media's focus on loss of husbands and brothers and destroyed hopes for domesticity (Toles Parkin 2004: 85–6). Thus, while the male terrorist 'is pictured as a "living weapon", ... the female terrorist is often suspected of joining the movement for emotional or social reasons' (84).

It is easy to dismiss as outdated the essentialist narratives of women as emotional and men as rational, but even in recent work the mother narrative appears and continues to locate a woman's quest to use violence due to a problem with her femininity. Thus the narrative carries with it the weight of gendered assumptions about what is appropriate female behaviour. Narratives of women's violence often centre around biologically determinist assumptions and arguments. In stories about violent women, their motherhood defines them – their inability/failure to serve as mothers is *so* dehumanizing (or dewomanizing) that it drives a woman to violence.

Within the mother narrative women are characterized as acting either in a support role (the nurturing mother) or out of revenge (the vengeful mother). The nurturing mother terrorist is fairly non-threatening. She is still a terrorist, revolutionary, genocidaire or criminal, but one does not have to worry too much about her personal violence. She is the 'domesticated' terrorist. Her instinctual desire to be maternal is seen as enough of a motivation for engagement in political violence. Restricting a woman's involvement to the acceptable socially scripted role of mother limits the female terrorist's involvement to behind-the-scenes work, such as work limited to the home (private). Therefore, the *non-violent* female criminal does not challenge Western notions of femininity. She still operates within the woman's 'field of honour' – tasks that have traditionally filled the private sphere (Elshtain 1987: 50; 1981). In this narrative, mothering violent men is mothering no less.

The nurturing mother narrative is particularly prevalent in the field of terrorism studies, where women have often been classified as mothers or housekeepers. One study defines the 'maternal self-sacrifice code', where a woman's involvement in political violence stems from a maternal desire to belong to and be useful to that organization; in other words, to be needed (Neuburger and Valentini 1996: 17). Neuburger and Valentini interviewed several female Italian Red Brigade members, who said: 'Yes, I knew that ... they were using me, but I was glad to be used because I was working for a worthwhile cause.' Another woman said: 'They needed me and I let myself be used. I was satisfied with that' (17). In these stories, women 'develop their experience in accordance with an affective model based on sacrifice, on caring for others, on responding to others' needs, and on protection' (81). In other words, women's psychological compulsion to assist and support others (specifically their men) extends to assisting and supporting, even mothering, terrorists.

The story of violent women as nurturing mothers is best represented by a story from the Weather Underground, a Marxist–Leninist organization in the United States that operated from 1968 to the late 1970s, which objected to US imperialism, the Vietnam War, and advocated violent revolution, among other objectives (Gentry 2004). In the Weather Underground, there was an account of a female revolutionary who returned to the shared house one day to find a list of things to do that ended with 'and don't forget to clean the fridge' (Taylor 2000: 303). This story signified the maternal, and subservient, role that female terrorists are seen as having within their organizations. Weinberg and Eubank question this idea of female-terrorist-as-housekeeper assumption. They cite a study that concludes 'women were help for their male counterparts'; in order to look beyond this, Weinberg and Eubank do examine women's role in the leadership of left-wing and right-wing Italian organizations (Weinberg and Eubank 1987: 243). Yet Weinberg and Eubank do not explore the other ways in which women participated. Instead, they emphasize the strong correlation between a woman's entrance into a terrorist organization and her already involved male relation (256). These chosen research priorities make it impossible for Weinberg and Eubank to refute effectively the female-terrorist-as-helpmeet assumption. Their work, by focusing on who got women involved rather than the motivations for and nature of women's involvement, implicitly endorses the nurturing mother narrative.

If the nurturing mother is the domesticated terrorist, the vengeful mother's onus is still maternal, but dangerously disturbed. The vengeful mother is driven by rage because of her maternal losses, maternal inadequacies or maternal incredulity. Her decision is not calculated retaliation but emotion-driven revenge. The vengeful mother is best exemplified in a recent *Newsweek* article which presents al-Qaeda female suicide bombers as acting out of a disrupted gendered path: women who have been frustrated in their marital and child-bearing roles become suicide bombers. The article describes the women's garments: '[Her] clothes also concealed the explosives strapped around her womb' (Dickey 2005: 1). This exploits the role the (mother) woman is supposed to play and places her innate womanhood into question by the political actions she has undertaken. In the article, Dickey also equates the woman's activity with her inability to 'have children' (1). Thus, her *raison d'être*, to have a 'successful' marriage and bear children, was denied to her and she became a vengeful mother. Much like Medea, the suicide bomber was disappointed in love. The disappointment in love made her a failure, because motherhood was her purpose for existence. This failure, her reason to live, caused her to act outside of the non-violent tendencies of normal women who are able to have children.

Indeed, many accounts of Palestinian and Chechen female suicide bombers have depicted them in a similar light – that they too have been disappointed in love and marriage and thus driven to violence. One author comments:

> Media coverage, particularly in the West, appears to actively search for alternate explanations behind women's participation in terror in a way that does not seem paralleled in the coverage of male suicide bombers, whose official ideological statements appear to be taken at face value. In the case of the relatively few female terrorists, media coverage profoundly emphasizes the emotional over the ideological. (Toles Parkin 2004: 85)

Several media accounts focus on emotional reasons for revenge. The accounts cite failed marriages, the inability to have children, humiliating experiences at Israeli checkpoints, loss of familial honour, and so on, as reasons these women blew up themselves and others (Toles Parkin 2004: 85–6; Jaber 2003: 2). An article in the *Sunday Times* includes both personal and political motivations[4] for the women; however, it places the personal reasons as the primary motivation (Jaber 2003). By dubbing the Chechen women desperate 'black widows', this designation continually points to their (typical or assumed) widowhood, which has led them to avenge their husbands' deaths.[5] Headlines related to women's violence in Chechnya and Greater Russia read: 'Hell Hath No Fury Like Chechnya's Ruthless "Widows of War"' (Jacinto 2002, 1), 'Widows with a Death Wish Spearhead Terror War' (McLaughlin 2003, 10), and 'Black Widows of Chechnya Take another Deadly Revenge' (Campbell 2003, 2). These are sensationalized accounts that directly link the women's violence to no other driving force (ideological or ethno-nationalist justifications) than their desire to avenge their husbands' deaths.

There has been extensive engagement in feminism and women's studies with the question of the relationship between motherhood, politics and political struggle. In nationalist discourses, women tend to be described in the private sphere and wrapped up in the domestic duties therein. Women in the private sphere are protected by men 'out there' while they are tied to the idea of the 'motherland' and the protection of that ideal (Cockburn 2001b: 19). The essentialist ideal-type of the peaceful mother ties into the mother narrative. Jacobs, Jacobson and Marchbank describe the 'maternalist position' which forges an 'essential link' between women, motherhood, and non-violence (2000: 13). In recent years, feminists have become more concerned with women's agency in violent conflict (Moser and Clark 2001). There is little analysis, however, of the relationship (or lack thereof) between the peaceful maternalist position and the association of motherhood and violence in the mother narrative. As Wight and Myers commented, a woman's sex is the primary lens through which any of her actions are digested; this cognitive priority trumps contradictions within the representations it produces. As such, the identification of women as mothers can contribute to a number of (even contradictory) ideal-typical images of women's differences from men.

MONSTER

While the mother narrative explains women's violence through characteristics essential to womanhood, the monster narrative explains their violence as a biological flaw that disrupts their femininity. As Susan Gubar explains, 'female monsters have long inhabited the male imagination' because this idealization of violent women 'masks the fear of the other sex' (1977: 380, 382). As such, 'when women commit crimes ... they are categorized and labeled as either "bad" or "mad"' (Berrington and Honkatukia 2002: 50). Because women are 'supposed to nurture and protect, not kill', women who do kill are characterized as inhuman monsters (59). Their 'pathological deviance from prescribed feminine norms' is 'identified as the prime cause' of their violence (65). Women's violence is seen as the result of 'mental abnormality' which 'increases the risk of women behaving violently' (Ballinger 1996). While violent women inspired by motherhood are not responsible for their actions because they are women, violent women in the monster narrative are not responsible for their actions because there is something wrong with their womanhood. Monsters are pathological because of either their insanity or their self-denial of womanhood.

A monstrous women's violence is characterized as quite different from male violence. A violent woman is more deadly; she is more of a threat. The West German GSG-9, a team engaged in counterterrorist operations, at one point employed the command to 'shoot the women first' because women were supposed to be more ruthless and aggressive than men (MacDonald 1992: 11). This is a process Morrissey calls 'monsterization', which characterizes violent women as necessarily inhuman because human/real women do not commit violence. Morrissey characterizes monsterization as the ultimate 'discrimination and prejudice against her as representative of women accused of violent acts' (2003; Knowles 2004). The monster narrative at once demonizes violent women (characterizing them as evil) and ridicules them (hyperbolizing their evil, like the story of the 50-foot woman[6]). This dual role that the monster narrative plays is further complicated by the element of sexual fantasy in the monster narrative, where popular culture fetishizes monstrous women (King and McCaughey 2002). The monster narrative is ridicule for women's non-conforming behaviour 'as a means of neutralizing the challenge [women's violence] poses to dominant, hegemonic, patriarchal norms' (Berrington and Honkatukia 2002: 57).

The historical roots of the monster narrative can be found in its close relation to the Greek Gorgon myth. H.H.A. Cooper characterized violent women, specifically female terrorists, as Gorgons (Cooper 1979: 150–57). Cooper writes that female terrorists possess an 'intractable' and 'cold rage ... that even the most alienated of men seem quite incapable of emulating' (Cooper 1979: 150). This violent woman 'delights in aping' soldiers and is 'childishly motivated to engage in violence' and should be 'dealt with after the fashion of the Gorgon' (153–4). In these accounts, violent women are supposedly so horrific that no chances can or should be taken with them – whereas one can apparently be more flexible dealing with violent men, who are more predicable and rational, even at their worst.

The Gorgon analogy is made in a number of current characterizations of violent women. 'Gorgon' is Greek, translated as either 'terrible' or 'loud-roaring' (Wilk 2000). In Greek mythology, Gorgons were vicious female 'dragonlike creatures with wings' and hair of living, venomous snakes (Hamilton 1940: 43, 143). An early description of the Gorgon sisters says they had 'scaly heads, boars tusks, brazen hands ... with protruding tongues [and] glaring eyes' (Wilk 2000: 21). They had fire coming out of their hands and could steal powers from the gods. They both ruled the underworld and could appear as innocent humans. Medusa, the queen of the Gorgons, was at once the most beautiful woman in Greece and a fierce monster that could turn people to stone with a stare. The Gorgons were known 'far and wide [for] their deadly power' and could turn a man to stone if gazed upon (Hamilton 1940: 143). Like other creatures of Greek mythology, beautified Gorgons have been popularized in modern times by fantasy books, comics and role-playing games. There, Gorgons are evil monsters whose biggest weapon is their appearance of normalcy and beauty.

Boudica[7] is another example of the monster narrative in historical accounts. Boudica was born *circa* 25 AD. She married Celtic King Prasutagus of the Icenis when she was in her late teens. In Boudica's time, Rome had been in Britain for almost a century and both sides welcomed the empire's presence because of the sheer wealth of trade. But in 43 AD, Rome imposed a harsher rule over the British Isle (Donsbach 2004: 51, 52). By the time Nero became emperor, the violence against Celtic tribes had reached Boudica and her family. Boudica's husband was killed. When the Roman general arrived to take over Boudica's land, she refused. In response, he flogged her and had her two daughters raped (Harbison 2006: 82; Donsbach 2004: 54). It is at this point that Boudica decided to mount her offensive against Roman forces.

In most accounts, Boudica's monstrousness is the key element of the tale of her violence. Dio's description of Boudica is the most influential: Boudica was 'very tall and grim in appearance, with a piercing gaze and a harsh voice' (Donsbach 2004: 54). She was known to wear a torque, a gold neckband worn by warriors to symbolize readiness to die for their tribe. Boudica is not described as a normal warrior, however. When she reached Londinium, the story recounts, 'she killed everyone she found' (55). Dio described the scene:

> They hung up naked the noblest and most distinguished women then cut off their breasts and sewed them to their mouths, in order to make the victims appear to be eating them; afterwards they impaled the women on sharp skewers run lengthwise up the entire body. (Donsbach 2004: 55)

It was in the Romans' best interest to present Boudica as far more threatening than she was, because she was a woman who dared to go against the empire: 'To the misogynistic Romans, Boudicca was everything evil they could imagine' (Harbison 2006: 82). For Romans, it benefited them to establish her as terrifying and monstrous.[8] As such, many inherited tales about Boudica do not emphasize her personal or political motivations, but the savage and unwomanly brutality of her actions.

Contemporary examples demonstrate that the monster narrative perpetuates across time, space and culture. Berrington and Honkatukia examine the recurrence of monster language in the story of Sanna Sillanpaa, a Finnish woman who opened fire on five men in a gun shop, killing three of them (2002: 50). As they explain, 'rather than considering her 'badness', there was an early assumption, in the media and criminal investigation, that she must be mentally ill' (Berrington and Honkatukia 2002: 50). Because Sillanpaa was aggressive in a way that women are not, she was perceived as a 'ruthless' killer (56). In Finnish media, 'a gendered picture of Sanna as a monster was emerging' (67). She was characterized as 'sick' and 'mad' and 'being the victim of a tragedy' was blamed for her madness (Ballinger

1996: 1). Sanna had walked into the shop and fired her weapon; she was evil (monstrous), but not responsible for her monstrosity, because she was mad.

Aileen Wuornos, the subject of the 2003 movie *Monster*, provides another contemporary example of the monster narrative. Wuornos was a prostitute who killed seven johns she claimed either raped her or intended to rape her (King and McCaughey 2002). After receiving her death sentence, Wuornos desired to be executed immediately and protested a number of appeals, which argued that she was not mentally competent to be executed. Wuornos explained:

> I killed those men, robbed them as cold as ice. And I'd do it again, too. There's no chance in keeping me alive or anything, because I'd kill again. I have hate crawling through my system.... I am so sick of hearing this 'she's crazy' stuff. I've been evaluated so many times. I'm competent, sane, and I'm trying to tell the truth. I'm one who seriously hates human life and would kill again. (Zarrella 2002)

Wuornos, whose sanity was the subject of the major controversy around whether or not to execute her, often protested descriptions of her as mad or insane. She contended that she had killed the first man because he had raped her, and the others because they had been about to do the same thing (Zarrella 2002). Still, Aileen Wuornos was often characterized as a mentally disturbed monster, incapable of judging or deciding for herself either her actions or her desire to die. Though she was described as 'cognizant and lucid' in her mental fitness interview for execution, and expressed a desire to be executed, media outlets and opponents of the death penalty emphasized her previous diagnosis as 'borderline psychotic' (Motion for Stay of Execution, 2002, Florida Case No. SC79484). Her madness was the focus of most stories about Wuornos, whose insanity had turned her into a monster (Russell 2002; Zarella 2002). Her monstrosity, then, was at fault for her serial killing spree, rather than her choices to pull the trigger. Wuornos had to be insane, because sane women, real women, are not killers.

Like a Gorgon or Boudica, a violent woman today is evil incarnate with an insane mission borne of anger. The comparison, directly or

NARRATIVES

indirectly, to a monster takes away not only violent women's agency but their very humanity by stripping them of rational thought. According to this narrative, women are involved in political violence for personal reasons that are obsessive or pathological in nature (Cooper 1979: 154). While it is valid to inquire into men's political violence, it 'is useless to inquire why women become terrorists' (Cooper 1979: 154). Their irrationality in the face of men's rationality makes them not only monsters, but horrific ones not seen since the times of Greek mythology. Violent women defined within the monster narrative are not real women because they are described as both actually evil and psychologically broken, two facets which the ideal-types of womanhood in gender norms exclude. Monstrous violent women are thus pathological, and therefore neither they nor their gender are responsible for their actions.

WHORE

Stories vilifying women because of their perceived sexual depravity are recurrent throughout ancient and modern history. Even biblical stories are interpreted to equate women's sexuality with their violence. Jezebel, married to the violently bloody King Ahab of Israel, is linked to idolatry and witchcraft. As the daughter of a priest and priestess dedicated to Baal and Ashtoreth, she opposed the Hebrews and their belief in one god. She killed many followers and prophets of the Hebrew God and also killed those who hampered her husband (*Life Application Bible* 1991: 591). Jezebel, upon hearing of Elijah's seizure and killing of the prophets of Baal (1 Kings 18:40), threatened him with death (1 Kings 19:1–2). When Jezebel's son was defeated in battle, her body was thrown from a building, whereupon it was trampled and then eaten by dogs (1 Kings 16:31; 2 Kings 9:35). In many ways, Jezebel's life was a *politically violent* struggle between the old ways and the new ways in the ancient kingdom of Israel. There is some mention of Jezebel and whoredom[9] in the Bible (2 Kings 9:22; Revelation 2:20), but the modern link of Jezebel and harlotry is quite strong. A Google search on Jezebel reveals biblical websites interlaced with lingerie websites. One biblical website goes so far as to deem Jezebel the 'mother of harlots and abominations of the earth' (Atkinson 2006: 1). When men do bad things, it is because there is something *evil* about them; when women do bad things, their evil is sexualized.

Another historical example of the sexualization of violent women is the story of the Amazons. The Amazons were described as having adopted many of the physical and sexual traits of men. The Amazons' supposed appropriation of masculinity, however, was not something to be honoured. Instead, these women of legend were described as beautiful and sexually enrapturing yet physically damaged. To be functional as warriors, they amputated their right breast (Crim 2000: 20). This practice brought the Amazons closer to men through the mutilation of their female bodies. Still, their beauty kept them as objects of lust. In other ways, the Amazons were like men – they were considered to be the female Spartans. The gender roles were reversed as the women took on the male role as described by Greek patriarchal society (Crim 2000: 20). The Amazons were the daughters of the 'peace-loving nymph, sweet Harmony' and Ares, the god of war (Hamilton 1940: 122). The Amazons followed the ways of their father and 'were not gentle foes' (Hamilton 1940: 122). They dressed as men in 'long trousers, midthigh-length coats, leather boots, and Phrygian hats' (Jones 1997: 6). The women carried shields, battleaxes, and swords, and, after observing the Greeks, they adopted the bow and the war spear (Jones 1997: 6).

Descriptions of the Amazons as sexually hedonistic dominate stories about them. They are said to have treated men as slaves and as expendable. They 'mated randomly' and as such displayed promiscuous behaviour (Jones 1997: 6). They did not marry (8), and they had no need for men after sex, if they needed them then. Much like the Greek patriarchy's attitude that women were inferior and no better than slaves or children, the Amazons treated the men as less than their ideal of woman. The Amazons crippled or killed their male children in order to limit their power and keep them as slaves, but raised physically healthy female children (6). Their beauty also figures in their war making accounts. In the *Iliad*, when Achilles kills the Amazonian queen Penthesilea he mourns 'for her as she lay dead, so young and so beautiful' (Hamilton 1940: 287). Other accounts add prettiness to the Amazon's battle – the magical beasts they rode into battle 'scattered gold and silver sands from the hooves'

(Jones 1997: 6). The Amazons, like Greek men, were willing to go to war for women.[10]

The Greeks believed that patriarchy was the natural way of the world. In this patriarchal world, the image of the Amazon way of life was used to represent the chaos of women who not only engaged actively in warfare and battle, but who ruled (Lane and Wurts 1998: 41, 48). The Amazons also represented 'the opposite of all that is good and right in women' because 'good Athenian women married, bore their husband's children, and lived safely and demurely' within the 'ordered world' of the patriarchy (Jones 1997: 7–8). In contrast to 'real' women, Amazons had sex freely and caused chaos in a disordered world. In the whore narratives of the Amazon, women who either could not or refused to please men were equated with danger and violence. If matriarchy were ever to overwhelm the patriarchy, Greeks believed, the world would immediately be thrown into chaos. Thus, the message of the Amazon myths is: 'women who step outside their assigned roles damage all of civilization' (Lane and Wurts 1998: 51). The Amazons are the beautiful ultimate outsider, 'a terrifying force for unmanaged change' (52).

Descriptions of the Amazons were used by the Greeks to 'delineate the roles of women in Athenian society' (Jones 1997: 7). Stories of women's violence operated to warn of the disorganization and a disruption of the natural order of things that came from women transgressing their expected gender roles. In this way, the Amazons are othered and treated as women who do wrong not only by engaging in battle but as women who have no need or use to *please men*. They are freaks not so much because of their warrior status, which is bad enough, but because they have *chosen* to reject the male-dominated lifestyle and create their own, where men are extraneous.

The trend of associating women's violence with their sexuality did not end in Greek culture. In early modern and mid-modern history, Gerald De Groot points out, one 'way of discounting the contribution of women to the military and thus limit their empowerment was to present them as dangerous sexual predators' (2000a: 16). In both early modern and mid-modern history, women and children as camp followers nursed, found food, made camp, carried ammunition and artillery, and were, essentially, pack mules when the camp moved

(Crim 2000: 27; Hendrix 2000: 34). Camp follower and prostitute have often been equated, but, as Brian Crim and Scott Hendrix both demonstrate, this is not necessarily the case. It is true that camp followers may have been distracting, especially if there was alcohol involved, but many camp followers were hard-working and often common-law (or something akin to this status) wives of the soldiers (Crim 2000: 27; Hendrix 2000: 36). The conflation of camp follower with prostitute came about mainly because 'many marriages, which were probably considered valid by the participants, were often judged unsanctioned and immoral by outside observers' (Hendrix 2000: 36). Additionally, many women were quick to take another husband when theirs died in battle – this was seen as shocking, without recognizing the women's dependency upon men (Hendrix 2000: 36).

In early modern European history, between 1500 and 1650, '[a]t no [other] time … were so many women engaged in warfare – as spies, foragers, artillery personnel, or soldiers' (Crim 2000: 27). During this time, many women would dress as men in order to fight. But, the involvement of women with war 'seemed to suggest that society was on the brink of disaster because the gender hierarchy was unstable' (27). This echoes the beliefs of the Greeks, that women associated with war, like the Amazons, led to chaos, and foreshadows Machiavelli's assumption that 'all women within an army were prostitutes, who pursued 'those vile avocations which commonly make soldiers idle and seditious' (28). Yet, this assumption by Machiavelli and historians' wilful ignorance of women's real role as camp followers have placed women engaged in warfare in the red light of harlotry. Descriptions of women who fight in or vigorously support war have been cast in the language of sexual impurity throughout history, a move which distances 'violent women' from the innocence and purity of the ideal-type of femininity. Women who fight or who are close to it historically have been assumed to be sexually depraved, and have frequently been described not only in the language of harlotry, but actually as whores.

More recently, women who served in the armed forces during World War II also struggled with sexualized characterizations of their roles. Within British society, at least, there was a fear of sexual impropriety both for and of the women who joined the Auxiliary Territorial

Service (ATS), the Women's Auxiliary Air Force (WAAF), and the Women's Royal Naval Service (WRNS) (De Groot 2000b, 101). De Groot highlights an expert opinion published in *The Spectator*:

> We have here ... multitudes of reckless, unstable girls who drink far too much and are determined to have a good time come what may.... Venereal diseases are, of course, spread by promiscuity, and this is promoted by principally by absence from home with only remote prospects of returning there. (2000b: 101)

ATS women were derogatorily known as 'OGS' (officers' ground sheet) (De Groot 2000b: 109); one woman's brother, upon hearing she was being sent to the Continent, begged her not to go, writing in letter that she 'would only land up as' such (103). The socially sexualized stigma of joining the ATS was heavier, mainly because it was made up of working-class women – and 'workers were known to have insatiable sexual appetites' (109). De Groot clearly links what he calls a 'whispering campaign', the false rumors and assumptions about the ATS, WAAF and WRNS women, and the larger public fear that women were beginning not only to dress like men (the uniforms) but to act like them as well (110).

An example of the employment of the whore narrative to describe women's proscribed violence is in Catherine Taylor's discussion of Bernardine Dohrn, a leader in the United States' Weather Underground. Taylor claims that Bernardine Dohrn used her sexuality to tie the 'male acolytes' of the Weather Underground to her. It was Dohrn's power: 'she would control them ... by keeping her blouse unbuttoned and breasts exposed during strategy meetings' (Taylor 2000: 300). Taylor writes: this 'stereotype ... combines sex and violence in a titillating erotic mix, and ... [it is] probably quite [an] accurate depiction of the role which female terrorists often play' (300). Certainly, a woman's sexuality is a part of her daily life, and therefore a part of her daily life as a terrorist, but no more than can be said about men (Ayers 2001). The sexualization of Dohrn downplays both her real reasons for being involved in the movement and any real leadership ability and position she had.

Women's integration into spheres of power and violence threatens patriarchy, until those women are dehumanized through sexualization. While women who participate in militaries around the world gain more acceptance, women who engage in proscribed violence (crime, terrorism, etc.) are reduced to sexual objects with increasing vigour in the discourse of global politics. Violent women are othered and made subhuman in part by the fetishization of their existence and their actions. A woman's violence is not just violence, and not even just a statistical or psychological outlier. Instead, a woman's violence is a *sexual* event; women who are violent are highlighted, exploited and fetishized (Gentry and Sjoberg 2007). Some argue that this can be explained by the popular adage that, when something goes seriously wrong, men always find 'a woman to blame'. There is more going on, though, than blaming either women or their femininity. Instead, discussions of women's violence *debase* women and reduce them to their sexuality.

Violent women are often characterized by their capacity (or lack thereof) to have sex with men; women's involvement in sexual activity is somehow always closely linked to women's violence. Women either commit violence because of their insatiable need for sex with men, men's control and ownership of their bodies, or their inability to have sex with men. Men who are the victims of women's violence are '*screwed' by the sexually depraved*; they are lower than low because they are susceptible to women's erotomania or women's erotic dysfunction.[11] In the 'war on terror', sexually demeaning stories of the victims of women's violence are a part of a racialized narrative of (white) American supremacy.[12]

Whore narratives characterize women's proscribed violence, or women's support for proscribed violence, as sexually deviant. The whore narrative's descriptions of women's sexual deviance can be divided into three categories: erotomania, erotic dysfunction and sexual slavery. Like the mother, monster and whore narratives, elements of each of these stories can be interspersed in a single sexualized tale about a violent woman. Still, they are distinct characterizations, held together by the commonality of sexualization of women's violence.

The first whore narrative about violent women is one that characterizes them as almost exclusively sexual beings. In this understanding, focused on erotomania, violent women are motivated by their overwhelming perversion. These women live for sex, while normal women have a discrete and controlled sex drive, if they have any at all. This sexual deviance explains the deviance of their violence: erotomania makes violent women *just crazy enough* to be violent. Actual erotomania (in psychological terms) is a rare disorder in which a person holds a delusional belief that another person, usually of a higher social status, is in love with them. It is also called de Clerambaut's syndrome, after French psychiatrist Gaetan Gatian de Clerambaut, who published a comprehensive review on the subject in 1921. The term's common usage, however, is the less specific clinical sense of the excessive pursuit or preoccupation with love or sex. The erotomaniac violent woman is unable to resist her sexual urges, and this inability to do anything but sex drives her violence.

An example of the erotomaniac narrative is that of Nannie Doss, a serial killer from Alabama who murdered six husbands and many members of her family with rat poison baked into pies and other foods between 1920 and 1954. Doss was characterized as a woman who 'got around' and had a mean streak that 'burned rabid inside her' (Geringer 2002). According to the stories, 'all she ever wanted was romance, a man to love her' (Manners 1995). When she realized either that the man was going to disappoint her or that someone was going to get in the way of the man satisfying her needs, she took care of the problem – literally. She 'killed because she liked it' and got off on the idea (Schechter and Everitt 1996). She was characterized as 'easy' and someone who had no regard for sexual faithfulness, having sex whenever she could (Geringer 2002). Still, she could not control her sex drive, and 'her built-up tensions exploded within her', causing her to kill. Her sexuality was included in most stories about her murders, and she was described as someone who read 'tawdry' books and knew how to 'entice' victims (Geringer 2002). She was said to have come on to investigators as they interrogated her and to have been 'sexual to the core' (Manners 1995).

The second whore narrative targets erotic dysfunction as an explanation for women's violence. While some whore narratives explain women's violence by their insatiable and uncontrollable need to have sex with men, others explain women's violence by insanity inspired by their inability to perform their basic function in life, providing men with sexual pleasure. In this narrative, women's destiny is bound up in their ability to please men. Many stories of violent women discuss their violence in terms of their *inability* to fulfil that biological destiny, characterizing violent women as somehow *sexually less than real women*. This section of whore narratives, which we call sexual dysfunction, explains violent women as lesbians or otherwise sexually deviant, as unable to have or rear children, or as sexually failing their men in some way or another.

One example of the sexual dysfunction whore narrative is that of Celeste Beard and Tracey Tarlton murdering Celeste's husband in 1999 (Krajicek 1999). Celeste and her husband, who was wealthy and older, were said to have had sex just twice (Krajicek 1999). Celeste, unhappy in her marriage and sexually uninterested in her husband, met Tracey at a mental institution. Celeste and Tracey were 'caught in a passionate love clutch' and 'buckets of ice water couldn't have kept them apart' during the time that they were institutionalized (Krajicek 1999). They began to plot to murder Celeste's husband, and, once they succeeded, the media told the story of a man killed by his wife's 'lesbian lover with a shotgun' (Krajicek 1999). Celeste's unwillingness to have a sexual relationship with her husband and the depravity of her lesbian affair are continuous themes in the stories about her role in the murder (Krajicek 1999).

Lesbianism is not the only 'sexual dysfunction' used to explain women's violence. The story of Leslie Nelson's killing several police officers staking out her house in 1995 implicates questions of sexual identity in motivating violence. Seamus McGraw describes Nelson as 'an awkward and mannish transsexual who had celluloid fantasies' (2002). Nelson, who grew up as a man and had a sex change operation, is discussed in terms of sexual inadequacy. Nelson had 'always wanted to excite a man' but could not because (s)he was 'a clumsy transvestite who looked more like a caricature than a real woman (McGraw 2006). Because she was unable to please men, Leslie was said to have fallen in love with her gun collection, and guns 'had become her children' (McGraw 2002). When the police officers threatened to take the guns that she used to compensate for her sexual inadequacy, Leslie opened fire on them, killing several. Both the stories of Celeste Beard and Leslie Nelson point to sexual deviance and inadequacy as a reason for women's violence and loss of control. Real women, the kind that can please men, would never commit these kinds of crimes.

The final whore narrative, focused on men's ownership and control of women's bodies, describes men as (actually or metaphorically) the owners and controllers of women's bodies, physically and emotionally choosing their violence for them. These women are described as whores in the most literal sense, sold to men to be used as pawns in political violence. In these narratives, the men who have dominion over women's bodies force them to engage in violence; the women never have a choice. Stories later in this book about Chechen women 'sold into suicide' fit this narrative of (sexual) slavery, as do stories about women figuratively sexually enslaved by men. In these accounts, the violence was men's choice and men's plan; the women went along with it because they were physically or emotionally forced.

An example of the sexual slavery narrative are the stories told of Myra Hindley. Hindley, with Ian Brady, lured five children aged 10 to 18, male and female, out into the moors where Brady could rape them and kill them for his own sexual satisfaction (Ritchie 1991). Hindley actively recruited the victims, distracted them in order to allow Brady to catch them off guard, and participated in the clean-up and cover-up of the murders (Goodman 1986). Though Myra's descriptions of the murders show that she had a key role in their planning and execution, many of the stories of her involvement emphasize that she, too, was only an object of Ian Brady's sexual control (Goodman 1986). While even Hindley's accounts struggle with questions of her agency, she acknowledges an active role in the murders (Ritchie 1991). Still, the sex slave/owned woman narrative comes through in stories about her role in the Moors murders.

The characterization of violent women as *less than women* because of their deviant sexuality has a prominent place in the history of dealing with women's violence. As Gilbert explains, 'perhaps one of the most deeply held myths about violent women involves lesbianism. If women exhibit violent tendencies, they are not women but rather masculinized' (2002; Hart 1994). Though we proclaim women's sexual equality even in the military, regular 'servicewomen continue to grapple with the sexual images of dyke and whore framing their participation' and women who commit violence are more likely to experience the wrath of these stereotypical understandings (Meyer 1992).

THE SIGNIFICANCE OF NARRATIVES ABOUT WOMEN'S VIOLENCE

Through the employment of the mother, monster and whore narratives, work on violent women attributes their motivation to a problem with a woman's biological make-up and rarely deals with a woman's intellectual capability to make deliberate choices. As Toles Parkin documents:

> Perceptions of women's motivations for terrorism continue to be colored by the notion that women are emotional and irrational, perhaps even driven by hormonal imbalances; rarely have their actions been interpreted as intelligent, rational decisions. 'The average depiction of women terrorists draws on notions that they are (a) extremist feminists; (b) only bound into terrorism via a man; (c) only acting in supporting roles within terrorist organizations; (d) mentally inept; (e) unfeminine in some way; or any combination of the above.' (Toles Parkin 2004: 82, quoting Talbot 2001).

All of the reasons that Toles Parkins cites target women at the core of their personhood – their womanhood, their cognitive ability and their sanity are called into question. This negates any cause for which violent women may be acting.

These narratives of women's proscribed violence tell different stories, but they share a number of characteristics. First, they characterize violent women as psychologically handicapped and therefore unable to make their own decisions. Second, either by biology or psychology, they distinguish violent women from 'real' or 'regular' women, contrasting violence and true femininity. Through these dual discursive moves, narratives characterizing violent women in global politics as mothers, monsters and whores deprive women of agency and maintain subordinating stereotypes of women.

Whenever the stories of female violent criminals or female terrorists are presented in mainstream media, it is as a way to explain away the possibility that they made a conscious choice to commit political violence. The mother, monster and whore narratives exclude the possibility that women can choose to be violent because violent women interrupt gender stereotypes. 'Real' women are peaceful, conservative, virtuous and restrained; violent women ignore those boundaries of womanhood. Instead, the women on the pages of this book are the enemy from whom others, often innocent men, need protection. Their stories contradict the dominant narrative about what a woman is generally and about women's capacity for violence specifically. Their existence falls outside the ideal-type of the feminine characteristics of a 'real' woman. Because their stories do not resonate with these inherited images of femininity, violent women are marginalized in political discourse. Their choices are rarely seen as choices, and, when they are, they are characterized as apolitical. Their tales are sensationalized and fetishized in the gendered narratives that replace or substitute for their actual accounts. Stories of women's violence through their own eyes necessarily interrogate the ideal-typical understandings of what women are, which threatens the gendered order at all levels of politics. Those with a political interest in the gender order cannot hear or tell those stories; instead, stories are produced and reproduced where women's agency in their violence is denied.

Sensationalized stories of women's violence do not show equality. Instead, these (apparently) counterhegemonic discourses might not be actually counterhegemonic at all, but circumstantial confluences of interest which allow the hegemonic to decrease the appearance of hegemony (and thus the dissatisfaction of the subordinate other) without losing any power or dominance, absolute or relative. This understanding is inspired by Derrick Bell's discussion of fortuity in United States' (apparently) race-emancipatory policies. Bell contends that fortuity plays a substantial role in determining when (apparently) race-emancipatory policies are made, enforced and abandoned. Accordingly, Bell (2004) lays out two rules about the role of fortuity in racial policies: that the interest of blacks in achieving racial equality will only be served when that interest converges with whites' interest in consolidating power, and that the service of blacks' interest will stop when it would cause whites to lose relative power (Bell 2004: 69). If the interest-convergence rule can be rewritten for gender in global politics, it would argue that the interest of women's advancement will only be served when it converges with the interest of men in power, and will stop when it threatens male dominance. In this understanding, narratives which keep expanding women's 'place' to the extent that it appears that there are no limits, while maintaining limits, serve the interest of masculine power. *Gendered* descriptions of women's 'equality' in the perpetration of violence serve such a role. As mentioned in the introduction to this chapter, these discourses, couched in terms that deny women's agency, actually matter in global politics. If formative discourses are employed in relation to one another, then we live in a world not of objective truth but of competing stories (Hall 1999). This idea seems egalitarian enough until we begin to try to uncover which stories compete, who tells the stories that are competing, and whose stories go unheard. Participating in discourses and arguments of political significance is a matter of licence. The presentation of speech is a privilege that has many complexities, and presupposes social power:

> Hence the efficacy of the performative utterance presupposes a set of social relations, an institution, by virtue of which a particular individual, who is *authorized* to speak and *recognized* as such by others, is able to speak in a way that others will regard as acceptable under the circumstances. (Thompson 1999: 8–9)

Deleuze and Guattari agree on this point, contending that 'linguistics is nothing without a pragmatics (semiotic or political) to define the effectuation of the *condition of possibility* language and the *usage* of linguistic elements' (1988: 85). In other words, what is said matters, but what is unsaid matters as well, and the context, the source and the knower of who speaks and who does not all matter in the telling of stories and the making of assertions. Feminists analyse the content of what is said in politics to find what is neglected. Hilary Charlesworth calls this method 'searching for silences' (1999). Charlesworth understands that 'all systems of knowledge depend on deeming certain issues irrelevant, therefore silences are as important as positive rules' (1999: 381). Feminisms, then, search for the things that the traditional study of political science does not see (Maynard and Purvis 1994). In the context of feminism, texts that *do not* mention gender are making a statement about gender as clearly as those that are focused on gender – it is a statement that gender is unimportant. Likewise, as the mother, monster and whore narratives demonstrate, it is not only attention to women but the nature of that attention which matters for its impact on the perpetuation of gender subordination or advocacy for gender emancipation.

Applying this understanding to narratives about women's violence, two crucial insights can be reached. First, women's violence is not the only 'development' in global politics which merits attention; collective understandings of that violence are inseparable from the actual meaning. Spike Peterson contends that a gender oppression on the international level is 'dependent on hierarchical dichotomies naturalized through discourses to collective meaning systems into symbolic order' (1999: 40). Dominant discursive rules which marginalize women and femininities are actual rules. These rules engender a state of rule which governs (and genders) behaviour in global politics (Prugl 1999). This concept of political order comes from Nicholas Onuf's rule-based constructivist interpretation of global politics (1989). Onuf contends that speech acts, rules, and rule are the central elements in a systematic and inclusive framework to explain global politics: rules create a state of rule which defines the content and processes of global politics. Discourses like the mother, monster and whore narrative are 'imperial hermeneutics', which are 'the kind of reading that attempts to control, govern, regulate, or discipline text(s) in terms of policing the boundaries of meaning' (Hussain 2000: 29). These imperial hermeneutics police meaning in global politics. Meaning, in turn, controls the content of international relations stories; which, in turn, limits policy choices and frames of reference. Against these dominant discourses, then, feminisms engage in projects of discursive destabilization, looking for and pointing out the gendered silences and oppressions inherent in the stories that get told (Gibson-Graham 1994: 216). This book is one such project of discursive destabilization.

The project of discursive destabilization begins with the question of gendered voices. Christine Sylvester recognizes that there are a number of voices which go unheard in the discourses of international politics, while other voices make the rules that the owners of those unheard voices must follow (1999). She explains that 'fictional and postcolonial narratives, which purport to tell us about the lives of local people sandwiched in-between imperial motives and statist international politics, are out of view in conventionally constituted social science in general' (Sylvester 1999: 250–51). Sylvester extends the feminist argument that abstraction can be materially insidious. She contends that the international relations discipline 'needs to travel physically into the societies it purports to paint away with a brush labeled "the state" or "the international system" [and] ... to notice and appreciate its own capacity for the hybridity that postcolonialism discovers' (259). Along these lines, feminists contend that, in the international arena, women's voices often go unheard, and women's narratives often go unconsidered, in the formation of international policy (Tickner 1992). Often, women's narratives are replaced by men's stories about women's lives. Even when gendered 'feminine' voices are heard, they are incorporated into dominant discourse (if at all) in a partial way which leaves the international political discourse community largely gendered male (Tickner 2001: 1992).

The insight that discourses of global politics are gendered, both generally and specifically, in terms of women's violence is important in terms of the stories that we consider in this book. As mentioned in the introduction, (select) women's voices are increasingly visible in global politics. In the first decade of the twenty-first century, the UN Security Council mandated women's participation in peacemaking efforts; Liberia elected a woman president; and the United States had a female secretary of state for the second time in two consecutive presidential administrations. While many men's stories (like the tale of Condolezza Rice as a 'warrior princess') (Sjoberg 2006) remain, women policymakers' voices are earning some recognition. This book, however, argues that, while women's narratives are gaining an audience in global politics, this prominence is limited in subject matter to women who either assume traditionally feminine roles or maintain femininity while filling traditionally masculine roles.

Against this background, we recognize that women's narratives of their violence continue to be marginalized and others' narratives of their violence tell their stories without their permission. The observation that the discourses of global politics remain gendered, and that such gendering has tangible effects, helps us discover both *why* violent women's narratives are marginalized and what the impact of that marginalization is. The mother, monster and whore narratives that exclude women's agency from proscribed violence are a signal, we argue, of the continued subordination of women who do not fit our inherited conceptions of acceptable femininity. Instead, narratives and metaphors are used to singularize and other violent women. As discussed briefly in the introduction to this chapter, the employment of metaphors (such as mother, monster and whore narratives of women's violence) serves a function of expressing cognitive content that would otherwise be too complicated (Debatin 1995). A metaphor both simplifies and organizes content, allowing for human understanding and rational anticipation. A metaphor also allows a certain cognitive content, or version of the truth, to assume supremacy while appearing to be the only version of the story. A metaphor, therefore, is a constitutive model for thought (Debatin 1995). The mother, monster and whore narratives serve an orientational and world-disclosing function as inherited, but personal, experience, bridging the gaps between experience and thought. The central moment of synthetic power is the iconicity of the metaphor, which evokes specific sensory perceptions and integrates them into meaningful constellations. In other words, a metaphor serves the dual function of assigning conceptual meaning and granting cognoscibility. The narratives in this book at once make violent women cognizable and define them as lacking agency, motivation or rational reason in their violence.

Metaphors, however, are not static but constantly changing. A metaphor evolves, creating re-descriptions, which expose the contingency and partiality of the 'old' metaphor, but which also introduce new conceptual contingencies and partialities. Metaphor analysis cannot reduce conceptual contingency, but can provide a specific, linguistic mode of analysis for the contingencies of social and political relations, broadening horizons and extending insight into otherness and difference (Debatin 1995).

The discursive gendering of women's violence, then, is changeable rather than static. The employment of gendered narratives and the exercise of the gendered stereotypes which they contain has tangible effects. First, discursive subordination combines with and produces the material gendering of international politics; both are necessary components to understand gender oppression. Second, discursive subordination is to be seen as a barrier to 'solving' material gender oppression. If the dominant discourses which shape political understandings are reliant on oppressive constructions, oppression will become less visible, but will never disappear. Third, discourses directly affect social practices. Nancy Isenberg explains that 'discourse theory examines how narrative codes and conventions used in speech and writing not only transmit ideology but mediate and create social and cultural practices' (Isenberg 1992: 450). A discursive frame, or paradigm, consists of 'intersubjective systems of representations and representation-producing practice' (Laffey and Weldes 1997). Discourses thus can be seen as a feature of reality, as constitutive of reality, and as representative of reality; so long as it is understood that discourses exist not in egalitarian community, but in hierarchical competition. The mother, monster and whore narratives of women's violence, however subordinating and/or inaccurate, are *real* in global politics: they create the sensationalized images of women, gender and individual violence in global politics, and perpetuate the gendered discourses of global politics more generally.

Narratives which 'other' violent women both represent the continuation of subordinating images of women in global politics and are complicit in that continued subordination. Functionally, 'narratives of belonging also relationally construct difference and otherness and there has been an explosion of interest in this issue' (Anthias 2002: 277). In dichotomous terms, narratives of group belonging construct an 'inside' and an 'outside', and assign membership relationally. A person is either a 'real woman' or not a 'real woman'; gendered narratives implicitly or explicitly describe people in these terms. Membership then has meaning for the political relationships between those 'inside' and 'outside' or a group, or between groups. If a violent woman is not a 'real' woman, this has implications for the meaning of womanhood for violent and nonviolent women alike, as well as for the meaning of manhood for all men. Because they have a discursive component, groups are 'shifting constellations of social actors, depending on the ways that the boundaries of a denoted category are constructed' (Anthias 2002: 278). In other words, constructions of violent women can shift and change with culture and interest.

The mother, monster and whore narratives, then, serve as systems of signification which are productive (or reproductive) of their subject women which shift but maintain shape across time, culture and political structure (Milliken 1999).[13] According to Milliken, 'discourses make intelligible some ways of being in, and acting towards, the world, and of operationalizing a particular 'regime of truth' while excluding other possible modes of identity and action' (1999).

As we progress through this book, we will see the discourses of mothers, monsters and whores serving as systems of signification that define and produce women's violence, women more generally, and the global political atmosphere in which they reside. These discourses make violent women intelligible while resisting disrupting images of 'regular women' as peaceful and innocent. Across the world, stories tell away, marginalize and trivialize women's violence.

THREE

TRIPLE TRANSGRESSIONS AT ABU GHRAIB

From the front page of the *New York Times* to the most serious discussions in the United States Senate, the United States was rocked by a scandal referred to in historical context only as 'Abu Ghraib'. At the Abu Ghraib prison in Iraq in 2004, an as yet unknown number of photos were taken of American soldiers abusing Iraqi prisoners.[1] These pictures were later discovered by both the United States military and the media. The photos depicted, among other things,[2] Iraqi prisoners in compromising positions: hooked up to electric-shock devices, naked, forced to perform sexual acts on each other, and in other (sexually) compromising positions. Even now, American media discussion is plagued by speculation about remaining unreleased photos, which might include more war crimes perpetrated by women.[3] Torture in wartime is not a new phenomenon. While there is a purported international norm against torture, the United States military has been involved in torture scandals, particularly during armed conflict, as have a number of militaries around the world.[4] What was different and novel about the pictures from Abu Ghraib was the faces of the abusers. Traditionally, most military criminals have been men;[5] the stereotype of a war criminal definitely has a male face. At Abu Ghraib, the abusers were not all men; instead, three of them were women in their twenties (often referred to in the news as 'girls') who were also soldiers in the United States military. This chapter traces the (almost paradoxical) development that women have come to be accepted in the United States military as 'soldiers' but not as agents of (proscribed) violence. Women who are involved in or accused of proscribed violence in the military have committed not just the double transgression of violating the law and the standards of femininity, but also of violating the idealized image of militarized femininity (Enloe 2000), where a woman is at once innocent and non-violent *and* a soldier. A soldier can engage in torture, but a 'woman soldier' cannot be a torturer. After all, by its very nature, the military does *allow* certain violence in certain situations. Still, the exclusion of women from combat arms positions decreases the amount of violence they are allowed compared to men, who are permitted to serve in combat arms positions. Women in the military are soldiers, but not *combat* soldiers; they have weapons, but are generally not expected to use them. In addition to the combat arms band, women, like men, are limited to military rules and regulations as to when the use of violence is permitted. Thus, even in an organization the primary task of which is violence, there is proscribed violence. This is not to say that the United States military embraces men who commit violence in violation of military policies or international laws. Quite the opposite, of course: the military has in place an intricate system of laws, trials and punishments to minimize these violations and redress them when committed. In other words, a certain amount of proscribed violence is expected by those who run the military – soldiers will sometimes fall out of line, require reprimand, and need to be reminded of the rule structure. Women's proscribed violence, however, is treated differently, and much more effort is put into emphasis on the singularity of women's war crimes. Both internal and media stories of women's proscribed violence *within* the United States military involve the mother, monster and whore narratives and draw a careful distinction between *singular* women's violence and carefully constructed militarized femininities.

Certainly, the women who were accused of war crimes at Abu Ghraib were not the first women in history to be allegedly involved in or convicted of proscribed violence in a military situation. A

Viking named Sela is described as an 'accomplished Pirate' who often 'took the biggest loot' in ship-robbing expeditions (Jesch 1991). In seventeenth-century France, a Mademoiselle La Maupin was known for killing men who refused her challenge to a duel (Baldick 1965). She was pardoned by King Louis XIV. Still, narratives of women's war crimes are sparse, likely caused by the limited roles women have been allowed in war and the extreme taboo of women's war crimes. This chapter focuses on women's war crimes within the United States military, including popular and institutional reactions. Chapter 6 returns to the question of women's war crimes in a somewhat different context: the perpetration of genocide. The differences between the women in this chapter and those in Chapter 6 are many, including membership of a highly structured military organization with professional rules and social norms. This chapter investigates the relationship between the gender of the perpetrators at Abu Ghraib, their crimes, and the responses of the United States military, as well as members of the public who saw them as members of that military.

FEMALE TORTURERS IN NAZI GERMAN FORCES

There were mother, monster and whore narratives around militarized femininity before those women accused of perpetrating abuses at Abu Ghraib. Though the offences were fifty years ago, the narratives around women members of Nazi forces during the Second World War include images of mothers, monsters and whores, much like those of military women involved in torture in the twenty-first century. One of the most prominent examples is the story told of Ilse Koch.

Ilse Koch was married to Karl Koch, the commander of the concentration camp at Buchenwald. Ilse's role in the torture and murder of prisoners at the camp was substantial. Several accounts describe a number of her torture tactics and terror-inspiring method. Koch is said to have collected tattoos from the skin of murdered inmates, and constructed household items from that skin, such as lampshades and other decorative household pieces (Weber 2003). Her family dinner table was decorated with the shrunken heads of her victims. She had a reputation for sadistic cruelty towards prisoners

(Pryzembel 2001). Because of this reputation, she was often referred to as the 'Bitch of Buchenwald' (Weber 2003).

Explanations of Ilse Koch's involvement in the German military cause often centre around her sexual relationship with Sturmabteilung (SA) soldiers – she is characterized as having been converted to the Nazi cause and methods through this involvement. Her story is told as one of a woman manipulated by the sexual prowess of the men: driven by her sexual urges to adopt their habits, and led by her erotomania to outdo their cruelty. This is consistent with the whore narratives which emphasize erotomania. When Koch is not presented as her husband's woman, she is presented as Hitler's; news and Internet articles depict her as Hitler's woman and pawn, reminiscent of the whore narrative that focuses on control by men and sexual ownership.

The little information that we have about the actual Ilse Koch contradicts that story. Her involvement with the SA seems to have been independent of her relationships with fellow prison workers. Before marrying Karl Koch, Ilse served as a guard at the Sachsenhausen concentration camp (Duncan 2004). Her husband was arrested for treason against the Nazi regime, but Ilse stayed behind, maintaining her position of power in the torture camp (Weber 2003). Her power over her subordinates has been characterized as 'absolute'; stories that 'she had a whip fitted with razor blades at the end, which she used on female prisoners' were confirmed in her later trial (Duncan 2004). The stories told at Koch's trial recognized that she had more agency than the inherited monster and whore narratives would attribute to her.

Other German women who were formally members of the German military during the Second World War were also accused of war crimes as a result of their actions. These include Elizabeth Volkenrath, Herta Oberhauser, Dorthea Binz and Irma Grese. Elizabeth Volkenrath served as a Schutzstaffel (SS) supervisor at several concentration camps during the Second World War. She worked at Ravensbruck, Auschwitz and Bergen–Belsen. She took part in the selection and abuse of prisoners and oversaw hangings. Volkenrath was sentenced to death and hanged on 13 December 1945. She was convicted of beating prisoners, denying them food, and personally delivering them to the gas chamber (Brown 2002). Stories characterize Volkenrath as a young woman (she was 26 when she was executed), desperate for male attention, who committed horrendous violence because she was still single and held out little hope of winning a man's affection in some other way. As a woman without male attention, she is 'less than a woman'. This tale places her in the erotic dysfunction stream of the whore narrative.

Other women in similar positions committed similar horrors and inspired similar stylized narratives. Dr Herta Oberhauser was the resident physician at Auschwitz (Weindling 2006). She killed children with oil injections, and then removed their limbs and vital organs. She rubbed ground glass and sawdust into wounds. She operated on healthy women for the purpose of medical experimentation. Oberhauser has been characterized as an extraordinarily vain woman (Brown 2002), as one who took her loneliness out on other women, as a mentally unstable monster (consistent with the monster narrative) incapable of normal social interaction (Weindling 2006).

Dorothea Binz, who also worked at Auschwitz, has been described as unyielding, leading torture sessions and training some of the most brutal guards in the Nazi concentration camps (Christie 2006). She was in charge of around 50,000 women and children prisoners. She is said to have supervised gas-chamber killings, shootings, starvations and freezings (Brown 2002). There is evidence that she beat, slapped, kicked, shot, whipped and abused women for long periods of time, in addition to setting a trained fighting dog on them (Christie 2006). Binz's violence is often explained by her romantic relationship with Edmund Brauning, who encouraged her to go with him on romantic walks around the camp to watch the abuse of women, after which they would walk away laughing. He is said to have indoctrinated Binz, who began her career as a maid, into violence (Brown 2002). Binz's violence is told as violence for 'love's sake', another example of the whore narrative. Along the same lines, Irma Grese, who was notorious for torturing female prisoners at a number of prison camps (all before her twentieth birthday), has been characterized as blinded by her sexual obsession with medical experimenter Josef Mengele and camp commandant Kramer (Duncan 2004; Christie 2006).

WOMEN'S CRIMES AND THE US MILITARY

There is very little documented history of proscribed violence by women within the United States military. There are a number of reasons for this dearth of coverage. First, the United States military has systematically excluded women from participation in combat activities (MacKnick 1999; D'Amico 1990), where the opportunities to commit proscribed violence are most obvious. Second, dominant narratives of American women's relationship with the military, even when women are soldiers, characterize men as fighters and women as those who are fought for (Sjoberg 2006; Brennan 1994). Third, women's violence is ignored or downplayed because it contradicts idealized images of militarized femininity, (discussed at the end of this chapter) (Enloe 1993, 1990). Finally, the violence women affiliated with the United States military did commit before Abu Ghraib was generally distanced from their roles as members of the military; it was described as coincidental, rather than on-the-job.

What history of United States military women's violence does exist echoes the characterizations of women in the Nazi forces and provides some foreshadowing for the treatment of the women at Abu Ghraib. One form of women's violence in violation of military rules is their participation in military operations without permission. There is a fairly significant literature which deals with women who participated both in the fighting of the United States Civil War and in the capture and torture of enemy prisoners in that war. DeAnne Blanton and Laurie Cook characterize Confederate women in the civil war as 'fighting like demons' (2002). Ellen Renshaw House, a woman who fought for the South, characterized herself as a 'very violent Rebel' who tortured and killed Union soldiers (House and Southerland 1996).

Other women members of the United States military who committed proscribed violence did so while they were soldiers but not on the job. Perhaps the most notorious of these women is Diane Zamora, a midshipman (*sic*) in the United States Naval Academy, who participated in the murder of another woman, Adrienne Davis (Verhovek 1996). Her case, dubbed the 'Texas Cadet Murder', made national news. The woman that she and her boyfriend, David Graham, killed was described as a rival for Graham's affection. Zamora was at once characterized as psychologically disturbed and easily manipulated – *bad*, but incapable of making such a decision *as a woman* (*New York Times* 1998). David Graham was described as 'her mother, her father, and her lover at once', and Zamora as a 'troubled young woman dominated by a controlling young man' (Bouchard-Kerr 2003). It is not enough to characterize Zamora as without control of her choices or her faculties, however. She is also said to have been 'psychopathically deviant and paranoid' and may have 'ordered David to kill Adrienne to prove his love' (Bouchard-Kerr 2003). A Lifetime television movie, *Love's Deadly Triangle*, characterized Zamora as unstable and monstrous (Carter 1997).

Though women in the United States military have been accused of violent crimes, and women in militaries around the world have been accused of war crimes, it was not until stories about the abuse at Abu Ghraib broke that women in the United States military were publicly implicated in war crimes. This chapter seeks to understand why that development was the benchmark in the development of American military culture that it was, and to place the narratives concerning the women implicated in the Abu Ghraib abuse within the broader narratives of militarized femininity and of violent women as mothers, monsters and whores.

THE STORIES OF GENDER AND ABU GHRAIB

The first woman commander in a combat zone in United States military history supervised a group of military police, including men and women, who systematically employed methods of sexual torture on prisoners and photographed each other doing so. The evidence of this alleged torture comes in the form of photographs and videos taken at an Iraqi prison called Abu Ghraib, which was a political prison during the Saddam Hussein regime and was utilized by the occupying United States military as a detention facility. The pictures show prisoners in compromising positions and American soldiers, often smiling, standing over them. The blame for this abuse has been laid everywhere, from the soldiers who interacted with the prisoners to the Pentagon, and in between. Whether the troops were following orders, as they have claimed, engaging in formally forbidden behaviour, as the military claimed, or possibly both, remains undetermined in the web of different stories. What is obvious is that the public tales about the three women soldiers implicated in the prison abuse scandal at Abu Ghraib and the general who commanded them have been filled with the stories of the mother, monster and whore narratives, layered over comparisons between their stories and their perceived inability to meet preconceived definitions of militarized femininity in the United States military.

FEMALE PERPETRATORS OF SEXUAL TORTURE IN IRAQ

> Her face is familiar to millions of people around the world as one of two smiling American soldiers seen in a picture standing behind a group of naked, hooded Iraqis stacked in a pyramid. ... Harman is accused by the Army of taking photographs of that pyramid and ... of Iraqis who were told to strip and masturbate in front of other prisoners and guards. (AP, 10 May 2004)

Scholars researching issues of gender in global politics have worked for decades to bring attention to wartime rape as a war crime. Judith Gardam observes that 'nowhere is women's marginalization more evident than in the attitude of the law of armed conflict to rape, an experience limited to women', and describes rape in war as a site where women's oppression can undoubtedly be documented (Gardam 1993b: 358–9; Buchanan 2002). While wartime rape is not per se limited to women (as the events at Abu Ghraib demonstrate), it both disproportionately affects women and feminizes those who are not women but rape victims (Hansen 2001: 59; Blanchard 2003). Gardam contends that the frequency and severity of wartime rape demonstrates an 'air of permissibility' about the treatment of women in war (1993b; Sjoberg 2007: 95). Gardam documents that 'it is difficult to find any support for the view that non-combatant immunity at any time in its development has included [effective] protection from rape' (1993b: 359). Spike Peterson and Anne Sisson Runyan argue that there are a number of distinctly institutionalized types of wartime rape, including recreational, national security and genocidal, which are all steeped in gender oppression (Peterson and Runyan 1999: 127). Gardam explains that, 'indeed, feminists have argued that in one sense; rape is never truly individual, but an integral part of the system ensuring the maintenance of the subordination of women' (Gardam 1993b: 363–4). Card discusses what she calls a punishment fantasy that men would actually suffer for the rapes they commit in wartime. She explains that she calls it 'a *fantasy* because until women have more political power, including military power (by which I mean martial power, the power to engage in war), such penalty has no chance of being implemented' (Card 1996: 16).

In various studies, feminists have described rape in war as terrorism (Card 1996: 6), aggression (Goldstein 2001: 364), dominance (Card 1996: 7), genetic imperialism (Card 1996: 7), strategy (Hansen 2001: 59), torture (Schott 1996: 23), and gender oppression (MacKinnon 1993: 38; Gardam 1993b: 363). Studies of wartime rape have illuminated a number of its negative consequences for women. In the 1990s, advocacy around the issue inspired specific international legal provisions making systemic rape a war crime, largely hailed as important protection for women, since rape is historically the least prosecuted war crime. Sexual abuse of men, though it has doubtlessly occurred, has been addressed less than wartime rape of women, most likely because it is much less frequent. Abuse by women has received even less attention, if it has ever happened before in the United States military. It appears unprecedented, then, that three military police officers convicted of involvement in the abuse at Abu Ghraib were women: Lynndie England, Sabrina Harman and Megan Ambuhl. The soldiers are accused of sodomizing prisoners, forcing them to masturbate, and forcing them to perform homosexual acts on each other (Smith and White 2005). Another photograph has a hooded prisoner attached to wires. As Karpinski describes, abuse of women also took place. She explains that there was a teenager that

> One of our female MPs [military police officers] had taken under her wing, tried to boost her spirits, and taught a bit of English. But while the MP was escorting the Iraqi woman in another part of the prison that day, somebody had told the MP to lift up the teenager's shirt and expose her breasts to the camera. The MP complied.
> (Karpinski and Strasser 2005: 18)

TRIPLE TRANSGRESSIONS 67

Underneath Karpinski's stylized narrative is a description of the sexual exploitation of prisoners for the purpose of (child) pornography. The photos and videos indicate that the MPs at Abu Ghraib, including England, Harman and Ambuhl, engaged in sexual abuse, torture and rape.

While the women who were involved in the abuse at Abu Ghraib received attention on the Internet and in alternative media sources, the accounts of their actions in the mainstream media were initially very limited. First, while the photos were on the front page of every American newspaper for several weeks, the women who were in them and took them were given unusually little attention *as individuals* and unusually high attention *as women*. If fact, as we will discuss later, where the women involved in the prisoner abuse at Abu Ghraib were most famous was the world of Internet pornography. Elsewhere they were characterized at once as monsters, victims, and whores: as helpless and inhuman.

LYNNDIE ENGLAND

In the coverage of the three women involved in the prison abuse, Lynndie England received the most press attention. Her 2005 trial was highly publicized, as a court found her unable to understand her own guilty plea. England was charged with conspiracy to maltreat prisoners and assault consummated by battery. On 30 April 2005 she entered a guilty plea. In pleading guilty to the charges against her, England said 'she knew she was committing wrongful acts when she took part in the mistreatment of Iraqi detainees', but the court accepted fellow MP (and ex-boyfriend) Charles Graner's testimony that England believed the photos were meant to be a 'legitimate training aid for other guards instead' (Badger 2005a). On 4 May 2005, England's plea bargain was tossed out because Graner's suggestion that she did not understand her own actions held weight with the court (Badger 2005a).

On retrial in September of 2005, England was convicted on all but one count, and sentenced to three years at Brig Miramar in San Diego, California (Harris 2005; Badger 2005b). In the press coverage of her trial, England's sexual relationship with Charles Graner has been the subject of much attention (Tetreault 2006). Because of her relationship with Graner, she was characterized as an 'undisciplined, sexually overactive' soldier (Atlanta Journal-Constitution 2004). England and Graner met prior to their deployment to Iraq and had a sexual relationship while stationed in Virginia (McKelvey 2006). Many media sources have found it important to describe that sexual relationship graphically, including certain positions and activities with which the couple experimented (Harwood 2004; McKelvey 2006). Others have speculated that England must have been sexually abused as a child in order to have committed the atrocities that she did, though no independent evidence of such abuse exists. England has merited such headlines as 'The small town girl who became the all American monster' (Riddell 2004). She was also the inspiration for the Rolling Stones song 'Dangerous Beauty' (Jagger and Richards 2005). In 'Dangerous Beauty', the Rolling Stones sing to England in very sexualized way, calling her the 'lady with the leash' and asking her 'was it funny on the midnight shift/ I bet you had your fair share of stiffs' (Jagger and Richards 2005). They praise her (sarcastically), telling her she's 'a natural at working with dogs' (Jagger and Richards 2005). The song flows from one sexual characterization to another, sensationalizing her 'dealing out electric shocks' and calling her a 'bit of booty' (Jagger and Richards 2005).

The publication of interviews with England did not seem to change the demeaning tone of public stories about her. In the article published as a result of the only interview England has given, the first paragraph describes her appearance in very gendered terms: she used to be the 'waiflike girl with a devilish grin', whereas now she is '30 pounds heavier' (McKelvey 2006). Throughout the article, England's femininity is constantly the subject of interrogation. She is characterized as having a 'pretty smile' but being a girl who 'wore her hair short and no makeup' (McKelvey 2006). The author finds it important that she 'hit softballs', 'joined Future Farmers of America, and played cops and robbers, firing off pop guns as she ran through the uncut fields around her home' (McKelvey 2006). Several times, the article mentions her being in love with Graner as an excuse for her behaviour. For example, 'Lynndie found out you're damned if you do and damned if you don't. And being in love with Graner, that made it even harder' (McKelvey 2006). The article is quick to point out General Janis Karpinski's characterization of England as 'a quiet girl' who 'didn't know anybody' until she met Graner. General Karpinski, her commanding general, also characterizes England as attention-starved and under Graner's control: 'She was blown away ... she felt like someone was finally talking to her. Paying attention. He seemed far more experienced and worldly than anyone she new. It only took a few short conversations. She was enamored with him' (McKelvey 2006; Karpinski and Strasser 2005). An article in *Marie Claire* characterizes her as his sex slave: 'Whenever Graner asked her to, England would strike a pose', and chronicles their pattern of taking pornographic pictures while characterizing her as 'a little plaything for him' (McKelvey 2006). Several reports use England's learning disability to affirm this version of the story (Badger 2005c). She is described as 'small', 'not assertive or aggressive', 'naïve', and 'young and innocent', exchanging sex for a feeling of safeness and protection (McKelvey 2006). McKelvey concludes that 'England was a small-town girl, not even of legal drinking age, when she found herself halfway around the world, in an amoral place, surrounded by violence and infatuated with a volatile, manipulative man' (2006).

The *Guardian* describes England as a member of the 'queens of violence, from Penthesilea of the Amazons to Uma Thurman in Kill Bill' who 'can attract awe', but asserts that 'Lynndie is no upmarket she-devil. Instead, the response to Abu Ghraib sandwiches her somewhere between Myra Hindley and Maxine Carr in an all-woman axis of evil' (Riddell 2004). This article describes England as of 'childish physique' and with 'terrible taste in men' (Riddell 2004). It laments that, 'back home, family and friends are trying to work out how a "sweet, down-to-earth" paper-pusher who wanted to be a weather girl turned into a preening sexual predator' (Riddell 2004). Riddell is quick to gender England's violence specifically and women's violence more generally:

> Nor are violent women the aberration they are sometimes painted. Mothers ready to defend their children to death are a common stereotype, while any notion that women are Stepford soldiers, caring and compliant, was challenged way before Boudicca headed the Iceni. But, though female warriors have a long history, their legends rarely dabble in gory detail, let alone the fact that bloodlust can be triggered by more role than gender. (Riddell 2004)

In the above passage and throughout the article, Riddell accomplishes exactly the task she complains others do: singularizing violent women and blaming everyone but them for their decisions (2004). Riddell blames motherhood and societal role, as well as the United States government, for women's violence generally and England's specifically. She explains, 'Lynndie England, however unpleasant, is not the villain of this debacle. She is what happens when politicians prosecute shambolic wars in the name of piety' (Riddell 2004). In other words, men's wars do this to weak women. England's violence is the fault of her womanhood or sexuality gone awry and of the men who made decisions for her, but could not have been her choice.

SABRINA HARMAN

A brief interview with Sabrina Harman was published after she was charged (CNN.com 2004). She claimed that she was not responsible for the abuses at Abu Ghraib because she was just following orders (CNN.com 2004). After that interview, very little mainstream publicity was focused on Harman, on her fellow female perpetrators, or on the crimes with which they were charged, save the coverage of England's trial. Harman gave an interview in early 2005 on *20/20*. When asked about the abuse, Harman claimed that she 'doesn't think she did anything wrong' (*20/20* 2005). Presented with the photos of her abuse, which *20/20* characterized as 'some of the prison scandal's most iconic photos', Harman said 'she never hurt anyone' (*20/20* 2005).

Harman is seen in one picture smiling behind a pyramid of naked prisoners, and is alleged to have been involved with causing a prisoner to stand on top of a box with wires attached to his arms for days. According to the *Washington Post*, 'Harman is accused by the army of taking photographs of that pyramid and videotaping detainees who were ordered to strip and masturbate in front of other prisoners and soldiers' (Spinner 2004). It was her camera that took most of the pictures which have been publicized. She also told her girlfriend about the abuse long before the media story or the military investigation, which suggests that she knew that something wrong had been occurring (Powell 2005).

Narratives about Harman emphasize both her femininity and her sexuality. In the first four months of her duty, Harman was stationed in Hillah, supporting the Iraqi police. She is characterized as 'especially popular with kids', and it is often written that she bought a refrigerator for a family that made her home-cooked meals (Delahoussaye 2005). These stories emphasize Harman's softer side, and focus both on her maternal instinct and on her need to belong, even in a faraway land. At her trial, a letter to her girlfriend was read into the record, where Harman said that 'these people are going too far' and 'Kelly, it's awful. I thought I could handle anything, but I was wrong' (MSNBC.com 2005).

An alternative narrative in the media centres on the fact that Sabrina Harman is a lesbian, who wrote letters home to her partner, Kelly Bryant (Powell 2005). While several news sources were careful to refer to Bryant as Harman's 'roommate' (Edgar 2005), others used their same-sex relationship as fodder to sensationalize their stories. Several Internet pornography sites published re-enactments both of Harman's lesbian relationships and of the abuse she was alleged to have committed at Abu Ghraib.[6] Several other lesbian porn sites have added Harman's name to their pages so that it comes up on a search engine. Harman and her partner are included in several Usenet porn stores, which link the hedonism of her lesbianism and the lesbianism of her abuse.[7] Stories which emphasize her lesbianism use it to describe Harman as hard and cold. They describe her as a lonely woman who 'didn't have anyone to turn to' and was therefore hardened (ABCNews. com 2005). In these stories, she went 'numb and completely detached from reality' because a lesbian has problems feeling appropriately (*20/20* 2005). These stories focus on her lesbianism as erotic dysfunction. Other media stories treat her sexual perversion as an extension of her lesbianism, calling her a necrophiliac, at once labelling her with erotomania and sexual inadequacy (Burke 2004).

Harman herself adamantly claims both that she did not do anything wrong and that, if she did, she did not know it (Coman and Freeman 2004). She describes herself as a scapegoat, and explains that she knew nothing about the Geneva Convention or any other prohibition that would have forbidden her behaviour (Spinner 2004; Coman and Freeman 2004). Harman was sentenced to six months in a military prison and given a dishonorable discharge from the military forces.

MEGAN AMBUHL

Megan Graner (then Ambuhl, and still Ambuhl in public appearances), the third woman implicated in the prison scandal, has sought media attention in order to tell her side of the story. She is a strong advocate of clemency for the involved soldiers. Megan Ambuhl was convicted of conspiracy to commit abuse and demoted within the military, but was not convicted of any direct involvement with the abuse. She points the finger at Maj. Gen. Geoffrey Miller, and contends that the United States government 'started at the bottom when what they should have done was start at the top' in assigning blame for the abuse (Ambuhl 2006). Ambuhl points out that 'soldiers sentenced to 3, 8, and 10 years for this is much more harsh than any other sentence handed down for about 70 similar cases where soldiers were facing the same or more prison time' (Ambuhl 2006). She insists that 'all the superiors knew, and you see how many of them plead the 5th at CPL Graner's trial', a statement that she believes 'speaks volumes' (Ambuhl 2006). Though Ambuhl does not contend that the soldiers at Abu Ghraib did nothing wrong, she argues that they did not have agency in their choices. Ambuhl runs a website, 'supportmpscapegoats.com', which is petitioning for clemency for the involved military police (MPs). She is careful to limit her public exposure to venues where she can advocate for clemency for the involved soldiers.[8] Ambuhl's requests are not specifically gendered, and she requests clemency for the men involved in the prison abuse as well, despite the fact that the men are often characterized as the ringleaders and the women the followers.

Despite Ambuhl's gender-neutral advocacy, public stories about her have been very gendered. In news articles about her behaviour, Ambuhl is characterized as someone who 'did not understand' what she had got into and 'asked few questions because she did not know what to ask' (White 2006). The paradox of the emphasis on her abuse and her humanity is visible is Stephen Welsh's (2004) account of her behaviour:

> Ambuhl reportedly was present during sexually humiliating abuse including the formation and photographing of a human pyramid of nude detainees, and was partially visible in a photograph of Pfc. Lynndie England holding a leash attached to a nude detainee.

At the same time, several detainees reportedly praised Ambuhl for treating them humanely, and she apparently came to the aid of a detainee who had difficulty breathing after being punched by another soldier. (Welsh 2004)

On the one hand, this account accuses Ambuhl of witnessing and participating in some of the crimes that have come to mark the notoriety of the soldiers at Abu Ghraib. On the other hand, it implies that she could not have been directly involved because she was kind, and even maternal, to the prisoners. Harry Volzer, Ambuhl's attorney, played the gender card in her defence, giving an interview to *Newsweek* where he said: 'I feel sorry for the women. I don't think there's much they could have done to control their situation' (Scelfo 2004). Volzer went on to comment that he felt especially sorry for England, who was 'such a tiny little thing' (Scelfo 2004). He describes Ambuhl as feminine, and claims that all of the soldiers and prisoners at Abu Ghraib knew her as 'loving and caring' (Scelfo 2004).

A different strand of stories about Megan Ambuhl emphasizes the role of sexuality during her time at Abu Ghraib. The National Coalition for the Protection of Children and Families has accentuated the sexual part of Ambuhl's involvement in the abuse, giving her a very public lesson in 'sexual morality' (2006). This, like several other accounts, emphasizes Ambuhl's sexual relationship with Charles Graner while he was involved with, and fathering a child with, Lynndie England. It characterizes her relationship with Graner, and their mutual abuse of prisoners, as evidence that she is a 'selfish nihilist preoccupied with pleasure (National Coalition 2006). Likewise, Powell characterizes her relationship with Lynndie England and Charles Graner as fodder for a soap opera, dramatizing the sexuality in the situation (2005).

PUBLIC REPRESENTATIONS OF THE FEMALE TORTURERS AS A GROUP

The three women accused and convicted of war crimes at Abu Ghraib had very little in common, but inherited common fame and blame for their roles in the abuse there. They were at once characterized as at fault for the abuse and lacking agency in their behaviour. They also shared fame in the world of Internet pornography, where their abuse is replicated for entertainment purposes. In May and June of 2004, a Google search, which is fast becoming the pulse of American culture, for Harman, Ambuhl or England turned up several million results. More than 99 per cent of these results were pornography sites promoting either the images taken at Abu Ghraib or actor recreations of the situations. Years later, their notoriety has died down, but there are still a number of sites which base their promotion on pornographic pictures depicting or mimicking the women at Abu Ghraib. Several prominent political figures, such as Rush Limbaugh and Representative Shays from Connecticut, have characterized the events at Abu Ghraib as pornography rather than torture, using phrases like 'good old fashioned American porn' (Gogola 2006). These characterizations imply both that there was nothing aberrant about these events at Abu Ghraib and that it is acceptable to present women and racialized others as sex objects for public consumption.

Several feminist anti-pornography advocates have criticized this assumption even when the making of the pornography is at least apparently consensual. Susan Brownmiller explains:

> There can be no 'equality' in porn; no female equivalent, no turning of the tables in the name of bawdy fun. Pornography, like rape, is a male intervention, designed to dehumanize women, to reduce the female to an object of sexual access.... Pornography is essence of anti-female propaganda. (Brownmiller 1975: 394)

Andrea Dworkin has called pornography 'a civil rights issue for women' (1986), and Catherine MacKinnon has classified pornography as harmful in production and consumption (2001). The pornographic aspect of the abuse at Abu Ghraib implicates these issues doubly, since many of the pictures involve people involuntarily photographed.

The problem with the narratives about the women who participated in the abuse at Abu Ghraib is not that the stories are stylized or false. The argument of this chapter is not that the behaviour was typical of women soldiers, or that it had anything to do with their being women that makes either these women or the narratives about their behaviour important. Instead, the media, the United States, and a world full of socially constructed and reinforced gender stereotypes *were not ready* for the reality of women sexual abusers (Sjoberg 2007). Rising rumours of these women's sexual perversion, necrophilia, and even nymphomania, provided an acceptable public discourse for their stories. This public discourse emphasizes the perversity of the relationships not only between the abusers and the victims, but between the abusers themselves. Much has been made of the fact that Lynndie England had Charles Graner's baby although he married Megan Ambuhl (Powell 2005). These relationships are fetishized, told as a story that there was *something wrong* with the sexuality of these violent women which at once explains their violence and allows them to be treated as sexual objects, porn stars. These women's violence has been explained by their sexuality in a number of accounts. Their actions have been characterized in scholarly accounts as sadism (Apter 2006), masochistic dominatrix games (Jagodzinski 2006), bestiality (Puar 2006) and nymphomania (Paul 2005). They were not *women who chose to commit violence*; they were whores who could not control their need for sex or violence.

GENERAL JANIS KARPINSKI

Only a few months into the war in Iraq, the United States military made history by appointing a female general to a command post in a combat zone. Janis Karpinski, appointed in June of 2003, was an army reserve general charged with heading sixteen United States military detention centres in Iraq. Karpinski was the sole female commander in Iraq. She had been to the Middle East before, as a military training officer and as an intelligence officer with the Special Forces in the First Gulf War (Karpinski and Strasser 2005). In the Second Gulf War, her command of sixteen prisons included 3,400 army reservists, mostly military police. Though the soldiers under her command had little in common, they were all undertrained in the business of running military prisons (Karpinski and Strasser 2005).

Karpinski's appointment was news; she described being treated 'as a novelty; even as something of a celebrity' (Karpinski and Strasser 2005: 166). She describes receiving attention on the basis of her gender at almost every turn, with soldiers, the command and the media (Karpinski 2006). An article in the *St. Petersburg Times* celebrated the addition of a feminizing influence, painting her as a 'caring' woman who 'loves' her soldiers like her children (Martin 2003: A8). Karpinski's femininity was extolled as a virtue as she took command of war prisons. In news stories, her maternal nature was emphasized. Still, she was at the same time treated as an object of fear. She explains that 'the male bias of the branch was probably sharpened by the insecurity' because MPs were already emasculated as the 'little guns' in military discourse (Karpinski and Strasser 2005: 61). Still, before deploying, Karpinski spoke with pride about her observation that the military has come to treat female soldiers like male soldiers (Martin 2003: A8). Her outlook would change during the time she spent in Iraq.

Excitement and fear over Karpinski's ability to break glass ceilings for women in the military did not last long. It was followed mere months later with front-page stories of prisoner abuse that happened under her command at Abu Ghraib.[9] Karpinski had made the decision to reopen the Abu Ghraib prison due to a shortage of suitable facilities, but it had only been open a few months when the prison became the subject of an official investigation, targeting, among others, Karpinski's MPs. In addition to evidence discussed earlier of individual participation in abuse, the military investigation uncovered systematic patterns of discomfort, shock, rape and sodomy (Taguba 2004).

While the military both performed its own investigations and commissioned external reports, queries into the abuse have been unable to discern whether the perpetrators were directed to engage in the abuse or made the choice on their own (Taguba 2004; Fay 2004). In fact, none of the MPs' individual trials reached a conclusion concerning the ultimate responsibility for the abuse. For her part, General Karpinski insists that she had no knowledge of the torture until it was investigated, and then was asked to keep quiet (Karpinski and Strasser 2005). In her memoirs, Karpinski contends that she was a convenient scapegoat as a woman (whom the army did not want) and a reservist (who is not respected) (Karpinski and Strasser 2005). She accepts her share of the responsibility for the abuse, but explains that 'I do not accept the aspersions cast upon the great majority of soldiers who worked at Abu Ghraib and other prisons. Nor do I accept my assigned role as the sacrificial lamb of the tale' (Karpinski and Strasser

2005).[10] Karpinski recognizes weaknesses in her leadership, but also points to the impossible nature of her task, since she inherited an inexperienced and disorganized force (Karpinski and Strasser 2005). She also contends that it is no coincidence that the scapegoat was a woman. In fact, she resents being used to produce a 'new image of what happens when women go to battle' and slow the gender integration of the military (Karpinski and Strasser 2005).

Karpinski is convinced that several members of the military command structure in Iraq were determined not to see her succeed, and broke several rules of investigation to hide from her the abuse under her command (2006). In our personal interview, Karpinski explained that her success in combat command would have opened the doors for her and other women to the most envied posts in the Pentagon, which require successful command in a combat zone for serious consideration (2006). Since a woman had never been in command in a combat zone, women individually and as a group were (and remain) considered unqualified for those positions (Karpinski 2006). Karpinski relates that, seeing what happened to her, other women eligible for combat command posts have not been eager to seek them for fear of ruining their military careers (2006).

In her book, Karpinski targets the military for intentionally blaming women for a systemic problem. She explains that 'the abuses at Abu Ghraib were indeed an aberration. But they were not the work of a few wayward soldiers and their female leader' (Karpinski and Strasser 2005: 5). 'Instead, they were the result of conflicting orders and confused standards extending from the military commanders in Iraq all the way to the summit of civilian leadership in Washington' (5). Though she never explicitly says so, Karpinski clearly feels that the way she was treated in the aftermath of the abuse at Abu Ghraib was an intentional manufacture of news in order to keep in place, and even lower, the glass ceiling for women in the command structure of the US Army (2006).

As Karpinski speaks, it appears impossible for her to separate tales of the gendered nature of her military experience and her gendered experience with the fallout from the prisoner abuse at Abu Ghraib. Karpinski describes life in the military as a very gendered experience from day one. She recounts sexual harassment, blackmail and unequal treatment. She remembers that 'some women played into the stereotypes' but that you could not 'just slide into any gray areas if you were a woman. If you had come through Fort McClellan ... you were rumored to be a lesbian ... if you weren't a lesbian, then you must be sleeping with every man in sight' (Karpinski and Strasser 2005: 78). Karpinski had the impression that 'the army might be opening doors to women, but the old boys network continued to have its fun at women's expense' (78).

Karpinski recounts that her leadership experiences were every bit as gendered as what she experienced when going through the ranks (2006). She describes commanding generals who made comments about her appearance and touched her without her permission, intentionally marginalizing her authority (Karpinski 2006). She recalls that 'the troops in the ranks treated me as a novelty, even as something of a celebrity' (Karpinski and Strasser 2005: 166). Karpinski experienced combat command as a woman, as a target, as an oddity, and ultimately as the 'fall guy' for the Iraqi prison abuse scandal (2006).

The treatment of Karpinski's story after the prison abuse scandal broke demonstrates the gendered nature of narratives about her and her command. The first reaction has been to believe Karpinski when she says that she was set up, blaming the men at higher levels of the military command for the abuse in the prison in Iraq (Bartz 2006). This image maintains the possibility that Karpinski, like the ideal-type of women discussed in the Introduction, is pure and innocent.

A second response has added another dimension to that story, accounting for Karpinski as pure, innocent and naive. These stories characterize Karpinski as a bad leader. While they do not explicitly make reference to her gender, they use gendered terms to describe Karpinski's perceived inability to lead a combat command effectively (Taguba 2004). General Taguba, who investigated the events at Abu Ghraib, characterized Karpinski as a poor leader who failed to establish rules for her command (2004). His report, which purports to be a comprehensive assessment of authorization and fault at Abu Ghraib, was authorized by the military only to analyse Karpinski's performance (Atlanta Journal-Constitution 2004). While a number of other generals, including the commanding general in Iraq, Ricardo Sanchez, have been characterized as failing in their leadership positions, Karpinski was the only one whose failures were 'leaked' to the public, and the only one demoted for the role her poor leadership played in the scandal.

A third reaction has been direct scepticism about a woman's ability to serve as a commander in a combat zone. An article in the *Washington Times* in May 2004 accused Karpinski of being the responsible party, telling readers to 'be assured that if Gen. Karpinski was a man, demands for his accountability would be loud and clear' (Wheeler 2004). The author of the article, Jack Wheeler, also accuses Karpinski of reacting to the scandal 'like a girl' by 'whining, making excuses and complaining that it's not her fault' (2004). Wheeler identifies the source of the problem as the feminization of the American military, when 'war is not woman's work. It is man's work – not because men are more brutal or stronger, but because they can endure the stresses of combat and be accountable for the failures those stresses inevitably create' (Wheeler 2004). In Wheeler's understanding, women's lack of endurance and accountability makes them unsuited to be military leaders, and the scandal at Abu Ghraib is the result of the military's choice to appoint an incompetent woman to a combat command.

A final story told of Karpinski's role in the crimes at Abu Ghraib has been less public, but is still politically and symbolically significant. While few stories have questioned Karpinski's assertion that she was unaware of the abuse as it happened, some accounts frame her as a ringleader. These tales[11] emphasize Karpinski as tough and masculine, lacking humanity. Very few stories have doubted General Karpinski's claim that she did not know what was happening. A small minority, however, tell the story that Karpinski did know what was going on at Abu Ghraib and organized it in some way. Internet searches turn up some five hundred results questioning Karpinski's sexual preference. More specifically, these blogs, newspapers and websites call her a dyke or a bull dyke. These references account for a dozen of the first fifty results in a Google search for Karpinski, indicating that they are frequently viewed.[12]

General Karpinski has been married to a man for thirty years, and nothing in our interview gave any impression she had any interest in women (2006). Karpinski's actual sexual preference, however, is irrelevant to the name-calling here (Sjoberg 2007: 89). These characterizations of her sexual preference are not about whether or not Karpinski sleeps with women. Instead, they imply that Karpinski is somehow less of a woman; less pure and therefore less female because she (allegedly) coordinated prisoner abuse. The depiction of Karpinski as a dyke because of her (alleged) involvement with prisoner abuse at Abu Ghraib implicitly characterizes *real women* as incapable of that sort of violence.[13] In the narratives, women with erotic dysfunctions (like lesbianism) are violent because they are *unable to please men*. Karpinski's alleged violence, therefore, must be a result of her flawed sexuality. Heteronormative international discourses provide space for the criminalizing of deviant sexuality and the sexualization of deviant violence.

Pearson argues that the feminist response to these claims has entrenched the gender subordination. She explains:

> Whereas they once described violent women as lesbian, maneaters and perverts, we have simply sailed to the other extreme, from whore to Madonna. The old fabric of misogyny blends seamlessly with new threads of feminist essentialism to preserve the myth that women are more susceptible than men to being helpless, crazy, and biddable. (Pearson 1997: 56)

Pearson mistakes a hybrid reaction for a progression, however. Reactions proclaiming Karpinski's innocence because of her gender would certainly entrench gender subordination. Reactions proclaiming women generally innocent of Karpinski's specific actions because of her sexual perversions also entrench gender subordination. If Karpinski is a woman, and committed war crimes, then women can commit war crimes – no sexual perversion can sufficiently exclude her from the category of woman. These characterizations, which try to maintain the perception of all women's innocence despite Karpinski's alleged actions by robbing her of her membership in the group of women, reduce Karpinski to a sexual object and narrowly define femininity to exclude people like her. These accounts do not only hurt Karpinski and her image, however; they also pigeonhole women in a purist category which denies their ability to act or be acted upon outside naivety, innocence and virginity.

MOTHER, MONSTER AND WHORE NARRATIVES IN THE ABU GHRAIB SCANDAL

The mother, monster and whore narratives permeate public discourses about the women allegedly involved in the prisoner abuse at Abu Ghraib. The mother narrative comes through in most of the discussions about these women's roles. Stories about Lynndie England emphasize her need for acceptance, and the pressure that she felt to please the men around her. Like the mother in traditional narratives about violent women, England is characterized as dependent on the men who protect and sustain her, 'attention-starved' and vulnerable to manipulation because 'someone was finally talking to her' (McKelvey 2006). Stories which characterize England as desperate for affection and approval, like stories which emphasize Palestinian women's failed marriages, frame women as dependent on men for their self-worth and use this to explain their aberrant behaviour.

Also, Lynndie England's status as an actual mother is emphasized in stylized narratives about her conduct and her punishment. England was pregnant with Charles Graner's baby at the time of the abuse, and media coverage often focused on her future, then actual, motherhood, both in sensationalizing her relationship with Graner and in describing her monstrousness. Stories soliciting sympathy for England focus on her status as a single mother who is spending the first years of her son's life in jail (McKelvey 2006). Stories which focus on her sexuality emphasize that she is mother to a child by Charles Graner, to whom she is described as a sexual slave. In these narratives, her motherhood is a reminder of how she was controlled and manipulated by a man who is responsible for her crimes, a feature that is also present in the whore narrative (McKelvey 2006)

Likewise, the discussions about Sabrina Harman fit with the nurturing mother narrative. Harman is described as especially good with kids, and her likeability and charity are emphasized. The story about Harman buying a family a refrigerator is replayed in the media – here is a woman who *took care of people*, and therefore could not be characterized as harming them. Elements of the more general mother narrative are present in her story too: Harman is characterized as 'lonely' and 'devoid of any sense', implying that her life is incomplete without a man in it, and that she is therefore less sensitive and less of a woman (capable of engaging in proscribed violence).

Characterizations of Janis Karpinski show elements of the mother narrative as well. Narratives about Karpinski's leadership ability question whether war is 'women's work' and imply that women should hold caretaking roles in the military rather than roles which require leadership or the ability to fight. They ask the question of whether women can abandon their maternal instinct enough to fight in wars. The stories before she was shipped out about her maternal love for her soldiers set Karpinski up as someone who had a maternal role vis-à-vis the soldiers under her command. This is a role that Karpinski accepts, either consciously or unconsciously, in her book and in our interview (Karpinski and Strasser 2005; Karpinski 2006). Karpinski describes the individual soldiers under her command, especially the women, as children in need of care (2006). Her self-identification with a maternal role can be juxtaposed with those accounts that characterize her maternal nature as a reason for her poor leadership (Wheeler 2004) and/or her desperate need for *actual* maternity as a reason for her violence.[14]

Elements of the monster narrative are also evident in the characterizations of the women at Abu Ghraib. The representation of Lynndie England as a part of the 'all woman axis of evil' characterizes her as intractably and irrationally evil (Riddell 2004). Riddell's characterization of England as a 'she-devil' and a member of the 'queens of violence' vilifies her as monstrous rather than as an actor who made choices in her violent behaviour (2004). The emphasis on the women smiling in the pictures highlights women's coldness, focusing on their delight in the injury of their victims. Stories which focus on the innocent appearance of the abusers at Abu Ghraib bring up a comparison with Medusa: the female abusers are monsters who can appear innocent and beautiful when they are really cold-hearted abusers and killers. Emphasis on Harman's claim that she 'went numb and was completely detached from reality' brings up the part of the monster narrative which separates women from responsibility for their violent actions by focusing on their alleged psychological handicaps. If Harman was unaware of right and wrong (insane), then her behaviour was not culpable. If she was not culpable, then women generally can remain outside of the realm of culpability for proscribed violence in international politics.

Finally, the stories of the women at Abu Ghraib include many elements of the whore narratives. Themes of sexualization run through most tellings of the stories of the women at Abu Ghraib. England and Ambuhl's sexual relationships with Charles Graner, characterized as the ringleader of the scandal, are emphasized. These sexual relationships are often described in graphic detail, even though they are secondary (if relevant at all) to the commission of the alleged crimes. The stories position the women as whores of manipulative men – they leave no detail about the women's sexuality private. Instead, the more polite stories stress the women's appearances and the less tactful stories highlight their sexual proclivities, tastes and partners. In the Rolling Stones song 'Dangerous Beauty', the references to the number of 'stiffs' that Lynndie England produces is a double entendre linking erections and dead bodies.

Pornography sites that feature the women implicated in the abuse at Abu Ghraib emphasize sadomasochism, necrophilia and nymphomania. New photos provide documentary evidence that guards performed sex acts in front of each other, the prisoners and a camera. Many of the pictures show these women as passive participants in sexual acts performed by American soldiers *on* them. McKelvey's characterizations of England as Graner's 'sex slave' and 'little plaything' sexualize her participation within the erotomania and ownership whore narratives (2006). McKelvey takes the analogy to prostitution even further than sexualizing England, however: she claims that England exchanged sex for a feeling of safeness and protection (2006). Hers and other narratives focus on Graner's sexual control of England as an explanation for England's behaviour.

Narratives about Sabrina Harman and Janis Karpinski resemble the whore narratives that conflate sexuality and sexual dysfunction. Most non-military narratives about Harman often include the fact that she is a lesbian, whether or not any other observations about her personal life are included. Many of the websites which discuss her behaviour or feature her as the centre of pornographic stories characterize her as a 'dyke' or question whether she is a 'dyke' or a 'bidyke' or a 'biho', discussing whether or not the prisoner abuse proves a secret sexual interest in men.[15] Characterizations of Janis Karpinski which implicate her in the prison abuse talk about her as cold, manly and calculating, and also include the language of lesbianism. The characterizations of Karpinski as a 'bull dyke' who 'needs to be satisfied' invoke the whore narratives.[16] When asked about these descriptions, Karpinski laments that the media and the military need to characterize her as a lesbian or a whore, lest she be understood and dealt with as a human being (2006).

IDEALIZED MILITARIZED FEMININITY

As mentioned in the introduction, in the United States military, as elsewhere in global politics, women seem to be filling 'male' roles with increasing frequency. While less than 1 per cent of the United States military deployment to Vietnam was female, 7 per cent of the deployed force in the first Gulf War was women (Goering and Woo 1997), and 15 per cent of the deployed force was female in the Second Gulf War (Karpinski 2006). The 'woman soldier' introduced a new gender-role expectation to the United States military. She was not just a gender-neutral 'soldier' but a special kind of solder, a 'woman soldier'. A 'woman soldier' in the United States military is still formally barred from combat participation, but can serve combatant functions like flying spy helicopters and riding in battle tanks so long as their jobs are not classified as 'combat arms' (Karpinski 2006).

The new 'woman soldier' was a fetish in American popular culture. Movies like *GI Jane* and *Courage under Fire* explored the ethical standards for the 'woman soldier' and her male colleagues. In *Courage under Fire* (1996), Captain Karen Walden, the female officer and protagonist, had died in the desert. The movie was about the investigation into whether or not she merited a medal of honour for courage in battle; she would be the first woman to ever to receive that honour. Walden is assumed to be the stereotypical passive woman, showed extraordinary bravery in combat, the likes of which emasculated her male colleagues. Captain Karen Walden represented the best of the 'women soldiers' as tough as men, but maternal and sexually appealing to them at the same time (Sjoberg 2006: 186).

The 'woman soldier trope showed that the seven percent of United States forces who were female in the first Gulf War and the fifteen percent in the Second Gulf War did not operate in a military that had suddenly abandoned centuries of militarized masculinity to accept their presence' (Sjoberg 2006: 186; Cockburn 1991; Cockburn and Zarkov 2002). Instead, these women were included in an organization still dominated by masculinities. As Karpinski notes, 'the army gave her a very tough job in an overwhelmingly masculine environment' (Karpinski and Strasser 2005: 234) She describes that women soldiers are often de-gendered and masculinized in the theatre (17). In fact, 'pornographic movies were still shown prior to the execution of missions; challenges to masculinity were still issued to inspire soldiers' (Sjoberg 2006: 187).

If a woman can meet the traditional requirements of masculinity while maintaining her femininity, she is allowed to be a part of fighting a war. Women's expected role in the United States military, however, is anything but gender-neutral or gender-equal. The military's idealized notions of femininity are encapsulated in the stylized narrative that the military told of Jessica Lynch, who was the ideal 'woman soldier' whose images captured many of the ambitions and fears that the military has about gender integration. The ideal military woman was a 19-year-old girl who went down fighting, was injured in battle, and was tortured in captivity (Ellingwood and Simon 2003). According to the official account, Lynch was just a country girl who became a hero and a household name (Gibbs 2003; Sjoberg 2007).

In the military's narrative, Lynch was a woman who could make it as a man, but could never escape the weaknesses of femininity. Her vulnerability to sexual torture and rape was emphasized in almost every official or unofficial story during her captivity. Even though the military trained Jessica Lynch and gave her a gun, they emphasized the remarkable singularity of a woman who fought; even a woman soldier is not a fighter or a warrior, but a guest and a tourist (Bragg 2003). Also, despite her status as a soldier, Lynch was fought for instead of fighting in most of the story – she needed soldiers to save her. The most publicized rescue mission in military history followed. Even when women are members of the military, war is about protecting innocent women. Jessica Lynch was presented at once as a glorified war hero and as an innocent woman – 'a Beautiful Soul who could not escape the mold, even with a gun and a uniform' (Sjoberg 2007: 56).

The military's 'woman soldier' story of Jessica Lynch was also further complicated by the fact that it was not true. Lynch herself protested the portrayal of her as a standout, and complained about being used as a symbol of gender roles in the military (Bragg 2003). The military, however, was less concerned with the actual Jessica Lynch than the one that they moulded into to the ideal-type of a 'woman soldier'.[17]

Today's militarized woman, like the story told about Jessica Lynch, is tough, but not wantonly violent. She is brave, but needs the men around her to survive. She is trained, but cannot be self-sufficient. She is fragile, but puts on her game face. She is sexy, but not sexual. She can fight, but the kind of fighting she can do is sanitized: she cannot engage in cruelty or torture. She is never far from her maternal instincts. She is a soldier and a participant, but fundamentally still innocent. The ideal-type of militarized femininity expects a woman soldier to be as capable as a male soldier, but as vulnerable as a civilian woman. As such, Jessica Lynch's hero story was plastered on the television, in newspapers, and even in a made-for-television movie; her gender-role story could be made to fit an ideal-type of militarized femininity (Sjoberg 2007: 97).

MILITARIZED FEMININITY AND ABU GHRAIB

Even though women now make up between 15 and 20 percent of the United States military generally and deployed forces specifically, the military does not have the same expectations for the men and women in its forces. Recruiting ads show women with make-up and nail polish, emphasizing their difference and femininity (Brown 2006). Rules against women shaving their heads, wearing men's uniforms, or occupying combat arms positions show that women are an uncomfortable addition to a men's military rather than truly integrated, and that women are expected to be like women even when they must be like men as well.

This image of militarized femininity excludes the women who were implicated in the prisoner abuse at Abu Ghraib, because they failed to behave like women should. The image of a woman standing over a pyramid of naked detainees does not resonate with traditional images of women as the innocent people that war protects. Instead, these women seem somehow guilty, defiled and impure, things that women are not, by definition.

In order to defend the stereotype of militarized femininity, then, the military tells the stories of the women who participated in the abuse at Abu Ghraib by characterizing their actions which fall outside of these norms as aberrant not only to their membership in the United States military but also to their womanhood. Women who commit proscribed violence in the military are not only bad people, but bad women and bad women soldiers. In other words, women who commit war crimes have committed a *triple transgression*: the crime that they are accused of, the transgression against traditional notions of femininity, and the transgression against the new militarized femininity and its role in supporting the existing gendered structure of the United States military.

FOUR

BLACK WIDOWS IN CHECHNYA

The typical understanding about female Chechen suicide bombers is that they are desperate and hopeless women who blow themselves up to avenge their husbands' deaths, as exemplified here:

> Tens of thousands [of Chechens] have died in nearly a decade of conflict, and the most desperate and hopeless survivors are said to be the young, childless women whose husbands have been killed, kidnapped or gone missing – hence the term 'black widows'. (McDonald 2003: A4)

Yet this is not the only story of female revolutionaries and suicide bombers in Chechnya, as demonstrated in this quotation:

> In Russia, such women are known as shakhidki, the feminine Russian variant for the Arabic word meaning holy warriors who sacrifice their lives. In the media, they are known more luridly as black widows, prepared to kill and to die to avenge the deaths of fathers, husbands, brothers, and sons in Chechnya. (Myers 2004: 1)

While the women involved describe their motives as political and religious, most public narratives ignore those motivations to emphasize personal desires and the private sphere. These characterizations fuse the mother, monster and whore narratives to describe the *shakhidki* as desparate, hopeless, and without a cause. These gendered descriptors in the Chechen case coalesce in the phrased used to identify the women martyrs: black widows. Identifying *shakhidki* as 'black widows' deflects the attention of the international community away from a war Russia perpetrates against civilians with massive human rights violations (Eichler 2006). It draws attention to the female suicide bombers as terrorists (and therefore illegitimate actors, instead of as part of a people fighting for national independence), and specifically to the elements of their feminitiy that can be described as having gone awry. By characterizing these women as avengers, stories can at once blame womanhood for their violence and take away the possibility of individual agency, all the while obscuring the tragedy of the conflict and the women's real reasons for political violence. Indeed, 'black widow' is a term that is skilfully used by the Russian government to convey a racialized, monstrous image of Chechen women.

THE CHECHEN CONDITION

As documented by such researchers as Mary Kaldor (2006) and Michael Ignatieff (1995), the 'new wars' of the 1990s were spawned by a desire for independence and self-determination. These 'new nationalisms' were important to international affairs in the post-Cold War era. The break-up of Yugoslavia was by far the most infamous new war, but new nationalisms extended from Yugoslavia into Africa and to the Chechen nation. The historical struggle between Russia and Chechnya is long-standing. Since the time of the tsars, Russia has had an interest in possessing Chechnya as a territory and subduing the Chechens as a population. Yet, at the end of the Cold War, the new post-Soviet Russian government could not contain the ethnicities it had subdued for so long. In 1991 alone, fifteen new countries, once part of the Soviet Union, all declared independence (Rosenberg 2007). These include, but are not limited to, countries surrounding Chechnya, such as Georgia and Armenia, and those in the Caucusus, such as Kazakhstan, Kyrgyzstan, Tahikistan, Turkmenistan and Uzbekistan (Rosenberg 2007). The Chechen nation, never happy under Russian or Soviet domination, wanted to be part of this phenomenon. Russia, however, was not willing to let go of its territory. The wars in Chechnya are emblematic of Russia's struggle to maintain its empire since the end of the Cold War. As Boris Yelstin said from his hospital bed towards the end of his presidency, 'Russians! Our country has more than once emerged with honour from difficult trials. Let international terrorists of all stripes remember this. And this time, we will not yield an inch of our land' (Caryl and Nivat 1999: 42).

Since the Soviet Union dissolved, two wars have been fought over Chechen self-determination. The Chechen conflicts are connected to the broader problems of post-communist transformation in the former USSR, and as such hold substantial symbolic value for Russia's state legitimacy and the content of its identity in the post-Cold War era. The first war lasted from 1993 to 1996 and the second from 1999 to the present. Perhaps 20 per cent of the Chechen population has been killed (the total number of deaths is estimated at between 180,000 to 250,000). This makes the Chechen conflict 'one of the deadliest conflicts in recent European history' (Khalilov 2003: 407). A significant number of Chechens, between 200,000 and 250,000, are refugees living primarily in Ingushetia (Kramer 2005: 214; Campbell 2003: 2). As a part of Russia's policy of 'normalization'[1] (which appears to be a policy of trying to maintain a civil society in the presence of one of the worst modern separatist wars, including holding 'democratic' elections), Russia forcibly closed refugee camps between 2001 and 2004 (Kramer 2005: 214; Prague Watchdog 2004: 6; Hargreaves and Cunningham 2004, 2000). Since the latest war began, most towns, the infrastructure and all services, such as water, electricity and gas, have been destroyed. Little effort has been put into reconstruction (Kramer 2005: 210).

As we have documented across the conflicts described in this book, militarization and war are gendered societal processes, no less so because the parties are the Russian government and Chechen separatists (Eichler 2006; Tickner 2001). Russia's staunch commitment to defeating Chechen separatism has been described as fuelled by a need to 'get macho' with adversaries near and far, to maintain government legitimacy (Lentini 1996; Wagner 2000; Eichler 2006). Eichler describes how the 'Russian leadership's use of war relied on the construction of and association with the idea of militarized, ordered and patriotic Russian masculinity and opposition to the racialized notion of aggressive, anarchical, criminal Chechen masculinity' (2006: 495).

The Russian war effort also depends on certain notions of femininity. During the first Chechen war, images of motherhood and femininity were crucial in turning Russian public opinion against the war. Russian and Chechen women together vocalized objections to the fighting, vilifying the military and pointing out that the most frequent victims of the conflict were simple soldiers and innocent civilians: their sons and daughters (Eremitcheva and Zdravomyslova 2001: 232; Pinnick 1997; Vallance 2000).

The rhetorical transformation of Chechens from rebels to terrorists at the beginning of the second Chechen conflict was crucial to the government's gaining and maintaining public support in Russia (Sakwa 2004). The emphasis on the 'black widows' as terrorists emulating Palestinians has at once silenced the powerful feminine opposition to the conflict (Eichler 2006) and provided support for the use of force generally in Chehnya (Eichler 2006) and specifically against Chechen women (Baker 2004).

Within this conflict, gross violations of human rights are commonplace: beatings, torture, killings, gender-based violence, and disappearances. Families of the detained sometimes have the option of buying back their relative, alive or dead, from the Russians. The price is determined by the family's resources – '[a] thousand dollars, weapons … , a golden necklace' (Conley 2004: 335). Detained men have reported electric shock torture, often used on their genitals as a way of decreasing fertility (334–5). Rape 'constitutes "normal" conduct' and many of the cases 'never come to court' due to the occupation and guilt of the Russian forces and the cultural norms of Chechnya (Parfitt 2004: 1291; Conley 2004: 335; Putley 2003: 2). Médecins Sans Frontières documented that 85 per cent of the torturers and rapists were soldiers or police officers with the Russian forces; the other 15 per cent being Chechen forces (Parfitt 2004: 1291). Women are increasingly becoming the subject of arbitrary detentions, torture, rape in custody, disappearances and extra-judicial killings (noborder.org 2006; Strauss 2004: A7).

These various violations of human rights occur beneath the umbrella of two different 'policies': *bespredel* and *zachistki*. *Bespredel*, as described by conscripted Russian soldiers, means 'no limits'; it translates literally as 'excesses' or 'atrocities' and carries with it the interpretation of 'acting outside the rules, violently and with impunity' (Conley 2004: 334). *Zachistki*, a better-known term, describes the cleansing operations that occur when a Chechen village is

> completely surrounded by armed forces in APCs, trucks, and other vehicles, so that no-one may leave or enter during the operation, which can last three weeks. And all the men and boys of the village except the very old and the very young are then removed for 'filtration' during which they are held in large, uncovered pits in the ground and subjected to questioning, tortures of horrific kinds, and 'extra-judicial killing' … which is often carried out with explosives in order to leave no evidence of the bodily disfigurements resulting from torture. While the men are absent, the women of the village, completely unprotected, are subject to the depredations of the soldiery. (Putley 2003, 2)

Conley describes *zachistkis* as 'free-for-all[s]' (2004: 334) and another author feels they are the reason for the increasing 'calls for revenge against Russia' known as *adat* 'under the traditional Chechen code of law' (Kramer 2005: 215; see also Blandy 2003: 431–2). Other tactics employed by the Russian military include shooting anyone who protests, even a 100-year-old woman; the killing of civilians in their hiding places by the throwing of grenades into cellars; and killing at point-blank range (Wood 2001: 131–3, 136). The soldiers involved in *zachistki* are *kontraktniki*, special-contract soldiers who are 'allowed to keep what they loot', which often includes women and their bodies (Wood 2001: 128). The Russian military uses the insurgency of the *shakhidki* as an excuse to target women, taking them out of the sphere of civilian immunity. Usually, women and children are seen as civilians, whether they are or not, both by combatants in civil wars and international conflicts, and by the media. In the conflict between the Russian government and Chechen rebels, the 'black widow' narratives about the *shakhidka* have helped the Russian government frame all Chechen women as combatants, taking away whatever protection they might have had from the conflict had they been considered civilians. As a result, many Russian leaders have developed a 'shoot first, think later' mentality about Chechen women. General Vladimir Shamanov dismissed the killing of the wives of Chechen fighters – 'How do you tell a wife from a sniper?' (Russell 2005: 109).

Using the *shakhidki* minority as a shield from responsibility, the Russian government claims to be attacking not civilians but potential combatants, in indiscriminate attacks against Chechen women. Sergei Yastrzhembsky, the Kremlin's chief spokesmen on Chechnya, characterized Russia as fully compliant with the immunity norm even though the women were targeted:

> I am familiar with these allegations – as a rule, these are lies spread around by the Chechens' Kavkaz website ... which is prepared by people outside Chechnya. This website is aimed at stirring up Western public opinion and the Western media. There is no documented evidence concerning the use of artillery fire against civilians. It's nonsense. (Wood 2001: 131)

The Kremlin and Russian forces and their commanders deny any wrongdoing on their part and cover their responsibility with gendered stories of 'black widows' and racialized tales of a connection between Chechen fighters and international Radical Islamic terrorists. The dual move of blaming the fighting on radical Islamic groups, primarily al-Qaeda, and identifying monstrous women as terrorists legitimizes Russia's war in Chechnya as a part of the 'global war on terror' and maintains inherited stereotypes of women while allowing the Russian government to attack them. In addition to using the mother, monster and whore narratives to rob the *shakhidki* of agency, the Russian government's association of their tactics with Middle Eastern terrorists is a racialized story to obscure any choice they may have made in their tactics. The Russian government subsumes the 'black widows', an 'artifical[ly] import[ed]' tactic from the Middle East (Weir 2003: 1), to this global phenomenon under the guise of the 'Palestinianization' of the Chechen war – Chechen women are inspired by Palestinian women and this accounts for the spate of female suicide bombers in 2003. Russia's denial of blame for the war is intimately tied up in the gendering and racializing of tales of the 'black widows.'

RUSSIA AND THE RACIAL OTHERING OF CHECHNYA

Imperial Russia, Soviet Russia and the current Russian state have employed pejoratives alongside excessive violence against the Chechens. Dehumanizing rhetoric is part of an explicit strategy to justify the violence against the Chechen nation by the Russians. Female suicide bombers and the label affixed to them, 'black widow', is simply the latest stage in this struggle. A history of racialized discourses in Russia's subordination of the Chechen population extends into gendered discourses through its most recent manifestation, which appropriates and manipulates the mission of the *shadhidki* in order to validate Russian strategy and tactics.

The conflict between Russia and Chechnya is long-standing, and past events have striking similarities to today's conflict. Imperial Russia conquered Chechnya, along with other states in the North Caucasus, in the 1800s. This conquest was marked by 'extermination and expulsions of the indigenous population' (Khalilov 2003: 410). Chechens were and have remained the primary target of government forces. Between 'the late 18th Century and 1944, not a single decade passed without Russian or Soviet authorities committing massacres in Chechnya' (Khalilov 2003: 410).

The Russian invasion of the Caucasus in the early 1800s employed brutal tactics (Russell 2005; Hoffman 2004). Russia's policy 'of total attack' left 'the natives no option but to resist as desperately as they could' (Hoffman 2004). When Russia tried to reach an 'agreement' with the Chechens in 1806, one of the terms was: 'if the Chechens do not refrain from carrying out raids, they must expect to be completely exterminated and destroyed' (Russell 2005: 104). To Russell the intent of this term is clear: 'abandon your old ways or die' (104). In 1818, Tsar Alexander II said 'he would 'find no peace until a single Chechen remained alive' because 'by their example they could inspire a rebellious spirit and love for freedom among even the most faithful subjects of the Empire' (Khalilov 2003: 410). Similarities between the early stages of this conflict and the present phase exist: in the 1920s and 1930s 'relatives were taken hostage in order to force suspected rebels to surrender. When they yielded, they were either executed or imprisoned. Just like today, [Chechen] operations were deliberately portrayed as acts of terrorism' (Khalilov 2003: 410).

Russell also outlines how popular perceptions of Chechens were reflected in Russian culture. In the mid-1800s, Tolstoy described the Chechens as resentful towards the Russians; it was a resentment that went beyond hate and manifested as a 'refusal to accept these Russian dogs as people' (Russell 2005: 103). Russell also uses Lermontov's 'Cossack Lullaby' as another source of Russia's view of the Chechens. While the Russians had a healthy respect for the Chechen's warrior qualities, it was 'always counterbalanced ... with the negative "bogeyman" image of the "wicked Chechen" who "whets his dagger keen"' (Russell 2005: 103; see also Russell 2002: 73).

Modern discourses continue the rhetorical construction of Chechens as fierce warriors. Russians adopted the Chechen national symbol, the wolf, as a way of creating a threatening image. The wolf is featured on the Chechen national flag and the image is incorporated into their national anthem. Chechen warriors were characterized as 'proud to be called a *borz* (wolf) and strove to uphold' this image (Russell 2005: 106). Yet Russians view the wolf as a 'fearsome, cunning, fierce and untameable opponent' and thus Chechens are 'worthy' but 'wild and dangerous' enemies who 'warrant only destruction' (Russell 2005, 106). Chechen leaders are also constructed within this context: 'Aslan Maskahov (President of Chechnya–Ichkeria from 1997) – "the wolf with a human face", Shamil Basayev – "the lone wolf" [terrorist leader, vice president of Chechnya–Ichkeria, killed 10 July 2006] and Salman Raduyev – "the looney wolf"' (Chechen field commander, d. December 2002) (Russell 2005: 106).

After Chechen attacks in greater Russia, the media have also used what Russell calls 'lupine epithets' (2005: 106) to describe the events. These include images of 'rabid wolves under the headline 'The Chechen wolves have been driven back to the lair, but for how long?"' (106). Other pejoratives are also used to describe the Chechen separatists. Soldiers will refer to them as *dukhi* (spooks) because they appear from nowhere, or as *chichi* (the name of a monkey in popular children's books in Russia). Monkey was 'quite popular among the troops' – General Mikhailov went 'on the record to foreign correspondents calling the Chechen fighters *obezyany* (monkeys)' (Russell 2005: 106). This corresponds to the historical use of the term *cherniye* (blacks) or *chernozhopy* (black arses) by the Russian population as a reference to Chechens. This is in spite of that fact that 'Caucasians (being Caucasians) are largely white-skinned' (Russell 2005: 106).

Historically, then, Russian governments have expressed a shared contempt for the Chechen population. In the first post-Soviet Chechen war (1993-96), Yelstin referred to Chechen separatists as "bandits" or "terrorists" and as the separatist leader at the time, Djokhar Dudayev, 'as "mad"' (Russell 2005: 105). Putin's recorded statements do not necessarily engage in the racist rhetoric, but his wording tends to be violent. Putin has referred to the fighters as '"terrorists" who "must be plucked from the basement and caves (where) they are hiding" and [be] "simply eliminated"' (Walsh 2003: 15). Other Putin statements include the phrases 'wiped out' (Eke 2003) and the '[promise] to "waste the terrorists in the outhouse"' (Russell 2005, 108). In addition to 'basement' and 'outhouse', Putin has also referred to Chechnya as a 'cancer' (Almond 2004: 9).

The status of Chechnya as the wanted but hated stepchild is apparently not enough to justify military measures against the breakaway republic; the Russian government has begun to point the finger at connections to global terrorism. Radical Islam has had ties to the Chechen conflict since the early 1990s. Global terrorism, in the guise of al-Qaeda, has found both a haven and a cause in the Chechen conflict. Yet 'Chechens have not signed on to the worldwide jihad vision of al-Qaeda' because they are still focused on the primary goal of self-determination (Weir 2003: 1). Whatever level of involvement and support various radical Islamic groups have in Chechnya, Putin and his government are very quick to emphasize it.

In the post-9/11 world, the link to al-Qaeda justifies whatever measures Putin wants to use against Chechnya – at least in the mind of his administration.[2] In 2003, Putin told his ministers, as reported by the presidential press service, that 'Chechen rebels "are not only linked with international terrorist organizations but have become an integral part of them, perhaps the most dangerous part"' (Mainville 2003). It was an intentional exaggeration to claim the Chechens as 'the most dangerous part'[3] of the global terrorism network. This exaggeration reflects the use of rhetoric to justify the language of 'wiping out', 'eliminating' and 'wasting' the Chechen fighters.

The government and the media's connection between the Chechens and radical Islam was evident even before 11 September 2001. Russell claims that this connection began mainly when a Jordanian-born 'wahhabite'[4] fighter joined the Chechens in 1995 and it was aided by Shamil Basayev's conversion to radical Islam during the course of the first war (2005: 108). Mahmoud Hannawi, a founder of the global jihad movement, also aided the Chechens (Al-Shishani and Moore 2005). As soon as female suicide bombers became an apparent and key part of the Chechen strategy, the Russian government began to speak of the 'Palestinianization' of the struggle.[5] Palestinianization refers both to the link between the Chechens and global terrorism and to the 'adopt[ion of] the tactics of Middle Eastern terrorists organizations' (Eke 2003). As Alexander Iskanderay, head of the Armenian-based Center for Caucasian Studies told Fred Weir of the *Christian Science Monitor*, 'As in Palestine, we see more and more segments of the population, including women and children, being recruited into terrorism' (Weir 2003: 1). This is disempowering to the Chechen cause because it refuses to recognize the Chechens' own political greivances and reasons for struggle. The Russians are deflecting the blame from their own heavy-handed policies and instead blaming outside factors for Chechen violence.

During the summer of 2003, four female suicide bombers attacked Moscow (Balburov 2003; Campbell 2003: 2; tkb.org). It was during this spate of attacks that the Palestinianization accusation first occurred, despite the fact that Chechen *shakhidki* began suicide bombing before Palestinian groups regularly employed women suicide bombers. This device is both opportunistic and rhetorical. It is opportunistic because Russia has now staged the Chechen conflict as something larger than Chechen self-determination; it is rhetorical because the use of hyperbolic and threatening language legitimizes the policies and actions of Russian forces in Chechnya. *Borz* (wolf), *dukhi* (spook), *chichi* or *obezyany* (monkey), *cherniye* (black), and *chernozhopy* (black arses) are all terms of dehumanization, which Bandura contends displaces moral responsibility and enables the legitimacy of harsh retaliatory military forces (Russell 2002: 76; Bandura 1998: 181). The use of the 'black widow' narrative falls into this category as a dehumanizing (monstrous) rhetorical device that 'allows' Russia to respond with (un)necessary force.

THE BLACK WIDOWS AND THEIR WAR

> Covered from head to toe in all-black Islamic robes with only their determined, kohl-lined eyes showing, they quickly came to be called the 'black widows' as a horrified world watched. (Jacinto 2002)

Because Chechen self-determination has not been respected by the Russians, the Chechens have relied more upon what is largely recognized as terrorist violence, because they direct the violence at civilians and other soft-security targets in addition to Russian military forces. Attacks extended from operations in Chechnya and surrounding areas into greater Russia. The first of the infamous attacks happened in October 2002. Forty-one Chechen terrorists, of whom eighteen were women, held as many as 800 hostages in a Moscow theatre for three days, until the Russian authorities pumped in an unknown sleeping gas.[6] The Russian forces shot all forty-one Chechens at point-blank range, all of whom were unconscious. In many ways, the idea of the 'black widow' as a veiled widow of Chechen 'rebels' dates from this event. Mysterious and faceless, 'black widows' are both exotic and terrifying. While some descriptions are subtle in presenting them as monsters, other accounts blatantly refer to the women as zombies.

The first female Chechen suicide terrorists acted on 7 June 2000. Khaya Barayeva and Luisa Magomadova drove an explosive-laden truck into a Russian Speical Forces headquarters in Chechnya. Between June 2000 and June 2005 Chechen women have perpetrated 'twenty-two of the twenty-seven suicide attacks (81 per cent of the total number). ... There were a total of 110 bombers in the period reviewed, forty-seven of whom were women' (Speckhard and Akhmedova 2006: 63).

In 2003, after the Moscow hostage-taking and during a long summer of multiple Chechen female suicide bombers, Chechen leaders claimed they had two battalions of 'up to 500 women prepared to "martyr" themselves in the cause of independence from Russian rule' (Bruce 2003: 8). Most are between 20 and 25 years of age (Argumenty y Fakty 2003). It is assumed that the women 'are relatives of the estimated 15,000 mujahideen fighters killed' by the Russians since 1999 (Bruce 2003: 8). The Kremlin believes the women are physically and psychologically trained by international terrorist groups in the Middle East and Southern Caucasus (Cecil 2003: 12; see also Zedalis 2004: 10). Others believe the women are trained by Shamil Basayev's organization Riyadhus Salikhin (Path of the Righteous) (Shermatova and Teit 2003: 27). Yet this information cannot be confirmed 'because the investigators are tight-lipped' (Argumenty y Fakty 2003). In the week before the attack, 'a pair of tutors remain with the suicide bomber at all times' and help with the final stages (Cecil 2003: 12). It is even believed that if the bomber has second thoughts, 'the device is always remote-controlled, so that one of the "supervisors" can press the button if necessary' (Cecil 2003: 12) – although this was not the case for Zarema Muzhikoyeva, who was detained before the bomb went off[7] on 10 July 2003 at a café in Moscow (Boswell 2003: A1).

One author writes 'little research has been done on [women's] motivations' but what has been done 'shows a high degree of support [among] women for taking up arms' (Eke 2003). The same article connects the degree of support with the 'absolute desperation of many Chechen women's lives' (Eke 2003). Most of the refugees are women. In a traditional Muslim society such as Chechnya, women have gravitated to private-sphere roles. Yet, as 20 per cent of the population is dead and many of the men are involved in the conflict, women are being 'forced' to be more independent. This may be as the main source of monetary support for the family or perhaps even the choice to become bombers themselves. A Chechen human-rights worker in Ingushetia, Eliza Musayeva, told one journalist, 'Something has changed in our society, in our psychology. So many terrible things have happened to these women that actions that once seemed unthinkable have somehow become acceptable' (Mainville 2003). According to an anti-war worker, women can only take 'so much humiliation and violence' before being driven to *adat* (Mainville 2003).

All Chechens have experienced the pain and trauma of war; if *adat* is as prevalent and as important as the authors claim, then surely all Chechens would feel an impetus to commit *adat*. Even though Chechen women have not been socialized traditionally to be a part of the fighting force in Chechnya and the notion that there are no men left to fight is suspect, the reliance upon the 'desperation' of the women as a step towards *adat* seems to have some credability (Isayev 2004; Dougherty 2003; Jacinto 2002). What is meant, however, by desperation – are the women desperate to commit irrational acts or are they desperate because of the circumstances in which they have lived for almost fifteen years? Are the women crazed because of their grief and pain or are they desperate to get Russia out of Chechnya, desperate to stop Russia's 'normalization' plan, and thus desperate for self-determination? This is an important distincation – 'crazy' desperate puts them in league with the monster narrative, as discussed in Chapter 2. But if they are desperate for self-determination, the women's actions then are more heroic. Yet the Chechen women's proscribed violence is rarely seen as heroic; instead it is pereived as frighteningly monstrous.

AVENGER, SLAVE OR ZOMBIE: THE MESSAGE BEHIND THE BLACK WIDOW

The fact that it is the female black widow spider that is poisonous and not the male and that, occasionally, the female spider may kill the male spider after mating, has led to the nickname of 'black widow' for women who are violent towards men in their lives. The 'black widow' ephithet automatically sends the signal that the Chechen women are poisonous and violent towards a certain population – here, the Russians. Clearly this description is part of the monster narrative, but elements of the monster and whore narrative are prevelant as well.

The vengeful mother narrative is particularly prominent in descriptions of the so-called 'black widows'. They are described as women out to avenge the humiliations that have been imposed on their families, specifically their men, by the Russian government. The name 'black widows', and many of the narratives about the *shakhidki*, imply that their violence is borne directly of a desire for vengeance for the deaths of their husbands and sons either in combat with the Russians or in unprovoked attacks by the Russians. Because the Russian government has taken their husbands and sons, 'black widows' are characterized as living life without meaning, having lost their primary purpose. The narrative characterizes the *shakhidki* as women who, having lost their men, have also lost their *raison d'être*, and seek revenge. This revenge is described in personal and emotional terms:

> The loss of family members is a corresponding link between Palestinian and Chechen female suicide bombers, though more apparent in Chechen women, due to the nature of the conflict there. 'Of course there is an influence from the Middle East, but the roots of Chechen actions are very different from those of

(Osama) bin Laden or Al Oaeda. Their actions are motivated by the fight for independence and, more and more, by the desire for revenge, which runs very deep in the (Chechen) tradition. Therefore, terrorist groups' recruiters lurk within an atmosphere of emotional fervor, and take advantage of personal loss. (Bowers, Derrick, and Olimov 2004: 268)

While there appears to be some legitimacy in the idea of *adat*, the sensationalized terms that are used to describe it overplay the irrational and emotional elements. Speckhard and Akhmedova found that almost 'all of those we studied lost close family members in air raids, bombings, landmines, [*zachistki*], and in battle. Many personally witnessed the death, beating, or other mistreatment of a family member at the hands of the Russians' (2006: 67). Additionally, the women were 'deep[ly] personal[ly] impact[ed]', which led to a psychological crisis (67). On 24 August 2004 two Russian planes were hijacked and brought down, and on 31 August 2004 a woman detonated herself at a Moscow subway station. One of the hijackers and the suicide bomber were sisters, Amnat and Rosa Nagayeva.[8] Their brother, Uvays, was disappeared during a *zachistki* in 2001 and subsequently killed.[9] In a later interview with Amnat and Rosa's older sister, Asma (who does not believe either sister is dead), she recounted the economic uncertainty and hardships they had all faced and the *zachistki* that started in 2000 (Walsh 2005: 6).

The mother narratives often told of these terrorists, however, leave out the elements of the stories that would humanize the women, and focus instead on their anger and desperation. By calling them desperate 'black widows', media descriptions emphasize violence born of desire to avenge. These women are characterized as having 'bombs around their tummies the size of babies' (McDonald 2003: A4), which they explode, often undetected, because they are mistaken for pregnant women.

Part of the vengeful mother narrative is the notion that the women have nothing left to live for. One of the Moscow hostages told McDonald, 'They told me when a Chechen woman's husband is killed, she can't marry again.... She has to put on a black mourning dress for the rest of her life. But by dying she gets closer to her beloved. That's why the women were so scary. They had no reason to live' (McDonald 2003: A4). These women are characterized, then, as vengeful mothers who use their capacity for motherhood to kill after their motherhood has been killed.

Descriptions of the women participants in the hostage-taking during Moscow Hostage situation in October 2002 echo the nurturing mother narrative. The women terrorists would bring in the medicine and the food during the siege, taking care of their victims even as they held them against their will (Groskop 2004b). One hostage described a Chechen female hostage-taker as 'very normal. She hid her feelings behind a mask of courtesy.... She would ask people about their children. She would always say, "Everything will be fine. It will finish peacefully"' (Groskop 2004a). This positions the women within the narrative as caretakers, nurturers, and as peacemakers.

Portrayals of the Chechen *shakhidki* as monsters are also present in accounts of their actions. According to most sources, it was the Russian press that 'dubbed' Chechen female suicide bombers 'black widows' after Salambek Mayigov, Chechen secessionist former spokesman in Moscow, 'said that most of them had lost husbands or sons in combat ... and were driven by a desire for vengeance' (Agence France Presse 2004a). Yet another says that the *shakhidki* were given this sobriquet 'because of their Islamic dress' (*Sunday Mail* 2002). This plays on the previously discussed convention of using rhetoric to demonize the Chechens. The Russian government and much of the press adopted this sentiment and furthered it by offering sensationalist descriptions of the women that made them something 'other'. The Chechen female suicide bombers are not women who have lived through decades of violence[10] – they are crazed avengers.[11]

For example, Williams and Thomas paint a portrait of black widowhood with these words:

> Each of the women was dressed in traditional black Arabic robes, only their dark eyes visible from behind their veil. They say they are the widows of Chechen rebels killed in the war with Russia and vow that they too are ready to die for the cause. (2002: 8)

The Chechen women are frequently introduced as 'black robed' (Voss 2004), 'veiled' (Davies and Hughes 2004: 12; Hall 2004: 2; Williams and Thomas 2002: 8), and 'kohl-eyed' (Jacinto 2002). Their names are 'exotic' (Groskop 2004a). The women in the Moscow hostage-taking were described in one source as 'shrouded under dark scarves, only their eyes peering out' (McDonald 2003: A4). This, again, reads similarly to the mother narrative and to the actions of the Middle Eastern female suicide bombers, as discussed in Chapter 5; however, the racialized language – 'shrouded', 'peering', 'black robed' – others the women. In reading this discourse, the reader is automatically engaged in the 'Palestinianization' of the conflict – these women are not Russians; they are not citizens. As 'the most terrifying tool yet employed' (Cecil 2003: 12), they are 'fanatical' (Bruce 2004: 4), 'warped', 'mad beasts', who represent Chechnya's 'mass psychosis' and play into the 'atavistic loathing' between Russia and Chechnya (Matthews 2004: 8). Even if the woman has chosen her 'mission, it is not because of a religious mission or a political cause, but for personal reasons' of revenge – 'they are pawns in a man's game' (Groskop 2004b). Such statements work together to deny women's agency and to pin their actions on something outside of their control – involvement of global terrorist forces and mental illness. The loaded, sensationalized language of Chechen female suicide bombers as fanatical (irrational), warped (irrational) avengers fails to contextualize the Chechen tradition of vengeance and the brutality of the war with Russia.

The whore narratives also play a key role in the descriptions of the 'black widows'. The characterization of the leader of the *shakhidki* is erotic and eroticized. It would appear that all of the Moscow female suicide bombers have had a handler known by the moniker 'Black Fatima' (the name given by detained suicide bombers is 'Lyuba') (McDonald 2003: A4; Parfitt 2003: 28). She is described as something out of a spy novel: wearing sunglasses, a fur coat, and with dyed blonde hair (Paukov and Svistunov 2003: 2; Parfitt 2003: 28). Her enticing mystery is overshadowed by her (monstrous) actions. She is said to drug the women – '[she] spikes the drinks of new recruits and sends them out to kill and maim' (Parfitt 2003: 28). 'Black Fatima' is also thought to be the 'mastermind' behind the bombing campaign of 2003 and answered only to Shamil Basayev, the leader of the Chechen fighters (Beeston 2004: 4; Parfitt 2003: 28; see also Myers 2003: 2). Her mysteriousness is prominent in eroticized narratives about her. This erotic mysteriousness is not limited to the leader of the Chechen *shakhidki*. Descriptions of the women involved as mysterious, faceless and exotic fetishize the women and their violence. These characterizations are present in almost every account of *shakhidki* violence.

The most prominent use of the whore narrative, however, is the description of the *shakhidki* as entirely under the control of others, usually men but sometimes mysterious women, who choose their actions for them. There are some stories which explain these women's lives as a trade-off, as if they have sold their bodies, either for debt forgiveness or for a price for their families. Most stories, however, describe the *shakhidki* as female pawns in men's games. The stories tell many of the Chechen *shakhidki* as raped, drugged or blackmailed into suicide missions (Agence France Presse 2004a). The term given to this practice is *zombirovaniye*, an expression meaning 'turned into zombies', which describes the women suicide bombers as men's pawns (Groskop 2004a). In an extensive study of Chechen women, Speckhard and Akhmedova (2006) found no evidence of this style of coercion:

> While some, mainly Russian journalists have written that Chechen women are kidnapped, raped, and/or drugged to encourage them to take part in terror activities, we have found no evidence for this. On the contrary, we find strong evidence of self-recruitment and strong willingness to martyr oneself on behalf of one's country and independence from Russia, to enact social justice (in their perspective) for wrongs done to them, and to avenge for the loss of loved ones in their families. (Speckhard and Akhmedova 2006: 70)

Even though there is no evidence of the use and abuse of women's bodies within the *shadhidka* movement, the story of women as pawns is perhaps the most prominent portrayal of these women who choose to give their lives for Chechen self-determination. Russian officials maintain that the women are 'brainwashed into their missions' and that the Chechen secessionist groups '"use hypnosis, drugs, anything to alter the minds of these simple village girls"', claimed one Russian security source' (*Express* 2004: 3). Not only are they characterized as brainwashed, officials allege the women are also drugged and that their families are blackmailed by showing them videotapes of their daughters or sisters being raped, which dishonours the women and their families (Groskop 2004a, 2004b; Walsh 2005: 6).

One example is Mareta Dudayeva, who, at 17 years old, was captured when her truck bomb failed to detonate. None of her family had died in the war and she was described as 'not very religious'. Thus her actions, Russian police concluded, stemmed from a video that Chechen terrorists had made of her 'being raped – making her unsuitable for marriage or family life in Chechen society – and then used the tape to blackmail her' (McDonald 2003, A4).

The narrative link between drugs, brainwashing, blackmail and *zombrirovaniye* is incredibly disturbing, and makes the women who are involved in suicide bombing appear to be involuntarily enslaved. Yastrzhembsky, Putin's senior adviser on Chechnya, told a *New York Times* reporter

> Chechens are turning these young girls into zombies using psychotropic drugs ... I have heard that they rape them and record the rapes on video. After that, such Chechen girls have no chance at all of resuming a normal life in Chechnya. They have only one option to below themselves up with a bomb full of nails and ball-bearings. (Myers 2003: 2)

A Russian journalist also links *zombirovaniye* with exploitation telling the *Guardian* that the women 'don't want to be involved in these attacks. They are drugged, raped, forced to do it' (Groskop 2004a). An advice columnist for a Moscow newspaper, Maria Zhirkova, also connects brainwashing to rape and 'zombification' (Groskop 2004b). Conley's account combines elements of the monster narrative and the stories of zombification:

> Many of the women involved in suicide bombings had suffered terribly. ... For more examples of explanations of the vulnerability of women, see Itar-Tass (2003): this report from a government news source states that 'Chechen gangsters are attaching much importance to the participation of women suicide bombers in the staging of acts of terrorism. ... They are trained for their missions, using psychological and psychotropic methods'. ... 'It's clear that the women who resort to such actions were born out of the madness that is going on in Chechnya.' (Conley 2004: 340)

If they are not drugged or blackmailed, Chechen women are often characterized as slaves who engage in suicide bombing to obtain money for their family. While monetary compensation to a suicide bomber's family is common practice,[12] it is held to be coercive by those who tell the *shadhidki* stories in a way that it is not in the stories of men in a similar position. Some compare compensatory money in Chechnya to slavery. Russia's Federal Security Service (FSB) 'suggests such women are recruited by criminal gangs who promise to forgive a family debt in exchange for their services' (Walsh 2005: 6). Vinogradova writes that the female terrorists in the Moscow theatre siege were 'hostages in a situation not of their own making' and equates suicide bombing with funeral pyre femicide in India (2003: 4). She claims that these women, among others, 'are little more than slaves' (4).

The allegation that women's bodies are prostituted to the cause of Chechen independence is fairly common in publicized stories about the *shakhidki*. Raisa Ganyev, sister of Rustam Ganyev, close to Shamil Basayev, testified that 'many of the women who lash explosives to their young bodies' have been 'sold into certain death by their own kin' (Vinogradova 2003: 4). The Moscow theatre investigation uncovered that Basayev paid Ganyev $1,500 for each of his two sisters involved and that Raisa went to the Chechen authorities to escape a similar fate (Vinogradova 2003: 4).[13] A hostage from the theatre told reporters that a female hostage-taker told her that 'her parents had sold her into it [terrorism]' (Groskop 2004a). Zulikhan Elikhadzhiyeva is said to have been kidnapped by her half-brother and taken to Moscow, where she later blew herself up at a concert, on 5 July 2003. An earlier source, however, reports that one of her brothers was an active, wanted terrorist and the other had been killed by the Russians six months before she joined the 'rebels in the mountains, where she passed a terrorist training course' (Paukov and Raskin 2003: 1).

Zarema Muzhikhoyeva is also described as having been prostituted to the cause of the *shakhidki*. She is one of the first Chechen female suicide bombers to be apprehended and face Russian custody. There are varying accounts of her story, but the basic plot is clear. Zarema was 22 when she backed out of her suicide mission in July 2003. She was a widow with very little power. Her in-laws had taken in her children, as is customary, after their son and her husband died.[14]

She felt beholden to them and without power so she stole $800 worth of jewellery for her escape. When this failed, she was shamed and now owed her in-laws for the jewellery. One journalist writes: 'Muzhikhoyeva said she decided to become a shakhid, or martyr, to repay her in-laws, as they would receive compensation of $1,000 from the rebels if she carried out a suicide bombing' (Saradzhyan 2004).[15] After she was sentenced to twenty years in prison in 2004, she told another reporter, 'What was there left for me to do? I was covered in shame. I went and asked to become a martyr' (Agence France Presse 2004b).

On 10 July, Zarema 'failed' in a suicide bombing mission. Different accounts explain that she was stopped by security forces (Boswell 2003: A1), that the detonator on her explosive device failed (Parfitt 2003: 28), that she lost her 'nerve' (Agence France Presse 2004b). The version of the story that maintains Zarema was stopped by security forces recounts that they asked about her handbag. She told them 'it was a suicide bomb belt and then challenged them to "press the button and find out"' (Boswell 2003: A1). When she was sentenced to twenty years, Zarema cried out, 'Now I know why everyone hates Russians!' She said she would 'come back and blow you all up' (Myers 2004: 1). Zarema's story identifies desperation over her circumstances with cultural shame and embarrassment. Yet some use her story to say that the women are not the ones who decide they will engage in these acts. The mother, monster and whore narrratives take away women's agency, obscure their real reasons for fighting, and legitimate the war effort against them while maintaining gender norms which require real women's conformity.

CHECHEN WOMEN DON'T KILL: GENDERED NARRATIVES AND GENDERED CONFLICTS

Chechens have watched atrocity after atrocity committed in their towns and cities; men and women alike have witnessed men being dragged from their homes at gunpoint, beaten and tortured, and even in some cases 'disappeared'. There is no argument taking place outside of Russia that policies there are considered crimes against humanity and cast serious doubts on Russia's status as a functioning and healthy democracy. Both men and women show signs of desperation. Since 2002, there has been a shift that has seen women participating on a greater scale. But the women's desperation over what they have witnessed is problematized not by acts that deepen their desperation, but the linking of that desperation by many to irrationality or to the women's exploitation by terrorists organizations.

Both linkages make the desperation out to be something that it may not be: the removal of a woman's own impetus from her actions by placing the onus outside of herself and on other factors, such as Palestinianization and exploitation. McDonald asserts that '[t]here are so many theories to explain the women's motivations that it's impossible to sort through them' (McDonald 2003: A4). But this merely echoes the government's agenda in finding any reason other than their war in Chechnya as the motivation for women's violence.

These narratives do not tell the world the Chechens' story. Instead, the narratives tell the world what the Russians want to portray about their war with the Chechens (the legitimacy of the Russian cause and the moral superiority of Russian masculinities and feminity). The media carry their own agenda – to sell newspapers and find readers – thus making their sensationalist language part of the competitive game to increase readership. As Fareed Zakaria wrote, 'We [the West] treat suicide bombers as delusional figures, brainwashed by imams. But they are also products of political realities' (Zakaria 2003: 57). The Chechens have legitimate political grievances that have created the momentum behind the extreme and brutal tactic of suicide bombing. Media and government narratives, however, gender the conflict and its participants and obscure the political reality.

The 'black widows' represent the latest stage of a discourse of Russian militarized masculinity aimed at legitimizing the Russian state enterprise (Eichler 2006). Whatever the effect of this narrative on Russian security, it has begun to undermine further whatever security women had available to them in Chechnya. Andrzej Zaucha, author of a book about the Moscow crisis, *Moscow: Nord-Ost*, is sceptical that there is anything behind the 'black widow' narrative. Zaucha remains unconvinced that there is any truth to women's blackmail, drugging and rape as motivating factors behind their martyrdom.

Instead, 'He believes all the women were there of their own free will – but had personal motives. "It suits the Russian government to say that drugs, brainwashing and blackmail are involved," he argues' (Groskop 2004b). Thus, force is necessary and the extreme rhetoric allows for extreme policies. In the continued use of extreme rhetoric that dehumanizes and demonizes the Chechens, women are the latest enemy.

Women's security in Chechnya has been in steep decline since the early part of this century. *Bespredel* and *zachistkis* reduced the security in the region, but in the past mainly targeted the men as the fighters in the war against Russia. Yet, as mentioned, women are now being killed, disappeared, tortured and raped in greater numbers. Murphey explains that 'the treatment of women is becoming harsher. They're not only being intimidated, blackmailed and threatened, in some cases they are being beaten' (2004). Widows are now being kidnapped by FSB agents simply because their husbands were killed in the fighting (Strauss 2004: A7). Most abducted women do not appear to have any connection to the terrorist organizations (Murphey 2004). In one family alone four women, a mother and her three daughters, were all taken during the night by men in military uniforms. They left behind six children, ranging in age from 4 to 18 (Strauss 2004: A7). In another case, a woman's husband disappeared in 2001; she was arrested four times. At one point she was 'hung by her ankles and interrogated'; a month after that (January 2004) she was taken from her house by men in masks and disappeared (Murphey 2004). A 59-year-old woman was taken with her three daughters and son. The women were finally released after three months; the son is still missing (Murphey 2004). These are only a sampling of the stories reported.[16] In other cases, women have been arrested because they were wearing hijabs or headscarves (Aliev 2003).

Women are attacking Russians, and Russians are attacking women in Chechnya with unprecedented force and frequency. Yet Weir tells a story of Chechen femininity which is at odds with this militarization and violence, as he explains that 'it is almost unheard of for Chechen women to fight. They are traditionally the heads of the household and the peacemakers in Chechen society' (Weir 2003: 1). A Chechen historian agrees:

'It's completely alien to our culture', rails an indignant Jabrail Gakayev, a Chechen historian at the Russian Academy of Sciences. Even during Russia's protracted war against the Chechens and their Caucasian neighbours two centuries ago, he says, 'women only took up arms when the men were killed and they had to protect their children'. (*Economist* 2003)

If Chechen women are unlikely to engage in tactics as radical as suicide bombing, then the public narratives fail by asking what is wrong with the women rather than what is wrong with the political and social context which has resulted in this (apparently) radical shift in Chechen women's choices and behaviour. After all,

Chechen women have been active from the first as suicide bombers. They do not appear coerced, drugged, or otherwise enticed into these acts. On the contrary, they are self-recruited on the basis of seeking a means of enacting social justice, revenge, and warfare against what they perceive as their nation's enemy. All the women in our sample had been deeply personally traumatized and bereaved by violent deaths in their near families or all about them, and we believe this formed the basis for their self-recruitment into terrorist organizations. Trauma alone, however, would not have motivated them into terrorism: it had to be coupled with a terror promoting ideology espoused by an organization able to equip the women to act. (Speckhard and Akhmedova 2006: 76)

Like most questions in gender and international relations, the issue of why Chechen women engage in suicide bombings is complex. It is taken up again in Chapter 8. The question of what impact the false but stylized narratives of these women have is also an important one. The narratives of the 'black widows' accomplish several important political goals for their Russian adversaries.

The instrumental use of language and terminology is an important factor in the narratives used against the 'black widows.' First, they vilify Chechen femininity and valorize the ordered, militarized Russian masculinity set up in opposition to what is held to be deranged, wild and irrational. Chechen femininity. The use of the term 'black widow', with its implication of threatening and irrational women driven to harm Russian society, creates a supportive audience for Russia's use of (il)legitimate force in Chechnya. By 'othering' the Chechen women as 'Palestinian', the successful association of Chechen women and terrorism breaks up the powerful coalition of Russian and Chechen women who are opposed to the Russian effort to maintain control over Chechnya by force. Defining the 'black widows' as having been 'Palestinianized' denies the Chechen women whatever citizenship they previously held (even though it was precarious at best) and contributes to the illegitimacy of their cause. The rhetorical construction of Chechen women as anything and everything but citizens who are seeking a solution to an incredibly violent war helps the Russian government ensure that the war efforts (the fighting and popular support for the war) go its way. The creation of such a monstrous image of Chechen women (and the men who either support or control them) allows the Russian government to justify whatever means it considers necessary to suppress the Chechen 'terrorists.' In the construction of the Chechens as terrorists and not as nationalists seeking self-determination, they lose their right to civilian immunity.[17]

Beyond the individual and social contexts of Russia's rhetorical construction of the 'black widows' as an illegitimate, disruptive source of change, there are international implications. The supposed Palestinianization of the conflict permits Russia to talk about Chechnya not as a civil war in Russia but as a part of the global war on terror, which gives the war effort legitimacy as well as gaining it national and international support.

The 'black widow' narrative, with its elements of the mother, monster and whore narrative, at once *blames women* for the conflict and absolves individual women of responsibility for their actions by describing them as at fault but out of control, insane or enslaved. Half a world away and part of a different conflict entirely, some of these same elements can be found in the discourses used publicly to characterize Palestinian and Iraqi suicide bombers, the subject of Chapter 5.

FIVE

DYING FOR SEX AND LOVE IN THE MIDDLE EAST

Even though women constitute a small percentage of suicide bombers in Palestine and Iraq, they receive a disproportionate amount of public interest and speculation.[1] Often female self-martyrs are seen as 'driven by emotions', a view which denies that women in the Middle East have legitimate political grievances.[2] Women make up almost 7 per cent of all Palestinian suicide bombers; they account for less than 1 per cent of suicide attacks in Iraq.

Since 2002, 15 women – 10 in Israel/Palestine, 4 in Iraq,[3] and 1 in Jordan – have completed 'successful'[4] suicide attacks in the Middle East (Schweitzer 2006: 8; tkb.org 2006; Fisher 2004: A23). These women have been profiled in international media and academic analyses, as well as by governmental and intelligence agencies. The resonance of the mother, monster and whore narratives is again apparent in the descriptions of these women's suicide attacks, even in different geographical (Middle Eastern), religious (Islamic) and cultural (often reputed as male-dominated) contexts.

WOMEN, ISLAM, WAR AND TERRORISM

Women's suicide attacks in the Middle East are described simultaneously as gender-liberating demonstrations of agency and as gender-

TABLE 5.1 SUICIDE BOMBERS 2000–2007

	1/9/2000–11/9/2001	12/9/2001–1/9/2003	2/3/2003–27/3/2007	Total	Female total
Israel, West Bank and Gaza	14	70	55	149	10
Iraq	0	1	609	610	4
Jordan	0	0	3	3	1

Source: tkb.org (accessed 27 March 2007).

subordinating evidence of men's control over women's bodies. Between the two different causes of Palestinian nationhood and al-Qaeda's radical religiosity, many narratives present women as pawns, subject to the whims of the men in charge. Others argue that women's participation in suicide bombings shows increasing gender equality in both the terrorist organizations and in the societies from which they draw members. The belief of some that women are gaining equality through their actions must be examined carefully, especially in light of historical examples. For example, Palestinian women are generally understood to have gained attention and equality by participating in the resistance movement during the first Intifada. Yet scholars and activists have been concerned that, after the conflict subsided, women would be sidelined and marginalized by the new Palestinian Authority, which attached less importance to the symbolism of gender equality and maintained traditional gendered expectations (Coughlin 2000). As radical Islam gained ground in the Palestinian Territories, a fear came to light, which still exists today, that women's socio-political autonomy would be obscured by increasing militant commitment to Palestinian independence (Coughlin 2000; Schulz and Schulz 1999; Hammami 1990). In the case of al-Qaeda, the group's affiliation with the misogynistic Taliban regime is well documented. Thus this attention focuses on the tension between whether women are being allowed to participate or if they truly want to participate, or on both. This is especially of concern in light of the manifestations of gender subordination as exemplified in the storied tellings of women's participation.

Still, these analyses treat women's participation in violent political struggle as an aberration in Islamic culture, a characterization which does not tell the whole story. While public space – political and social – is notoriously unavailable to Middle Eastern women,[5] there is precedence for women's involvement in political struggle in Islam and Middle Eastern cultures. One early Islamic sect, the Khariji, mandated that women, along with men, should participate in jihad (waging war) as a religious duty like prayer, pilgrimage, fasting and almsgiving (Ahmed 1992: 70). Many of the accounts of Muslim battles before and after Muhammad's death recall women warriors by name, including many of his wives (70). As veiling and the seclusion of women within Islam became prevalent, female fighters became more irregular (69–70).

In spite of the perception that women behind veils do not fight, many twentieth-century conflicts have prominently featured Islamic women. During the First Gulf War, a quarter of Iraqi soldiers and half of Kuwaiti soldiers were women (Sjoberg 2006). Both the United Arab Emirates and Yemen maintain trained women's fighting forces (Karpinski 2006). Women were heavily involved in the Algerian revolution against the French; women fought against the Taliban in Afghanistan during their rise to power; and the Iranian Mujahideen have all-female combatant units (Coughlin 2000: 226). In 1981, Mu'ammer Qaddafi opened Libyan military schools and colleges to 'Libyan Arab girls [and] ... all the girls of the Arab nation and Africa.' In addition, Qaddafi's Republican Guard and his personal bodyguards are women (Coughlin 2000: 232). Throughout the past thirty years, and especially during the past decade, women have become increasingly involved as warriors in the global jihad (Ali 2006). Female jihad fighters, or 'mujahidaat' (Ali 2006), and their successes have forced conservative organizations like al-Qaeda to reconsider the value of women as warriors.

While the position of women in Islamist revolutionary movements specifically and in Islamic societies more generally cannot be covered in the span of a few pages, there are several salient observations that can help to guide us. The apparent tension between women's public exclusion and their participation in resistance organizations is essential for analysing the stories told of Middle Eastern women suicide bombers. Second, not all Islamic cultures are the same, and women's situation varies individually, locally and within the groups that they join. Third, several Islamist women have critiqued the Western feminist notion that women in Islamic states and radical Islamist organizations are universally the victims of patriarchy. Instead, some have argued for a middle ground, recognizing that Islamic women's roles, like those of women around the world, are both in constant flux and set in the context of historical and current gender subordination (Coughlin 2000). This middle ground recognizes that, like women everywhere, Islamic women are affected by gender subordination, but also, like women everywhere, gender subordination is not the only salient narrative in their personal and political lives. It is in this hybridized context that we analyse women's entry into the Palestinian resistance organizations and al-Qaeda and the public narratives of their involvement in suicide terrorism.

WOMEN IN THE PALESTINIAN RESISTANCE MOVEMENT

Coverage of female self-martyrs in the Middle East gives disproportionate attention to the motives, training and processes behind Palestinian women's attacks, while less has been written about the women involved in suicide attacks by al-Qaeda. This is likely because of the duration and intensity of the conflict over Palestinian independence. The Palestinian Resistance Movement (PRM), along with some of its women members, has been active for the better part of half a century. The PRM grew out of the Arab defeat in the Six Day War. The PRM can be seen as the merging of two already existing movements of Fateh and the Arab Nationalist Movement (ANM). Although they both came together under the Palestine Liberation Organization (PLO) umbrella, they still have unique and distinct identities. Fateh and the Popular Front for the Liberation of Palestine (PFLP), the eventual outcome of the ANM, were religiously secular and, to varying degrees, supportive and encouraging of the inclusion of women. Resistance organizations are typically referred to as those under the PLO umbrella but may also include Hamas and Palestinian Islamic Jihad (PIJ).

Narratives concerning the enlistment of women in the Palestinian resistance movement and self-martyrdom focus on how women became involved in these organizations. According to these stories, Palestinians have relied upon family ties and men's relationships with women in order to involve women in the struggle. PFLP policy encouraged participants to bring in their family members, and especially for brothers to recruit sisters, as it was often easier to mobilize girls and women whose male family members were active in the Resistance (Peteet 1991: 119; see also Cunningham 2003: 184). Because these women have been exposed to politics and political arguments in the home, they are already more politicized. Additionally, 'the parents are acquainted with Resistance members and feel their daughters have a protected status' (Peteet 1991: 119). Honour is famiy-based in Palestinian culture; thus parents and older brothers protect the sisters' status. Therefore Palestinian families must be reassured that while daughters or sisters are doing something worthy for the community, their personal and familial honour is not being compromised.

Once they have joined Resistance organizations, women are often placed in traditional roles. Yet, as the conflict has continued, women's integration into roles previously reserved for men became increasingly accepted. First, women moved from household and private service to public activism and volunteering. From the late 1970s and into the 1980s, women's activism concerned literacy, small-scale production training, nurseries and kindergartens, and health education (Giacaman and Johnson 1989: 159). While these tasks may seem feminized, the performing of these services integrated women into the organizations and normalized their appearance as the public face of the Resistance.

During times of crisis, such as the first Intifada, women were allowed to participate in the defence of the nation. What had previously been prohibited (active participation in violence) was revisited and 'filtered through a nationalistic lens' (Peteet 1991: 3). Women's involvement in the military arm 'awakened [them] to their potential equality to men' (150). As the women proved themselves able, physically and emotionally, the stereotype that women were incapable lost some of its influence (150). New female recruits often 'demand[ed] military training and service', especially the women who were self-mobilized (150).⁶ The rigours of military training proved a woman's commitment to the cause. Once the crisis subsided women's participation on this new level did not (150). Therefore the crisis expanded women's roles.

The advent of Palestinian female suicide bombers demonstrated just how far women's participation had evolved. When the second Intifada began in 2000 the implementation of suicide bombers became more widespread and was less dependent upon religious motivation, as it had been when religiously motivated Hamas introduced it to the Palestinian territories in the 1990s. Even though martyrdom is now a secular strategy, women's participation in suicide bombings is a contentious issue. Yet the fact that Palestinian culture in the West Bank and Gaza is completely saturated by the idea of martyrdom serves to help us understand the phenomenon of suicide bombing and women's participation in it.

Posters, portraits, videos and music that praise the martyrs inundate the Palestinian territories (Rubin 2002: 15–16). It is so pervasive that one English teacher in the Aida refugee camp near Bethlehem commented: 'in the fourth grade you have kids who are Fateh, Hamas, Islamic Jihad, and the Popular Front for the Liberation of Palestine' (Rubin 2002: 16).⁷ A 2002 History Channel documentary (*Inside the Mind of a Suicide Bomber*) showed footage of school-aged children dressed in the uniforms of their paramilitary organization of choice. A Palestinian psychiatrist in Gaza City, Dr Iyad Sarraj, believes self-martyrdom attacks are a systemic problem: 'They are creating a new kind of culture.' He added that Palestinian children are beginning to equate self-martyrdom attacks and death with power (Bennett 2002b: 1).

This drive for power is ultimately political. Dr Emanuel Savin believes the 'Israeli occupation' and its dire socio-economic consequences are the 'main motivation[s] for the Palestinians' readiness to commit suicide attacks' (Victor 2003: 39). This affects people of both genders. Andalib Audawan, a feminist from Gaza, said,

> I believe that suicide actions are the outcome of despair.... And women are just as desperate as men, so why exclude them from taking these actions just because they are women? There should be no difference and no rules that prevent women from doing the same as men. (Victor 2003: 236)

The acceptability of self-martyrdom among Palestinians surfaces in personal reactions to male and female suicide attacks. Ayat Akras was the third Palestinian female suicide bomber. When journalists asked her best friend's younger sister, Shireen, what she thought, she smiled and said 'It's great ... It's sensational. Anyone would want to be in her place. ... If I had the means', she said, 'I would have done it yesterday' (Rubin 2002: 15).

Personal feelings of injustice also inform the resistance organizations' decisions to use martyrdom attacks, but it is also highly strategic. Hoffman finds that the 'rivalries between the various Palestinian terrorist organization groups has often spawned intense competition' (Hoffman 2006: 163). Each organization deployed suicide bombers to maintain public support. As a secular organization, Fateh was on the losing side of the competition for Palestinians' loyalty until they decided to deploy suicide bombings. Al-Aqsa Martyrs Brigade,[8] associated with Fateh,[9] was also the first to include female suicide bombers – a move that was seen as giving them a competitive edge. The first four and the eighth Palestinian women suicide bombers were associated with the al-Aqsa. Not to be outdone, the fifth, sixth and ninth bombers were trained by Islamic Jihad[10] and the seventh and tenth by Hamas[11] (Brunner 2005: 31).

Hamas was initially opposed to female suicide bombers; its former leader, Sheikh Ahmad Yassin, 'argued that a woman's appropriate role in the conflict was to support the fighters' and they were unnecessary at that stage in the conflict (Bloom 2005a, 60). He 'renounced the use of women as suicide bombers' following the martyrdom of Wafa Idris (the first female); but, as support grew, 'Yassin amended his position, saying that a woman waging jihad must be accompanied by a male chaperone' and must not be away from home for more than twenty-four hours (Bloom 2005a, 60). When the first female member of Hamas[12] blew herself up, Yassin said:

> The fact that a woman took part for the first time in a Hamas operation marks a significant evolution. ... The male fighters face many obstacles on their way to operations, and this is a new development in our fight against the enemy. The holy war is an imperative for all Muslim men and women, and this operation proves that the armed resistance will continue until the enemy is

TABLE 5.2 FEMALE PALESTINIAN SUICIDE BOMBERS[13]

Name	Age	Date	Group	Place	No. killed (besides herself)	No. injured
Wafa Idris	28	27/1/2002	al-Aqsa	Jerusalem	1	150
Dareen Abu Aysheh	21	27/2/2002	al-Aqsa	Ramallah	0	4
Ayat Akras	18	29/3/2002	al-Aqsa	Jerusalem	2	28
Andaleed Takafka	18	12/4/2002	al-Aqsa	Jerusalem	6	104
Hiba Daraghmeh	19	19/5/2003	Hamas	Afula	3	93
Hanadi Jaradat	27	4/10/2003	PIJ	Haifa	19	50
Reem Saleh Al Riyashi	22	24/1/2004	Hamas	Erez	4	0
Zainub Abu Salem	19	22/9/2004	al-Aqsa	Jerusalem	2	17
Mervat Masoud	18	5/11/2006	PIJ	Beit Hanoun	0	1
Fatima Omar al-Najar	55–68	23/11/2006	Hamas	Beit Hanoun	0	5

driven from our land. This is revenge for all the fatalities sustained by the armed resistance. (Bloom 2005a: 60; see also Victor 2003: 32–3)

According to Yassin, because men face 'many obstacles' women are like a 'reserve army' that can have better access to targets (Zedalis 2004: 7). In this understanding, jihad is a way for both sexes to seek revenge against Israel, Hamas's enemy. Many researchers isolate female suicide bombers' motivation as the seeking of revenge for a traumatic event. But, as Sheik Yassin implies, and as male suicide bombers have affirmed, post-traumatic revenge is not just a woman's motivation. Men's motivations are also often intimately tied up with revenge, even when suicide bombing is a strategic political move. Likewise, even when women have personal motivations, women's violence also carries with it their own strategic logic and that of those in command.

Specific profiles of the Palestinian women suicide bombers, however, downplay any role that politics had in their motivation to act. Many accounts that generalize their motivations claim the women were seeking to regain lost honour, either for themselves or (mainly) for their families. All but one of the Palestinian women were under 30 years of age (the one being between 55 and 68). The Palestinian women suicide bombers came from a variety of backgrounds; some were married with children, others divorced and childless; a few of the women were highly educated, others were not.

We have some information about these women's self-identified reasons for their choices, because, unlike many of the other women featured in this book, Palestinian women suicide bombers frequently leave messages and martyrdom videos. While the women's martyrdom statements often focus on their politics, the coverage and analysis of their behaviour often focus on their personal lives and feminine shortcomings. Female suicide bombers are 'portrayed as the chaste wives and mothers of revolution' (Bloom 2005a: 56). An Egyptian newspaper referred to Idris as 'the Bride of Heaven', while another compared her to the Virgin Mary: 'From Mary's womb issued a Child who eliminated oppression, while the body of Wafa became shrapnel that eliminated despair and aroused hope' (Bloom 2005a: 56–7).[14]

Wafa Idris took part and was politicized by the first intifada and died as the first Palestinian female suicide bomber (Victor 2003: 40). A popular account of her suicide attack uses Idris' divorce to rationalize the first female Palestinian's suicide bombing: 'Wafa had been a constant target for mocking after her husband divorced her' (41). Idris's husband is said to have divorced her because they had been told she could not have children; once divorced, a Palestinian woman does not typically remarry (41). Idris is said to have felt she was a financial burden to her already strained and impoverished family and wished to return to her now remarried ex-husband as his second wife in order to regain her honour (48–51). This familial desperation featured in explanations of her suicide attack. These ideas contribute especially to the mother narrative.

The second Palestinian female suicide bomber, Aysheh, wanted to become an English professor and resisted marriage. She was a student at Al Najah University in Nablus (Victor 2003: 97). One of her brothers was already a martyr and another was in prison for attempting a suicide attack (100–101). Victor writes that Aysheh was frustrated the university could not offer her more of a challenge and implies that she was seemingly too bright for her own good (104). Aysheh's honour was tainted when she was forced to kiss her cousin at an Israeli checkpoint (107). According to Victor, this experience motivated her to become a *shahida*.[15]

Ayat Akras takes on the Arab countries in her martyrdom video: 'I am going to fight instead of sleeping Arab armies who are watching Palestinian girls fighting alone' (Copeland 2002: C01; Toles Parkin 2004: 85). She was a journalist who wanted to communicate about the Palestinian cause and was described as more political than her fiancé (Victor 2003: 201, 203). She may also have been motivated by the death of two family friends, one killed by Israeli soldiers while he was planting a bomb near Bethlehem, the second a child playing with Lego in his home (Rubin 2002: 16; Victor 2003: 206).

The fifth bomber, Hiba Daraghmah, was the first to be sponsored by PIJ along with al-Aqsa. She was an English student and a single woman. Family interviews allege that she was raped by an uncle when she was 14 and subsequently became very religious (Brunner 2005: 33–4; Toles Parkin 2004: 85). Reem al-Riyashi, the Hamas female suicide bomber, has perhaps the most troubling story; her humiliation involved both familial and personal honour. It has been speculated that her husband drove her to the Erez Checkpoint to commit a bombing that would atone for her supposed adultery (Brunner 2005: 34; Associated Press 2004: A5). Stories about her attack raise the questions of her willingness to kill and die, and of Hamas's true support for female *shahidas*. Al-Riyashi said in her martyrdom video:

> God gave me the ability to be a mother of two children who I love so. But my wish to meet God in paradise is greater, so I decided to be a martyr for the sake of my people. I am convinced God will help and take care of my children. (Toles Parkin 2004: 86).

She was ready to die out of apparent religious dedication (martyrdom) but also 'for the sake of her people' (Moore 2004: A22). Al-Riyahsi also claimed, 'I always wanted to be the first woman to carry out a martyr attack ... That is the only thing I can ask God for' (A22). Nevertheless, accounts focus on her sexual sins more than her religious/nationalist dedication. Through these statements al-Riyashi contributes to a nationalist discourse that is clouded by the gendering of her actions.

A similar focus can be found in accounts of Zina, an imprisoned Palestinian woman who is said to have helped plan suicide attacks after becoming pregnant out of wedlock. According to stories about her, her family said the only way for her to regain acceptance was through involvement with Hamas; but she also found fulfilment through her participation (Victor 2003: 131–3). She demonstrated a profound political commitment to the cause of Palestinian independence:

> Her whole demeanor changed. Her face lit up. She was exuberant. 'For the first time in my life', she said, 'I was free and doing something meaningful for myself and for a political cause. I could study and not have to worry about what people thought. But I also realized how difficult life was under occupation. A lot of people I knew were injured, and several had even been killed.' (Victor 2003: 133)

Zina was inspired by doing something for her people and for a political cause. She was seeking justice for the Palestinians. Another woman told the *Sunday Times* about her desire to seek justice, for similar reasons:

> [W]e have waited long, heard a lot of poetic words, make-believe, promises and talk of peaceful solutions, justice and fairness for the Palestinians, but look around you, tell me what you see.
> We have nothing – nothing. Just empty, meaningless words that have brought us nothing. So it is time we abandon the talk and take our destiny into our own hands. Dramatic maybe, violent maybe, but there is no other way. Our acts are cries of desperation in the hope that someone will eventually heed us. (Jaber 2003: 2)

A number of Palestinian woman martyrs, and prisoners after unsuccessful attempts, have mentioned religious commitment as their motivation for involvement. When a woman in Israeli custody explained why she crossed into Israel from Gaza wearing 10 kilogrammes of explosive, she said, 'My dream was to be a martyr'

(*Record* 2005: A6). Another Palestinian woman (who was apprehended by Israelis before detonation) told an Al Jazeera reporter: 'I was very, very happy, happy on the inside. I tried to grow closer to my parents so they wouldn't be mad at me. I might have been a little confused, but not too much. The joy that filled me overcame everything else' (MEMRI 2005). The women's own focus is on political rationale or on religious joy intermingled with some personal statements, however, media accounts focus on personal reasons, such as divorce, rape or adultery.

Family-based motivations are also featured prominently in stylized narratives about Hanadi Jaradat, a trainee attorney, 'was said to have taken revenge for the loss of a male relative, in this case her brother' (Brunner 2005: 34). Jaradat's message is religious, but has strong elements of wanting to hurt and kill Israelis. As she trained, her religiosity increased, and in her martyrdom video she declared:

> By the will of God I decided to be the sixth martyr who makes her body full with splinters in order to enter every Zionist heart who occupied our country. We are not the only ones who will taste death from their occupation. As they sow so will they reap. (Toles Parkin 2004: 86)

Jaradat's desire for justice is downplayed in media accounts of her attack, while family is emphasized. In the narratives that analyse women suicide bombers *as women*, women's family, fantasy and fancy are the focus while their politics are ignored.

Brunner points out that the media paid decreasing attention to the bomber's sex as each event happened (Brunner 2005: 33–4). Accordingly, there is less written about the later bombers. Even so, the sensationalism surrounding Fatima Omar al-Najar's 23 November 2006 suicide bombing has brought media attention back to women self-martyrs. Characterized in the media as 'suicide granny' and 'hamas hag', al-Najar has broken another stereotype of suicide bombers: age (Farrell 2006). Those incredulous narratives about al-Najar's choice and agency in the attack emphasize the special tenderness of grandmotherly love (Farrell 2006). Many of the elements that recur in narratives about Palestinian women suicide bombers also recur in narratives about the women of al-Qaeda.

WOMEN IN AL-QAEDA

Al-Qaeda[16] used to advise its male members 'not to use women in the 'jihad business" and excluded women from membership and participation (Kelley 2002: 1). Since 9/11, al-Qaeda has made the decision to include women, both as support personnel and as jihadic fighters. Al-Qaeda has begun to recruit women as jihadis both inside and outside the Middle East and the Caucusus (Kelley 2002: 1). Al-Qaeda sees the strategic value of female involvement because women are less likely to be suspected as terrorists in airports and other public places. In 2006 Tufts' Fletcher School's Jebsen Center began investigating al-Qaeda female suicide bombers. They have since come to the conclusion that women as suicide bombers is a strategy specific to Abu Musab al-Zarqawi and his organization al-Qaeda in Iraq, and not indicative of the entire organization. They broadened their investigation to examine women's involvement in various roles within the al-Qaeda organization more generally (Dow 2007). Women from across the globe now participate in the organization, in one way or another. A Belgian woman who converted as an adult to Islam, a Pakistani woman educated at the Massachusetts Institute of Technology (MIT), and a British woman charged in the London airline bombing plot in August 2006 are all known or suspected al-Qaeda operatives. The organisation has even gone so far as to publish an internet magazine, *Al Khansa*, to train women to be better fighters.

In 2002, US law-enforcement officials announced their concern that 'al-Qaeda has begun recruiting Afghan and Middle Eastern women to distribute money and messages to its operatives around the world' (Kelley 2002: 1). At this time, women were limited to support roles, the typical entry point for women's involvement in Islamic or Middle Eastern terrorist groups (Peteet 1991: 110; and Jawaad 1990). So while the development signaled a sea-change in al-Qaeda's organization, it still limited women's role. Women's involvement may be explained as a strategic move – confounding the stereotype of al-Qaeda members as Arabic *men*. Women slowly came to play larger roles in the organization.

The women members of al-Qaeda who have received the most attention are those from outside the Middle East. In 2003, a Pakistani woman in America garnered her own fair share of headlines. Aafia Siddiqui, an MIT graduate and mother of three, is wanted by the FBI (Thomas et al. 2004: 3). Her brother's American Civil Liberties Union (ACLU) attorney described Siddiqui as a soccer mom: just a 'woman with children, wearing a hijab, [and] driving a Volvo' (Ragavan et al. 2003b: 50). It came to light that in mid- to late 2001 Siddiqui had filed for divorce in Karachi from her husband, Mohammad Khan, citing abuse of her person and her children. Her family claims Khan used Siddiqui's email address to purchase night-vision goggles, bomb-making books, and body armour (Thomas et al. 2004: 3; Ragavan et al. 2003a: 33). He also allegedly used her address to send emails to friends and family to maintain a happy-family pretence (Ragavan et al. 2003b: 50).

This image of the husband's exploitation, however, does not seem to tell the whole story. It was Siddiqui's name, not her husband's, given to American intelligence, by captured Khalid Sheikh Mohammed (al-Qaeda's operations chief), that identified her 'as a "facilitator" for future [al-Qaeda] attacks' (Thomas et al. 2004: 3). It was her name that was on a post-office box used to help an al-Qaeda operative in the plot to blow up 'gas stations and underground fuel-storage tanks in the Baltimore–Washington area' (3). She lived in Boston until late summer 2002, when she, her estranged husband, and three small children disappeared after the FBI expressed interest in them; they are now thought to be in Pakistan (Thomas et al. 2004; Ragavan et al. 2003b).

By 2003, the FBI was expressing concern that 'al Qaeda may be recruiting and training women to carry out terror attacks', in order to 'regain an element of surprise' (CBS News 2003: 1). As noted in the article, this represents a shift away from Taliban politics (1). One source claimed that al-Qaeda would implement female jihadis over the course of three phases (APS Diplomat News Service 2004: 1). According to the FBI, the first phase began with Chechen women – the 'black widows'.[17] The second phase was to have women operatives in Saudi Arabia and Iraq. The third phase would 'focus on Muslim females and children in the West as well as in Asia and other parts of the world' (APS Diplomat News Service 2004: 1).

Just as the Palestinian cause is being steeped in martyrhood, the al-Qaeda group mission revolves around it (Pape 2005). From an interview with a woman who identified herself as Um Osama (mother of Osama) in an Arabic newspaper, American intelligence learned that 'al Qaeda was setting up training camps ... to train women to become martyrs' (CBS News 2003: 1; Bell 2003: A7; see also Bloom 2005, 61). The training camp would establish a woman-only structure that would train 'female mujahedeen affiliated with al Qaeda and the Taliban' (CBS News 2003: 1). The existence of separate training camps and structures would mean that women and men would not have to interact, ensuring social safety and purity for both sexes. Um Osama said al-Qaeda was influenced by the success of Palestinian and Chechen female suicide bombers, who garner more media attention and have slipped past security forces with more ease than their male counterparts (CBS News 2003: 1; Phillips 2006: 2).

Al Khansa is a magazine produced by the al-Qaeda Women's Information Bureau which instructs women on the strategy and tactics of jihad. It is named after a seventh-century Islamic poet favoured by Muhammed. All of her four sons were killed in the battle of Qadisiyah, and Al Khansa celebrated their martyrdom.[18] The launch of *Al Khansa* also demonstrates al-Qaeda's intent to recruit and train more women, as it targets Saudi, Sunni Iraqi, and Sunni Arab women and children (APS Diplomat News Service 2004: 2). In an *Al Khansa* editorial, the author proclaims:

> We will stand up, veiled and in abaya (black cloak), arms in hand, our children on our laps and the Book of Allah and Sunnah of the Prophet as our guide. The blood of our husbands and the bodies of our children are an offering to God. (APS Diplomat News Service 2004: 2)

The *Al Khansa* website says that a female '"mujaheeda" ... must learn the Koran by heart, have basic first aid training and be able to prepare an emergency kit' in addition to knowing how to shoot, carry munitions, be willing to give her own money, and be content 'with what is strictly necessary' (Phillips 2005: 1).

In a translated summarization of *Al Khansa*'s various articles, it is made clear that jihad is a 'compulsory individual duty imposed by Allah' that both men and women must participate in: 'Women are at the same level as the men and for that they share the same responsibility in the continuation and the success of Jihad' (Silm 2004: 2). Another article focuses on the internal and external obstacles a woman may face in trying to carry out jihad. Internal obstacles can be both personal (lack of religious knowledge, weakness of belief, ignorance of physical fitness) and social (family, husband, environment and society) (Silm 2004: 3). External obstacles are politics, location, weather, and lifestyle, and health (3). Sex and gender roles are notably absent from the list of obstacles.

As al-Qaeda is no longer one centrally controlled organization, the reasons behind women's involvement are complicated. For example, while *Al Khansa* makes it clear that al-Qaeda intends to train women fully to become martyrs for their cause, the Jebsen Center cannot support the idea that all al-Qaeda organizations support female martyrs; instead, it maintains that only al-Qaeda in Iraq does so. Still, there are strategic reasons behind women's involvement. Zedalis says that women are used in attacks for four reasons: (1) it provides tactical advantage; (2) it bolsters the number of combatants; (3) it increases publicity and thus also recruitment; (4) it is a form of psychological combat (2004: 7). Saad Al Faqih, a Saudi Arabian dissident living in exile, believes female suicide bombings are increasing in Iraq, because

> Firstly, a large number of women are ready to join jihad. Secondly, women want to exact revenge for assaults against them and their families. This is particularly the case in Iraq where civilians have borne the brunt of the fighting. (Abedin 2005: 3)

Al Faqih also does not believe this represents an 'ideological shift by the jihadis' because 'there are no Islamic injunctions against women fighting on the frontlines of jihad. Moreover, jihadis have been training their wives or sisters for combat and jihad since the early 1980s' (Abedin 2005: 3). As the Iraqi situation deteriorates, the presence of women is growing, especially those with ties to al-Qaeda organizations.

There have been at least two female al-Qaeda martyrs since 2005.[19] In the fall of 2005 al-Qaeda female operatives were involved in two separate attacks in the Middle East. A Western woman blew herself up in Iraq and another female suicide bomber's explosive pack failed in the attack on three Amman hotels. On 28 September 2005, a Belgian-born woman, Myrium (who changed her name from Mireille), blew herself up in Tall Afar, Iraq killing six others (Browne 2005: 1; MITP Terrorism Knowledge Base 2005: 1). Myrium, raised as 'a good Catholic girl', converted to Islam before marrying her second husband (Smith 2005: 2). She came into contact with Radical Islam through her husband, a man of Moroccan descent (Dickey 2005: 1). As the first al-Qaeda female suicide bomber in Iraq, Myrium was described in maternal language in the press following her attack. Her clothing 'concealed the explosives strapped around her womb' (Dickey 2005: 1). By using the word 'womb', the article exploits the role (mother) women are supposed to play and places Myrium's innate womanhood in question due to the political actions she has undertaken. Myrium's actions are linked to her three 'failed' marriages. That Myriam 'couldn't have children' was the only quotation from the Belgian prosecutor's office included in the article (Dickey 2005: 1). Much like Medea, Myriam was disappointed in love and this disappointment caused her to act violently. Her *raison d'être*, to have a 'successful' marriage and bear children, was denied to her, and thus Myriam sought (maternal) revenge. This is the only known white Western woman suicide bomber – even though al-Qaeda is said to be recruiting white converts for their lower security profile (Browne 2005: 1).

While Myrium is the only known white Western al-Qaeda suicide terrorist, she is not the only woman who has performed an attack. In the Amman hotel bombings on 10 November 2005, Sajida Mubarak Atrous, aged 35, sister of al-Zarqawi's senior aide killed in 2004 by American forces in Falluja, tried to detonate herself in a joint suicide attack with her husband. In her confession to Jordanian security forces she gave details of how the plot was organized and 'was seen ... as likely to yield significant intelligence into the methods and plans of Mr. Zarqawi's group, al-Qaeda in Mesopotamia', which claimed responsibility (Fattah 2005: 1). While her statement – 'He [her husband] taught me. He taught me how to pull, what to do, and how to control it' (Sauer and Osman 2005: 1) – was amplified by the media, Atrous provided detail to the Jordanian authorities that validated her part in planning meetings. The overuse of that statement diminishes her wilful choice to be involved and unfairly subjects her to her husband's command.

MOTHER, MONSTER, AND WHORE NARRATIVES

Brunner also takes 'Western journalists' to task for 'looking above all for clues' in female suicide terrorists' private lives in order to 'find some rational arguments to explain what to them was inexplicable' (2005: 32). Brunner points out that by focusing on these suicide bombers' marital and child-bearing status, the accounts miss any other motivation. Toles Parkin belives that the media 'search[es] for alternative explanations behind women's participation in terror' that are not pursued 'in the coverage of male suicide bombers, whose … ideological statements appear to be taken at face value' (2004: 85). Instead, the media's emphasis on the 'emotional over the ideological' (Toles-Parkin 85) in describing women's violence is as prevalent in the characterizations of Middle Eastern female suicide terrorists as it is in the other narratives presented in this book. The media concentrates on gendered and sensationalist accounts, telling partial and marginalizing stories about who the female suicide bomber is and why she acts. Elements of the mother, monster and whore narratives are evident in the stories of Palestinian and al-Qaeda female suicide bombers.

Many researchers and journalists claim that a woman chooses martyrdom to avenge some form of personal trauma or regain a semblance of honour for herself or her family.[20] These emotional and personal factors are modern echoes of the classical private/public sphere divide.[21] The assumption that women are motivated by the personal dominates, and accounts ignore or make little mention of any political agenda. By characterizing women's actions within the mother narrative as maternal revenge makes a woman's participation different and apart from a man's participation.[22] Indeed, the language of domesticity and motherhood is particularly strong in the case of Palestinian and al-Qaeda female suicide terrorists. This gendered presentation ignores the culture of resistance that exists in the Palestinian territories and in al-Qaeda's recent commitment to involve more women.

Even though the women involved in these suicide attacks are alternately single, married or divorced, have children or are childless, have family members killed by opposing forces or not, and are educated to varying degrees, their stories are often told in terms of their actual or potential motherhood. An article in the *Sunday Times* places emphasis also on domestic disappointments: it quotes one Palestinian suicide bomber in training, 'my heart aches ... for my dead husband' and cites an Israeli expert's estimation that these women acted because they had been 'disappointed in love' (Jaber 2003: 2).

The language of motherhood is not new to the Palestinian cause. Women in the Palestinian conflict give birth to future martyrs – this has consistently been their place (Brunner 2005: 35–6; Amal 1993). But now 'multi-birthing' mothers can give birth to martyrs and become one themselves. Their bodies are a threat on all counts (Bloom 2005a). Instead their story is told as one of female honour being bound up in ideas of domesticity, maternal duty, and filial love.

Several media accounts focus on emotional reasons for revenge (Ward 2004: A6; Jaber 2003: 2),[23] which can be grouped in two ways: domestic dreams destroyed (pertaining to marital status and children), and humiliation and loss of familial honour. As a result, women's political violence is not seen as driven by ideology and belief in a cause, but instead is seen as a perversion of the private realm.[24] Female terrorists are depicted as avenging lost love and/or a destroyed happy home. Just as Medea's violence was directed towards (either to achieve or destroy) the feminine 'virtues' of preserving marriage and rearing children, so the female terrorist's violence takes on the same dimensions. Maternal revenge lacks political impetus, thus removing political onus from the women. Women 'are willing to become martyrs if by doing so they can erase a particular stigma attached to themselves or their families' (Knight 2005: A16). If a woman's actions are not political, then technically the women are not terrorists.

For example, one account of Hanadi Jaradat's actions relates them solely to her single and childless status; these aspects create 'an unenviable status in Palestinian society' for Jaradat (Hermann 2004). According to Hermann she was motivated by 'personal loss' and 'unhapp[iness] at home' ('unlike men, who tend to be motivated by national pride') (Hermann 2004). After eating her final meal in a restaurant crowded with families, 'she paused near a group of [empty] baby carriages and blew herself up' (Hermann 2004). This article implicitly links her childless status with some deeper sadness within her that led her (unconsciously) to blowing herself up. This ignores the political motivations that she declared in her martyrdom video. As noted, the language of motherhood has long played a role in the conflict, but even when this language is used it is not devoid of a political agenda. For example, Aysheh's message to Israel is politically strong and emphasizes her desire to be a martyr:

> Let Sharon the coward know that every Palestinian woman will give birth to an army of martyrs, and her role will not only be confined to weeping over a son, brother or husband instead (sic), she will become a martyr herself. (Palestinian Women Martyrs Against Israeli Occupation, 2004; in Toles-Parkin 2004: 85)

Nevertheless, narratives focus on her and others' actual and potential motherhood more than on the political choices, even when they deny motherhood in favour of politics. Perhaps it is only to be expected that images of motherhood and domesticity have been extended to female suicide bombers as they are embedded in Palestinian resistance and now radical Islam. From the first Intifada, to Idris as the Bride of Heaven, to Um Osama, motherhood and the duty (honour) women have to their family and community in the Middle East are resonant themes. They are aspects that Western media can easily grasp in order either to deny the true capability of these women or to prolong Western notions of what it means to be a woman in the Middle East. Their martyrdom videos are not filled with maternal images; indeed one mother says it is more important to be a martyr than to be a mother. The focus on motherhood serves to deny the women's part in the glorification of martyrs in these cultures of resistance.

The nurturing mother narrative is also evident in a number of descriptions of female suicide bombers and members of Middle Eastern terrorist organizations. When women were first integrated into the structures of the Palestinian Resistance Movement and al-Qaeda, they were placed in subservient, care-taking roles. The acceptance of women's participation in actual violence is described as evolving much more slowly than their permission to *serve* these radical Islamic men as they perpetrated suicide attacks. Further, the nurturing mother narrative can be found in recent coverage of the 'suicide granny', whose story cannot be told without reference to her nine children and forty-one grandchildren, whom she let down by engaging in actual violence rather than support (Farrell 2006). The monster narrative is also present in stylized stories of Palestinian women suicide bombers. Rachel Bronson, Director of the Middle East Studies at the Council on Foreign Relations, said 'I think [Sajida Mubarak Atrous] will be seen as a twisted, horrible woman who is going to hell.... Suicide is against Islam and she targeted Muslims, another taboo' (Sauer and Osman 2005: 1). Anne Marie Oliver, in her article 'The Bride of Palestine' (2006), compared Palestinian women suicide bombers to the monstrous bride of Frankenstein. Suicide terrorists, male or female, have been described in several accounts as being akin to a monstrous woman. According to Beres, 'the terrorist threat now facing Israel resembles the mythic Hydra, a monster of many heads who was difficult to kill because every time one head was struck, two new ones arose in its place' (1999: 1). This link between femininity and monstrosity others female participants in terror as well as members of society more generally.

Elements of the whore narrative are also used to describe women in Palestinian and al-Qaeda suicide missions. The sexualization of Middle Eastern women terrorists is not new – it dates back to women's participation in the 1960s and 1970s. The new bible of pop culture, Wikipedia, claims that Leila Khaled, two-time hijacker for the PFLP, was the inspiration for Leela the Savage Warrior in the British television show *Dr Who*. Leela was a scantily clad character whose prehistoric-looking costume and demeanour reflected that she was an uncivilized brute. There are obvious undertones of racism and sexualization in this pop culture 'homage' to Leila Khaled's political agency (Wikipedia 2006a). When women are assigned responsibility for their actions, they are described as 'femme fatales' (Ragavan et al. 2003: 33), imbuing in them a certain level of sexuality and even charm.

The sexualization of women suicide terrorists in the present day is equally obvious. Sheik Tantawi, a Cairo mullah who is regarded as the highest religious authority among Palestinians, endorsed women as self-martyrs, proclaiming that female attackers were allowed to disregard the code of modesty as they carried out their attacks (Margalit 2003). There is one mock *Playboy* cover that claims to feature the women of al-Qaeda: a (white) woman in a bikini with her head covered by the top of a burqa (Internet Weekly Report 2006). The racialized anonymity of the burqa on a scantily clad (but white) body demeans participants in suicide attacks as well as the other women in their societies.

The sexualization of women's attacks also exists in American media accounts. Several accounts explain how sex sold terrorism to female suicide attackers. In February 2005, Ayat Allah Kawil, an unsuccessful suicide bomber for Hamas, responded to questions about the female equivalent to the male suicide attacker's promised seventy-two virgins in paradise. She explained that as a woman suicide attacker she would have been rewarded with the right to be the 'head virgin', the 'fairest of the fair' (Oliver 2006: 1). Women interested in becoming Hamas suicide attackers are shown a romantic, sexualized video of Sana'a Mouhaidli's suicide attack in Lebanon in order to convince them to join the movement, because 'the fastest way to sell anything, an iPod or death, is to sexualize it' (1). There are also a number of accounts comparing the death of a female martyr and a wedding, where the dowry is blood and the husband is Palestinian liberation. All such characterizations sexualize female participants in suicide terrorism, and play into the whore narrative.

Accounts of violent women as prostitutes also appear in analyses of Middle Eastern female suicide bombers. The fourth Palestinian bomber, Andalib Suleiman Takafka, was, according to Victor,

> the only one of the four women who was not the subject of lengthy reports in the Israeli media. The reason perhaps is that she had no sensational story. She was just a young woman who was easily swayed and who got caught up in her own fantasy of stardom.
>
> In another society, Andalib might have ended up like countless other women and girls who fall in with the wrong crowd and become addicted to drugs or involved in prostitution or a life of petty crime. (Victor 2003: 247)

Yet Toles Parkin makes it clear that Takafka 'was concerned with the suffering of the Palestinian people' (2004: 85). While Takafka had avidly collected 'movie magazines and poster of celebrities ... in the months before her bombing she replaced those with posters of martyrs, especially Wafa Idris' (85). Victor's equation of martyrdom with drugs, prostitution and fantasy is disturbing. It removes the political implications of Takafka's choice and locates it in a deeply troubled, personal (private) realm, characterizing her as a metaphorical (and perhaps actual) whore rather than a political actor.

THE GENDERED STUDY OF SUICIDE TERRORISM

Media accounts are not the only stories of female terrorists that gender their bodies and their motivations. A number of mainstream academic studies of suicide terrorism[25] highlight the strategic nature of the act. At its very core, 'suicide terrorism is a strategy for national liberation from foreign military occupation by a democratic state' (Pape 2005: 45). Terrorist organizations make a strategic choice to engage in suicide attacks in order 'to intimidate and demoralize the enemy' (Bloom 2005a: 3). Suicide terrorism is described as a highly effective form of political violence because 'suicide terrorist campaigns ... are associated with gains for the terrorists' political cause about half the time' (Pape 2001: 64). If suicide terrorism has some political success in half of the documented cases, it can be characterized as a politically influential strategy.

According to this research, the strategic act of suicide terrorism is intended to gain political concessions. Therefore, in analysing individual acts of suicide terrorism, the consciousness of the individual cannot be ignored. If a suicide terrorist did not have a political motivation, s(he) would simply be a violent criminal who could be viewed as individual and isolated. Because suicide terrorism is a group political decision, in Pape's view suicide terrorists are 'rarely socially isolated, clinically insane, or economically destitute individuals, but are most often educated to have a good future. The profile of a suicide terrorist resembles that of a politically conscious individual' (Pape 2005: 200). In other words, this literature describes suicide bombers in the Middle East as rational political actors.

This is not to say that studies of suicide terrorists ignore personal motivations for suicide attacks. In a study of fifty Palestinian suicide bombers' autobiographical profiles, all cited personal trauma as their motivation to engage in suicide terrorism (Saleh 2005; Bagnall 2005). Nearly half of the fifty 'indicat[ed] a traumatic experience in the first intifada' (Saleh 2005: 2). Furthermore, 'evidence suggests that personal grievances have considerable weight in motivating attacks' (3). Thus, in at least half of the cases personal grievances combined with political causes to motivate political action on the part of the Palestinian suicide terrorists. A study that included suicide terrorists from inside and outside of the Middle East found that individuals 'have social, cultural, religious, and material incentives' (Bloom 2005a: 85). An example of a religious incentive is the desire for promised heavenly rewards. Material incentives include the promise of celebrity and cash incentives for the families of suicide terrorists. Humiliation, the 'loss of a loved one', or an abstract 'personal connection' to broadcasted images of death and destruction are also described as motivating factors (85–7). These personal grievances are characterized as playing a part in raising or in furthering political consciousness. In other words, personal grievances politicize suicide bombers, and their political consciousness motivates the choice of suicide attacks.

These studies appear gender-neutral at face value, but either explicitly or implicitly gender their subjects while ignoring the more general gendering of their specific political contexts and of the international political arena. We are warned by the feminists Hilary Charlesworth and Cynthia Cockburn to recognize the omission of gender in supposedly gender-neutral work or to recognize when gender identity is being manipulated (Charlesworth 1999; Cockburn 2001b). The application of both scholars reveals genderings in the academic literature analysing Middle Eastern women's motivations to engage in suicide attacks.

According to Charlesworth, studies silent about women, femininity and womanhood are not immune from gendering (1999). Pape includes the relatively few women suicide terrorists in his more general study of suicide terrorists' motives (2005). The study is careful to depict both men and women as politically conscious individuals. Therefore the profiling does not touch on the narratives of desperate mothers, cold monsters or erotically driven whores. Yet Pape's treatment fails to account for the differential treatment of gendered suicide bombers either before or after their missions. Saleh's study also includes both men and women without taking account of them as gendered actors in gendered contexts. Because both the terrorists themselves and the governments they attack operationalize gender, terrorist attacks *are* gendered and cannot be fully explained without reference to gender discourses.

Still, as Cockburn warned, taking account of gender discourses is not the same as accepting or perpetrating gender-marginalizing discourses about women's participation. A number of analyses of women terrorists *as women* do the latter, rather than seeing gendered discourses through gendered lenses. Bloom, for example, sets a woman's motivation apart from a man's in sexual terms:

> Why? Motives vary: revenge for a personal loss, the desire to redeem the family name, to escape a life of sheltered monotony and achieve fame, and to level the patriarchal societies in which they live. What is incredibly compelling about delving into how and why women become suicide bombers is that so many of these women have been raped or sexually abused in the previous conflict either by the representatives of the state or by the insurgents themselves. (Bloom 2005a, 143)

In her subsequent articles, Bloom highlights rape, sexual abuse, feelings of powerlessness, alienation, and revenge for family members or lost honour as women's motivation to engage in suicide terrorism. She emphasizes that sexual abuse is common to Kurdish, Tamil and Chechen women (Bloom 2005b: 2, 2005c: 59). For example, Bloom focuses on the report that Dhanu, the LTTE woman who blew herself up along with Indian Prime Minister Rajiv Ghandi, was raped by a gang of men and her brother was killed by peacekeepers (Knight 2005: A16; Bloom 2005c: 59). While gendered violence may be among women's (and men's) motivations for the perpetration of some suicide bombings, the reduction of women's reasons for political violence to the personal (and even sexual) sphere is problematic. These accounts emphasize women's motivations for engaging in suicide terrorism as different to men's, as associated with their femaleness rather than humanity, and as personal rather than political (Bloom 2005a).

Barbara Victor, author of *Army of Roses*,[26] also focuses on gender-differential motivations for suicide terrorism. According to Victor, a woman's decision to become a suicide bomber is due to something deeply personal and emotional. She links the decision to the relationship the woman has with her family. Specifically, Victor emphasizes women's participation as related to her family's honour. Even though she quotes researchers who place a woman's motivation in the same category as a man's (2003: 39–40, 236), Victor persists in treating women differently. To Victor, Palestinian female suicide bombers are marginalized, divorced, ridiculed and isolated, and influenced by the death and/or humiliation of a male relative (Victor 2003: 199). Like many media depictions of Middle Eastern female suicide bombers, Victor entrenches the mother narrative (emphasizing the women's dependence on men), the monster narrative (focusing on pathology and mental illness), and the whore narrative (directing attention to the role of sexuality).

At the beginning of her book, Victor's focus on women's pathology is particularly striking. She explains women's involvement in suicide bombing as mental illness, while men's involvement is a natural result of an insult to their pride. According to Victor, in the second Intifada:

> There are two different dynamics.... When an adolescent boy is humiliated at an Israeli checkpoint, from that moment, a suicide bomber is created. At the same time, if a woman becomes a shahida, one has to look for deeper, more underlying reasons. There are obviously cases where mental illness plays a part, since not all marginalized women within the Palestinian society kill themselves. Pathology plays an important role in these cases. Not all people who try to kill themselves and kill others are desperate to such a degree that they simply cannot tolerate their pain. Often there are other, more personal reasons. (Victor 2003: 28)

Apparently men can be sane and suicide bombers, while clearly women must be insane to be suicide bombers. These academic studies of the motivation for female suicide terrorists in Iraq and Palestine either ignore gender altogether or take account of gender without seeing *genderings*.[27] Instead of seeing women as agents making choices in relation to their socio-cultural situation, each produces a stylized, gender-marginalizing narrative of women's participation in these movements that denies agency.

Experts and the media keep pointing to honour and trauma as reasons behind a *woman's* involvement. This reasoning sets her apart, does not allude to political motivation, and thus denies her political agency. These characterizations make the triple move of denying women's agency in their participation, contending that women's involvement is gender-emancipatory, and feminizing the blame for the attacks.

Even though women suicide bombers in the Middle East are no longer anomalous, a large number of accounts question the validity and even existence of women's choice to engage in suicide terrorism in Iraq and for al-Qaeda. Uncertainties remain over the recruitment, training, and deployment of women in both the Palestinian territories and the al-Qaeda movement. Bloom questions if the recruitment of women is an insult to masculinity and therefore a call to action:

> Before Ayat Akras blew herself up in Israel in April 2002, she taped her martyrdom video and stated, 'I am going to fight instead of the sleeping Arab armies who are watching Palestinian girls fighting alone', in an apparent dig at Arab leaders for not being ... proactive. (Bloom 2005a: 57)

Bennett explains that a would-be Palestinian suicide bomber, Arien Ahmed, was neither trained nor questioned by 'her recruiters about why she wanted to kill and die' (2002: 1). This and a number of other accounts imply that Middle Eastern suicide bombers are being used by the organizations they represent. It has been claimed that female martyrdom training is shorter and less intense than men's and that women's missions need less technical training (Toles Parkin 2004: 80–81, 87). Others contend that women are less valued because their compensation for the deed is lower than men's (Toles Parkin 2004; Victor 2003). Yet, as cited ealier, Zedalis makes it clear that women as active participants stems from a strategic choice. Terrorists value the propaganda of the deed – the publicity that comes from an action is necessary to impart an organization's message and instil fear in society at large. The novelty of women's actions and the heavier (at first) media coverage of female suicide bombers explain, in part, why al-Aqsa deployed women, and why al Aqsa was followed by Hamas and Islamic Jihad (and why each organization engages in a tit-for-tat game). The idea that women are 'used' removes the possibility that either their choice is fully independent or that they wanted to participate.

The story of women being used and subordinated by Middle Eastern terrorist groups is juxtaposed with the argument those groups make that their women's participation is emancipatory. Gnosis, an Italian spy service, says that 'Al Khansa could indicate that ... Osama bin Laden has made a strategic choice in favor of "women's emancipation through martyrdom"' (Phillips 2005: 1). But Gnosis also doubts this new take on 'emancipation' and wonders if it is 'rather 'a tactic to involve all components of the [Islamic community] in the global jihad' (1). Indeed, some authors' terminology plays into this belief. At least three al-Qaeda women have 'been used' in Iraq, including the aforementioned Belgian woman (Phillips 2006: 2). Additionally, 'Al-Qaeda affiliates ... have used women in suicide attacks in Egypt and Uzbekistan' (2). Yet Saad Al Faqih's own words and the existence of *Al Khansa* problematize this belief and may actually indicate women's own choice to participate in al-Qaeda.

A closer look at the discourses that describe women terrorists as subordinated and emancipated sees them as a part of a larger political game, where Western sources generally characterize female martyrs as men's pawns in a patriarchal society. Middle Eastern resistance organizations combat those discourses by emphasizing both how liberated and how equal women are in their organizations, as opposed to in the organizations and governments they are combating. Of course, in the end, women's equality is neither a yes/no question nor one that should be fought on the battlefield of competing masculinities in international politics. Instead, it is a question that is very complex and reliant on many intricate details of the political context. Simona Sharoni (1997) tackles in an academic context the question of whether the Palestinian conflict and women's involvement in it has positive or negative ramifications for women's emancipation. She observes that large-scale military mobilization of women has not been characterized as a challenge to social stability, but as a necessary and valuable contribution to the nationalist struggle (1997: 24). Still, this does not mean that women participating in suicide terrorism has magically affected either their own or other women's equality.

Cultural war over the meaning of (dead) women's bodies occurs in the context not of a gender-neutral conflict, but of one fraught with many genderings of war generally and of their wars particularly. Even though the very existence of women's agency is questioned, directly or through the use of the mother, monster and whore narratives, the blame for the conflict and death in Palestine (and, in different ways, al-Qaeda)[28] is placed squarely on the shoulders of femininity.

SIX

GENDERED PERPETRATORS OF GENOCIDE

The task of analysing reactions to women's participation in genocide is qualitatively different from the other analyses in this book. The prevalence of genocide since the end of the Cold War has been a source of horror and embarrassment in international politics (Power 2002). Even male perpetrators of genocide are described in monstrous and horrified terms. The employment of the mother, monster and whore narratives in the case of genocide perpetrators is aimed specifically at dehumanizing involved women. Further, the scale of people affected by those who plan and perpetrate genocide is exponentially greater than the other crimes we have discussed: a suicide bomber, terrorist or sex abuser can count their victims in tens and maybe hundreds; a perpetrator of genocide can count victims in the tens or hundreds of thousands, if they can count them at all.

The women who are the empirical focus of this chapter, Bijana Plavsic and Pauline Nyiramasuhuko, are alleged to have played leadership roles in genocidal movements. These women, in some ways, lived very different lives and participated in very different conflicts, but it is what they have in common that makes them of interest to this chapter: each allegedly played a leadership role in the commission of genocide and each was the subject of very public stories which implicate the mother, monster and whore narratives. Their actions also raise another subject, new to this book: widespread woman-on-woman sexual violence. These two women, and many others who played similar, if less visible, roles, are accused of perpetrating not only genocide, but genocidal rape. Despite the difference in both type and scale of the conduct of the women in this chapter, striking similarities can be found between the public and popular narratives of their behaviour and those of other violent women, across time, culture, language, ethnicity and national borders.

THE CONCEPT OF GENOCIDE

There is no universally agreed upon definition of the word 'genocide', much less of the concept of genocidal rape, and many scholars speculate that there is likely never to be one.[1] William Rubinstein suggests a 'common sense' definition as a working framework for communicating what we mean by genocide (2004: 2). He explains, 'genocide might then be defined as the deliberate killing of most or all members of a collective group for the mere fact of being members of that group' (2). Article 2 of the Convention on the Prevention and Punishment of the Crime of Genocide (CPPCG) provides an operational definition of genocide:

> Any of the following acts committed with intent to destroy, in whole or in part, a national, ethnic, racial or religious group, as such: killing members of the group; causing serious bodily or mental harm to members of the group; deliberately inflicting on the group conditions of life, calculated to bring about its physical destruction in whole or in part; imposing measures intended to prevent births within the group; and forcibly transferring children of the group to another group.

The question 'Is it or is it not a genocide?' has surrounded a number of conflicts in recent years, including the current one in Darfur.[2] While this is an important question, this is not the place to examine it deeply, for two reasons. First, to the extent to which the word 'genocide' is a rhetorical tool used to sensationalize a particular conflict (or, in its denial, to encourage ignoring it), it is part of the rhetoric that this book attempts to examine and reconstruct. Second, the cases focused on in this chapter, in the former Yugoslavia and in Rwanda, have been labelled genocides with little controversy in the international community. In its focus on women's participation in genocide, this chapter notes that, however loose and controversial the classification of genocide itself is, the analysis of gender and genocide is even more underdeveloped and unknown. This is not to say that some (feminist and non-feminist) analyses of gender and genocide have not made important contributions. It is only to point out that they have thus far not formed a coherent dialogue, and that many of the projects on gender and genocide focus narrowly on a single aspect of gender and genocide – for example, the rape of women or the killing of men – rather than on gender and genocide more broadly.

Although international law has not traditionally recognized gender dimensions to genocide and mass killing, gender issues in genocide have gained increasing recognition in international legal and media discourses over the last decade. One distinctive characteristic of genocide, according to Rubinstein, is the targeting of groups usually considered to be *by definition* non-combatants, such as women, children and the elderly (2004: 2). International law has increasingly prohibited rape, along with other acts of violence against women, under a variety of human rights instruments (MacKinnon 2001: 897; Fitzpatrick 1994; Dietz 1996). Rape during war generally and during genocidal war specifically has been punished under international law, albeit inconsistently. As MacKinnon documents, 'in the Tokyo trials after World War II, individual Japanese generals were held responsible for rapes committed by their subordinates' (2001; Chang 1997). Additionally, courts and governments are increasingly recognizing a qualitative difference between *rape* and *genocidal rape*, where genocidal rape is actionable as genocide as well as rape. Whereas rape can be considered an assault against an individual body in the larger context of sex discrimination, genocidal rape is the systematic rape of women and girls in wartime as a tactic to subdue and conquer a people (Bennett 2002a).

In a precedent-setting lawsuit, Muslim and Croat women victims of genocidal rape during the Serb 'ethnic cleansing' in Bosnia and Herzegovina sued the former leader of the Bosnian Serbs in United

States' courts for rape as genocide (MacKinnon 2001; *Kadic* v. *Karadzic* 70 F.3d 232, 2nd Cir. 1995). The women plaintiffs, whom the court awarded $745 million dollars in damages, were found to be victims of genocidal rape, 'with the specific intent of destroying [their] ethnic-religious groups' (*Kadic* v. *Karadzic* 70 F.3d at 232). The International Criminal Tribunal for Rwanda found a similar offense actionable under international law (*Prosecutor* v. *Akayesu*, Case No. ICTR 96 4T (1998)). The court found that:

> The central elements of the crime of rape cannot be captured in a mechanical description of objects and body parts.... The ... Convention Against Torture ... does not catalogue specific acts in its definition of torture, focusing rather on the conceptual framework of state-sanctioned violence ... rape in fact constitutes torture when it is inflicted by or at the instigation or with the consent or acquiescence of a public official.... With regard, particularly, to the indicted acts of rape and sexual violence, ... they constitute genocide in the same was as any other act so long as they were committed with the specific intent to destroy, in whole or in part, a particular group, targeted as such.... The rape of Tutsi women was systematic and was perpetrated against all Tutsi women and solely against them. (*Prosecutor* v. *Akayesu*, ICTR 96 4 T, 694, 731)

Given the prominence of the rape of women as a weapon of genocide in both Bosnia-Herzegovina and Rwanda, the question of the gendered explanations for genocide has received more attention in recent times (MacKinnon 2001; Lindsey 2002; Card 2003). Several gender questions have arisen: Why is rape seen as essential to the extermination of a racial or ethnic group (Card 2003)? Why are men more often targeted for death and women more often targeted for rape (Carver 2004)? What gendered understandings of the world are necessary for genocide to occur (Carver 2004)?

The mother, monster and whore narratives around women's perpetration of genocide deny at once women's agency (in their own violence and otherwise) and gender genocide. Given the complexity of the subject matter, several points need to be made clear. First, the argument that women participate in genocide and genocidal rape *with agency* does not detract from others' arguments that most genocides are very gendered processes, which often disproportionately affect women and always have different impacts based on gender (Allen 1996; Hansen 2001). Second, this chapter does not use 'gender' as a substitute for 'women' and is concerned equally about the impact on women and men of subordinating images of women (Carpenter 2003a). Finally, rather than attempting to judge or vilify *women* participants in genocide specifically, this analysis leaves judgement and punishments to international criminal tribunals and the courts of public opinion, choosing to focus instead on the gendered nature of the public presentation of these women's actions. With those assumptions in mind, it looks at the question of how women participants in genocide or genocidal rape are portrayed in public and publicized narratives.

WOMEN PARTICIPANTS IN GENOCIDE AND GENOCIDAL RAPE

> The blood of blacks runs like water, we take their goods and we chase them from our area and our cattle will be in their land. The power of al-Bashir belongs to the Arabs, and we will kill you until the end, you blacks, we have killed your God. (Rubin 2006, quoting a song women called Hakama sing as Janjaweed men rape black Sudanese women)

In the last three years, at least 400,000 people have been killed, and 2 million displaced in a deadly conflict in Darfur. Since early 2003, Sudanese armed forces and a Sudanese government-backed militia known as 'Janjaweed' have been fighting two rebel groups in Darfur, the Sudanese Liberation Army/Movement (SLA/SLM) and the Justice and Equality Movement (JEM). The rebels' mission statement forces the government of Sudan to address economic underdevelopment and political marginalization in the area. The Janjaweed have targeted the civilians who support the rebel groups.

This conflict has been recognized widely as one of the largest humanitarian problems in the world. The Sudanese government and the Janjaweed militia are responsible for the burning and destruction of hundreds of rural villages, the killing of tens of thousands of people, and the rape and assault of thousands of women and girls.

A number of media accounts of the conflict have emphasized women's role. Even though the only evidence that women are participants in the genocide is one sentence in a 25-page, two-year-old Amnesty International report, a Google search for 'Janjaweed women' produces half a million results. The participation of women which Amnesty International documented involved their support for rape and other crimes by singing, cheering and passing messages between the male aggressors. Amnesty International explained:

> The songs of the Hakama, or the Janjaweed women as the refugees call them, encouraged the atrocities committed by the militamen. The women singers stirred up racial hatred against black civilians during attacks on villages in Darfur and celebrated the humiliation of their enemies, the human rights group said.... Amnesty International collected several testimonies mentioning the presence of Hakama while women were raped by the Janjaweed. The report said: 'Hakama appear to have directly harassed the women who were assaulted, and verbally attacked them.' (Sudanwatch.org 2006; Vasagar and MacAskill 2006; Amnesty International 2004)

This report is repeated in tens of thousands of news sites and Internet blogs, and included in academic accounts of the conflict. Phyllis Chesler adds that a number of the women cheer their men on and 'utter racial insults to the women being raped' (2004). Chesler, a psychologist who focuses her attention on deviant women, attempts to explain the motivation behind women's participation in the Sudanese ethnic conflict. She explains that she is 'not surprised by the behaviour of the Janjaweed women' (Chesler 2004). Chesler explains that, 'like men, women also internalize sexist values [and] ... cling to the status quo; even to one that demeans them' (2004). This explanation passivizes women's participation and fails to evaluate their motivations critically.

The disproportionate attention paid to women's roles in genocide (however expansive or limited) is not a new development limited to the conflict in Sudan. Several prominent genocide cases in the 1990s featured women who played leadership and/or other important roles in planning, inciting and carrying out mass murder. As tales of Pauline Nyiramasuhuko and Biljana Plavsic's roles in genocides made cover stories in national and international media, Askin noted the importance of recognizing women's participation in genocide:

It is important to note that women are increasingly recognized as actors, enablers, and even perpetrators, instead of simply as victims of wartime violence. As more women participate as combatants and government officials, women are being accused of responsibility for war crimes, crimes against humanity, and genocide, including crimes of sexual violence. (Askin 2003: 513)

However, recognizing women as actors in the commission of war crimes, crimes against humanity, and genocide, is not enough. Most acknowledgements of women's participation in war crimes are accompanied by gendered assumptions about how those women came to be involved in the movements and the cruelties that they committed, and emphasize the singularity of particular women participants as well as women participants generally. Many stories about women's participation in genocide employ the mother, monster and whore narratives to deny women's agency in their own heinous violence. For example, Strickland and Duvvury explain women's participation in genocide as women's alienation from their appropriate gender role as mothers (2003). Engle explains:

> At the same time they recognize women's participation in war, though, Strickland and Duvvury suggest that when women act as perpetrators they are not necessarily acting as women; rather, they have subordinated their gender identity. As examples, they discuss Biljana Plavsic and Pauline Nyiramasuhuko, and explain their crimes by saying that women's self-identification with their ethnicity was more powerful than their identities as women (Engle 2005: 812).

Naomi Wolf takes a different approach, choosing to emphasize elements of the whore narrative (2004). She argues that 'women are just as capable as men of taking part in a sexual spectacle' (2004). With this argument, a reader believes that she is talking about gender equality, but the remainder of the article makes it clear that Wolf is not arguing that women *naturally* are as capable of men, but that sexuality has corrupted women, thereby making them capable of violence unnatural to femininity. She argues that this generation 'is more likely to engage in certain kinds of semi-public sex, and perhaps even torture, under the right conditions, than previous generations might have been – because of the desensitizing effect of pornography'

(Wolf 2004). Wolf is arguing that women's exposure to base sex, specifically pornography, desensitizes women's otherwise non-violent tendencies, creating (whores who have) a capacity for (genocidal) sexual violence.

Several references to women involved in or perpetrating genocide emphasize their 'madness', akin to the monster narrative detailed in Chapter 2. These women are compared to the likes of Medusa and Boudica. Even narratives that appear to recognize women's equality entrench the stereotypes in these narratives. For example, in an analysis that appears as if it will give women equal treatment, Barbara Ehrenreich correctly recognizes that 'a uterus is not a substitute for a conscience' (2004). Ehrenreich, however, goes on to blame feminists for the purist images of women which make them by definition incapable of this violence. Ehrenreich fails to recognize that feminism, in its attempt to win both women's agency in global politics and recognition for that agency, would, carried to its logical conclusion, recognize that some women commit senseless violence because some people commit senseless violence.[3]

Other accounts emphasize women's sexuality and sexual competition between women. For example, Adam Jones focuses on women's participation in the Rwandan genocide to explain: first, that the genocide was 'targeted' against men at least in part by women; and, second, that women's sexual competition with each other can largely explain any energy they put into attacking other women (2004: 122, 123). Jones ignores the fact that 80 per cent of the Tutsi population, men and women, died in the Rwandan genocide, and that a majority of the female victims were not only killed, but raped, at the command of and by their male *and* female torturers. Also, as Terrell Carver notes (2004), Jones is conflating the very thing that needs explaining (the greater urgency of killing men) with the explanatory variable (that it is *about* men), when killing men first is all about gender-subordinating images of women as sexual objects incapable of posing a political threat. The conclusion of this chapter brings together both denials of women's agency and an emphasis on male victimhood as a new, more subtle perpetuation of old gender oppressions. While this chapter cites some of the empirical information that Jones and others collected, it does not support his conclusions. Further, while the gendered implications of genocide itself are not the focus of this discussion (though the gendered implications of reactions to and coverage of women's participation are), the authors are committed to the view that genocide is a very *gendered* phenomenon: that is, it affects men and women differently, and it does so because of its situation in a world in which femininities are subordinated to masculinities, and women to men.

The sexualization of women's participation in genocide has another side too. The women discussed in these cases have been accused not only of perpetrating acts of genocide but also of doing so through sexual crimes against other women, namely genocidal rape. Biljana Plavsic, former acting president of the Bosnian Serb Republic, has been accused of having incited the genocidal rape of Muslims and Croats. Pauline Nyiramasuhuko has been charged with genocide, with specific charges that include mass murder, allegedly demanding that soldiers rape women before they killed them, and espousing a system of sexual slavery for Tutsi women. The following sections provide some background to the conflicts these two women were involved in, and then explore the employment of the mother, monster and whore narratives in the presentation of these women's participation in (sexual) genocidal violence.

THE CASE OF YUGOSLAVIA

The war in Bosnia and Herzegovina was precipitated by the dissolution of Yugoslavia following the end of the Cold War. Yugoslavia had been governed by a Presidency with equal representation from all of its provinces. As the Soviet Union collapsed and immediately after, Slobodan Milosevic tried to consolidate Serbia's influence by asserting control over two smaller Yugoslav provinces, Kosovo and Voljovdina, and obtaining their votes in the Presidency, a body which included representatives from each of seven provinces. As a result, in 1991, both Slovenia and Croatia declared their independence. These declarations produced a short armed conflict in Slovenia and a war in Croatia.

Bosnia, the most ethnically diverse part of the former Yugoslavia, with 43 per cent Muslims, 35 per cent Serbs and 18 per cent Croats, had been governed by a multi-ethnic coalition which divided power fairly evenly between the ethnic groups. The parliament authorized a referendum on independence, and a referendum was held to determine whether or not Bosnians wanted to declare independence from Yugoslavia. While the Bosnian Serbs urged a boycott of the referendum, two-thirds of Bosnians voted in it, more than 99 per cent of whom favoured independence. Consequently, on 5 March 1992, Bosnia declared its independence from Yugoslavia. As a result, Bosnian Serbs declared an independent Bosnian Serb state within the borders of Bosnia. The Serb state, 'Republica Srpska', was established with the stated aim of preserving the Yugoslav federation. Almost immediately, the Bosnian Serb army began a practice of targeting civilians and ridding their territory of non-Serbs, which was 'euphemistically dubbed *etnicko cscenje*, or ethnic cleansing' (Power 2002: 249). As Samantha Power relates:

> Bosnian Serb soldiers and militiamen had compiled lists of leading Muslim and Croat intellectuals, musicians, and professionals. And within days of Bosnia's succession from Yugoslavia, they began rounding up non-Serbs, savagely beating them, and often executing them. Bosnian Serb units destroyed most cultural and religious sites in order to erase any memory of a Muslim or Croat presence in what they would call 'Republika Srpska'.... Yet despite unprecedented public outcry about foreign brutality, for the next three and a half years the United States, Europe, and the United Nations stood by while some 200,000 Bosnians were killed, more that 2 million were displaced, and the territory of a multiethnic European republic was sliced into three ethnically pure statelets. (Power 2002: 251)

The fighting in Bosnia continued for almost a decade. The Bosnian Serb army has been accused of systematic attempts to exterminate Muslims and Croats in Bosnia. Serbia, in its capacity as supporter of and adviser to the Bosnian Serb army, has been arraigned in the International Court of Justice by Bosnia and Herzegovina on charges of genocide. Among these is the accusation that Serbia was complicit with a programme of genocidal rape, in which Serb soldiers intentionally impregnated Muslim and Croat women and/or defiled them to make them unacceptable to their husbands. The

GENDERED GENOCIDE

International Criminal Tribunal for the Former Yugoslavia (ICTY) has prosecuted almost eighty cases of war crimes committed during the war in Bosnia. Though the ICTY has indicted a fairly large number of alleged war criminals in connection with the war in Bosnia, women are rarely mentioned as having played a political or military role in the war. Even though several sources document deep genderings in both the prosecution and the result of the war,[4] 'the ICTY brought no charges against women other than [Biljana] Plavsic' (Engle 2005: 811; Mudis 2003). Engle is concerned that this lack of indictments against women 'facilitates the perception that women, with few exceptions, were victims rather than perpetrators of the war ... focusing on women as victims – if only as victims of the "propaganda machinery" – could deflect attention from any extent to which they might have been responsible for the war' (Engle 2005: 811). The ICTY's indictment of Plavsic, then, is worth exploring both for the extent that it did (or did not) assign women responsibility for the war, as well as for its uniqueness among ICTY prosecutions.

BILJANA PLAVSIC

Bijana Plavsic was a member of the Presidency of the Republika Srpska, and served as Acting President of that political organization both in 1992 and between 1996 and 1998 (Mudis 2003). She has been described as 'renowned throughout the 1990s as an uncompromising apologist for ethnic cleansing' (BBC News 2003). Plavsic was the Dean of Natural Sciences and Mathematics at the University of Sarajevo (where she published almost a hundred scholarly papers in biology before becoming a charter member of the Serbian Democratic Party (SDS)) (Fitzpatrick 2000; BBC News 2003). During her political career, Plavsic used her knowledge of biology in order to convince people to share her ethnic hatreds, as she argued that Bosnian Muslims were 'genetically deformed Serbs' (Fitzpatrick 2000). She is also infamous for having goaded men into committing war crimes. In a speech in Bosnia in 1996, she was quoted as having said, 'when I saw what [Arkan] had done in Bijeljina, I at once imagined all his actions being like that. I said, "Here we have a Serb hero. He's a real Serb; that's the kind of men we need"' (Fitzpatrick 2000). She also has a reputation for recognizing sex as a source of ethnic purification and ethnic corruption. Between her presidencies, she explained that, as a government,

> We are disturbed by the fact that the number of marriages between Serbs and Muslims has increased ... because mixed marriages lead to an exchange of genes between ethnic groups, and thus to a degeneration of Serb nationhood. (Sarajevo's *Oslobodjenje*, May 1994)

Plavsic was described as proud to be called 'Madam Thatcher' by journalists and other media people – 'I have to be an iron lady' (*Telegraf* 1996). Even though Plavsic's toughness is often emphasized in media coverage of her behaviour during the Bosnian war (for example, most articles use her nickname 'iron lady' (Kuthjaklvokovic and Hagan 2006; Combs 2003)), her femininity is always present in accounts of her personal and political choices. Notably, most of the articles about Plavsic, both during and after the commission of the crimes to which she pleaded guilty, call her 'Mrs Plavsic', despite the fact that the titles 'Doctor' and 'President' would have been used if Plavsic were a man, a former president, and the possessor of a doctorate.

Plavsic's sexuality has been also a consistent theme in news coverage and academic analysis of her crimes. Her support for militant groups involved in the genocide has often been described in amorous, rather than political, terms. A BBC News article emphasized her capacity for affection even in the direst of circumstances when it observed that, 'in 1992, a widely-circulated photograph showed her stepping over the body of a dead Muslim civilian to kiss the notorious Serb warlord Zaljko Raznjatovic, known as Arkan' (BBC News 2003). In fact, much is made in media accounts of Plavsic's supposed Oedipal relationship with Arkan. One article states that, 'when the delegation met Arkan in front of the municipal offices in Bijeljina, Biljana Plavsic kissed him on the cheek. She called him "my child"' (Suljalic 2003). Indeed, stories of her supposed affair with Arkan are as frequent on the Internet as stories of her war crimes. Further, comments about Plavsic's 'closeness' to many of her male colleagues in government are frequent, while mentions of her husband are impossible to find.[5]

Equally prominent in the press was the characterization of Plavsic as a madwoman. BBC News, mimicking a number of Bosnian and

GENDERED GENOCIDE

Serbian newspapers, carried her mental health as a theme in discussing her case:

> Even Slobodan Milosevic regarded her as a radical. Her outbursts led him to question her mental health, while Mr Milosevic's wife, Mirjana Markovic, dubbed her a 'female Mengele' in reference to the notorious Nazi doctor. (BBC News 2003)

Slobodan Milosevic is not a popular source of character references, either positive or negative. The attention given to this particular judgement, I contend, is because it provides an explanation for a woman's heinous violence outside of her agency: here, her madness and poor mental health.

The gendered narratives about Plavsic only increased in frequency and visibility when she was arrested for war crimes. Plavsic voluntarily surrendered to the ICTY in response to an indictment. Askin recounts the war crimes that she was accused of:

> Biljana Plavsic, former acting President of the Serbian Republic of Bosnia and Herzgovinia, was charged with genocide, crimes against humanity, and war crimes for a series of crimes, including rape crimes, committed by the Serb military, political, and government authorities and agents. (Askin 2003)

Because Plavsic was the first to surrender to the ICTY, her case received substantial attention from the press. This attention was compounded when Plavsic voluntarily entered a guilty plea to the charge of crimes against humanity in exchange for the prosecution's agreement to drop genocide charges. Her guilty plea is universally acclaimed as an important factor in the healing process in Bosnia, though its sincerity has been questioned by a number of sources (Mudis 2003).

In questioning the sincerity of Plavsic's confession, BBC News recounted a number of her racist statements about her crimes, and then noted that 'a decade later, she pleaded guilty to crimes against humanity, and apologized to "all the innocent victims of the Bosnian war – Muslims, Croats, and Serbs alike"' (BBC News 2003). Some contend that this was a political move to lessen her jail sentence, while others believe that it was a demonstration of genuine remorse.

Because of her guilty plea, the only aspect of Plavsic's trial which was consequential was the sentencing phase, wherein the ICTY was charged with finding mitigating and aggravating factors in her commission of the crimes against humanity in order to choose her sentence. Plavsic, then 72, was eligible for life in prison. One of the oddities surrounding the sentencing phase of Plavsic's trial was the high-profile witnesses and attendees. As Mudis recounts:

> The parties called several high-level witnesses, in part reflecting the fact that the accused had contact with several senior international personalities, and also in recognition of the gravity of the offense and the important role of the accused in the commission thereof due to her political position. For example, Madeline Albright, Alex Boraine, Elie Wiesel, Carl Bildt, and Robert Frowick all testified. (Mudis 2003: 718)

Another oddity was the places where gender was (and was not) emphasized. The prosecutor and defence counsel emphasized Bijana's womanhood to register her humanity. They described her in feminine terms (pliable and polite, for example) when discussing her willingness to cooperate with the Western world after the war ended. While a number of the witnesses at the sentencing emphasized the rape charges against Plavsic, including Elie Wiesel and Madeleine Albright, neither attorney discussed Plavsic's responsibility for or complicity in sexual violence. Additionally, the question of rape did not come up in the formal sentencing process. Instead, in sentencing Plavsic, the ICTY found six relevant mitigating factors: the entering of a guilty plea and acceptance of responsibility, remorse, voluntary surrender, post-conflict conduct, previous good character, and age (Mudis 2003: 717). Gender was used to 'mitigate' her offences, but not to analyse their severity or their impact in Bosnia. Plavsic received a sentence of eleven years, generally considered to be light, which is understood to be the result of her choice to plea-bargain. Several victims of the Bosnian Serb ethnic cleansing have expressed their dissatisfaction with the sentence that Plavsic received:

> Upon learning that if they cooperate with the prosecutor, the severity of penalty is plea-bargained, I realized that everything is just a farce. Can you imagine Bijana Plavsic was sentenced to only

11 years of imprisonment to be served in the conditions of a high standard of living that an average Bosnian cannot afford even outside of prison and with a lot of hard work? (Kuthjaklvokovic and Hagan 2006)

MOTHER, MONSTER AND WHORE STORIES OF BIJANA PLAVSIC

Even though Plavsic's personal life is almost entirely omitted from news stories and journal articles about her career, elements of the mother narrative still permeate stories about her whenever her personal life is included. In all of the articles about Plavsic, the only hint that she is or ever was married is that she is constantly referred to as 'Mrs Plavsic'. These references themselves are a manifestation of the underlying stereotype of the mother narrative: women as mothers and wives first, and as individuals second. This is because, as mentioned above, whether or not Plavsic was married, both 'Doctor' and 'President' are the proper titles; 'Mrs' is no longer the most appropriate term. Indeed, her male fellow members of the Presidency and other leaders of the movement are described as 'Doctor' and 'President' or by their full names in the same articles where Plavsic is consistently identified as 'Mrs Plavsic' (Engle 2005). These descriptions demonstrate a conscious or subconscious attempt to push Plavsic away from the domain of the professional and political and back into the private domain of wifehood and motherhood.

Another element of the mother narrative found in the stories about Plavsic is the consistent reference to her as 'goading' or 'coaching' men into being 'real men' who can fight for the Republica Srpska (Ansah 2005). These narratives cast her in the role of nuturing mother: one does not have to worry too much about her personal violence. Instead, she is caring for and coaching the men who are engaging in violence while still serving in her socially scripted role as mother, not only to her sons, but to the sons of her country. In these stories, her involvement in political violence stems from a maternal desire to belong to and be useful to a political organization; a psychological compulsion to assist and support others. This stems from images of women as 'bearers of the collective' who pass on us–them boundaries and serve as biological and cultural reproductive agents; peaceful, but producing war (Yuval-Davis 1997: 22–3, 26). Women, this narrative relates, make war not by *fighting directly*, but by challenging men's masculinity such that they have no choice but to fight. The mother, in this story, Plavsic, then, plays the role of the supervisor of the standards of masculinity.

A third element of the mother narrative in the stories about Bijana Plavsic is that of her affair with the militia leader known as 'Arkan'. Plavsic's relationship with Arkan is the subject of a number of media stories and gossip mills. While we will discuss the sexual element of these narratives below when we discuss the whore narrative, it bears mentioning here that, although the stories imply that Plavsic and Arkan had a sexual relationship, they also emphasize a mother–child relationship. These stories imply that Bijana is the ultimate mother gone wrong: the mother who engages in mother–son incest, at an advanced age. This questioning of Plavsic's womanhood contributes to an image of Plavsic as *less than female*, which allows the related image of female innocence to remain intact.

Stories about Biljana Plavsic also contain the monster narrative. Emphasis on her toughness and her nickname 'iron lady' hint at a monster characterization, but these images are much more obvious in the emphasis on the view that Plavsic is lacking in mental balance. These narratives keep intact the image of a 'normal' woman's innocence by casting Plavsic as an 'abnormal' woman, one who is insane. This is because casting a violent woman as a monster or a madwoman singles her out of the category of peaceful women more generally, and allows for the maintenance of the image of women's general peacefulness.

This conclusion is reinforced by the emphasis in the sentencing hearings on Plavsic's womanhood. While it was never explicitly said, the lawyers for both sides (urging a lighter sentence) implied that, because she was a woman, Plavsic was less dangerous and more human than a man accused of her crimes would be. Stories which vilified Plavsic, then, emphasized her monstrousness, while stories which sympathized with her emphasized her womanhood as an argument that she could not possibly be monstrous.

Several elements of the whore narrative are also present in the stories about Bijana Plavsic. Though Plavsic apparently gave several hundred racist speeches, the most often quoted were those which emphasized either her sexuality or that of her victims. A number of the accounts put particular emphasis on her belief that Serbs should neither have sex with nor intermarry with either Croats or Muslims on the grounds of racial impurity. Her planning of genocidal rape for the purpose of biological corruption of the other racial groups in Bosnia is also a headline in several stories.

When Plavsic's opinion of the sexuality of her victims is not being emphasized, her own sexuality becomes a focus. While there is no information about her husband, many of the stories about Plavsic feel free to speculate about her other sexual involvements. As mentioned above, speculation about her relationship with warlord Arkan, whom she kissed in public on more than one occasion, was rampant. Additionally, a number of stories mention her alleged 'closeness' to male members of the government of the Republica Srpska as a reason both for her political position and for her criminal choices. Describing Plavsic at once as a sexual predator and as manipulated by sexuality draws attention away from questions of her culpability for her actions and her motivation for those choices. Because women's integration into spheres of power and violence threatens patriarchy until those women are dehumanized through sexualization, sexualized stories about Plavsic can be used to take away the threat she poses to male dominance.

A final element of the whore narrative in the stories of Biljana Plavsic is the scarlet-letter-like discussion of the punishment she received. As the first to plea bargain with the prosecutor in the ICTY, Plavsic reached a deal whereby she would plead guilty to crimes against humanity in order to have other charges, including genocide charges, dropped. While there was no official reference to her sentence in the plea-bargain, many believe she received a light term because she pleaded guilty to crimes against humanity. Many victims of the Bosnian Serb ethnic cleansing felt that her eleven-year sentence was too lenient, characterizing the ICTY as giving a break to a woman because she appealed to the court.

THE CASE OF RWANDA

The conflict between the Hutus and the Tutsis in Rwanda has substantial historical roots. The division between these groups is a unique one: they share a language, a religion and cultural traditions; they have always lived intermingled within Rwandan society. Hutu and Tutsi can best be described, historically, as caste divisions rather than ethnic groups. The Tutsi minority in Rwanda has historically been seen as the higher caste, while the Hutu majority was constituted largely by Rwanda's poor and marginalized citizens. Historically, people were 'demoted' from Tutsi to Hutu when they lost their fortunes or the good graces of those in political power. The caste system implications of these distinctions has been a source of tension throughout Rwandan history (Sperling 2006: 640). Rubinstein describes the situation in Rwanda leading up to the 1994 genocide:

> As is well-known, Rwanda's population consists of two distinct groups, the Hutu and the Tutsi, who between them comprise 99 per cent of the population. They are not precisely distinctive 'ethnic groups' in the normal sense of the term, as they speak the same language and are not separate tribes … In some respects, they correspond more to separate castes, with, traditionally, the Tutsis being dominant. (Rubinstein 2004: 287)

On 6 April 1994, Rwandan President Juvenal Habyarimana's jet was shot down with the president inside, along with the president of Burundi, Cyprien Ntaryamira (Power 2002: 329). While some believe this was an accident, most contend that the president was assassinated by extremist Hutu groups within Rwanda, with many pointing at the president's wife, Agathe Habyarimana, and her political group, the Akazu (Prunier 1995; Gourevitch 1999). Shortly after the president's assassination, a group of Hutu extremists consolidated governmental power in Rwanda.

As a result, 'decades of conflict between the Hutu majority and the Tutsi minority erupted into a full-scale genocide' (Power 2002: 331). After the President's death, group of Hutus immediately implemented a program of ethnic cleansing, trying to eradicate the Tutsi population of Rwanda. According to Power, 'within hours of

GENDERED GENOCIDE

Habyarimana's death, armed Hutu took control of the streets of Kigali' (332). Before the genocide, Hutus comprised about 80 per cent of the population of Rwanda, and there were between 900,000 and 1 million Tutsis in the population. At the end of the summer of 1994, only 130,000 Tutsis survived; between 70 and 80 per cent of the Tutsi population had been killed. Power explained that 'lists of victims had been prepared ahead of time ... many early Tutsi victims found themselves specifically, not generally, targeted' (2002: 333). As Sperling documented, 'nearly all the victims were killed in the first ninety days of the Rwandan genocide, making the rate of the genocide five times as swift as the Nazis' extermination of the Jews during the Holocaust' (Sperling 2006: 639). The Rwandan genocide was the 'fastest, most efficient killing spree of the 20th century' (Power 2002: 334).

The conflict died down in late summer 1994 when a Tutsi army began taking control of substantial parts of Rwanda. The United Nations Security Council created the International Criminal Tribunal for Rwanda (ICTR) on 8 November 1994 to prosecute the individuals responsible for this terrible genocide. The ICTR is vested with jurisdiction to prosecute persons responsible for genocide and other violations of international humanitarian law committed in Rwanda in 1994 (Miller 1994: 357–9).

The ICTR prosecutions have included both men and women. Unlike women in the Yugoslav conflict, women who participated in the genocide in Rwanda have received substantial media attention and have been subject to intensive prosecution. Pauline Nyiramasuhuko, whose case is discussed in more detail below, is not the only woman implicated in the genocide in Rwanda (Sperling 2006: 653). Other 'powerful women in Rwanda also assisted in the planning and incitement of genocide, just as women participated in carrying out the genocide in the former Yugoslavia' (653). Sperling details:

> Two women receiving international attention for their roles in the genocide are sister Gertrude Mukangango and Sister Maria Kisito. The two Benedictine nuns stood trial in Belgium for their role in the murders of thousands of Tutsis who took refuge in their convent in Suvu, Rwanda. Over seven thousand Tutsis ... were killed. (Sperling 2006: 656; Simons 2001)

Additionally, as mentioned above, 'Agathe Habyarimana, Pauline's close childhood friend and the former president's wife, is widely accepted as one of the people with direct responsibility for the genocide' (Sperling 2006: 657). Rwanda would like to bring Habyarimana to trial, but she has been granted asylum in France. In fact, more than 3,000 Rwandan women are being tried in Rwanda for genocide (Itano 2002; Powley 2003; Drumbl 2005). Carrie Sperling documents that 'women, girls, and mothers also willingly and enthusiastically played important roles in the Rwandan genocide. As a female perpetrator of mass violence, Pauline is not an anomaly' (2006: 638).

There is a tendency, however, to sensationalize women's participation in the Rwandan genocide. For example, Adam Jones consistently notes that 'the Rwandan holocaust is unique in the annals of genocide for the prominent role that women played as organizers, instigators, and followers'. He tells the stories of woman participants, including Rose Karushara, who 'beat up refugees herself'; Odette Nyirabagenzi, who 'took an active part in selecting men who were to die'; Anhanasie Mukabatana, who 'went into the hospital with a machete'; and Julienne Kizito, who 'worked directly with killers ... to burn people alive' (2004: 120–22). These stories are not false, but the choice to sensationalize them above and beyond the stories of the majority of (male) genocidaires creates a skewed gender picture of the genocide in Rwanda.

This bias is obvious in Pauline Nyiramasuhuko's case, which has received the most media attention. In media accounts, the terrible stories of her actions are often generalized to make women responsible for the horror of the genocide, which likely disproportionately affected them. Pauline Nyiramasuhuko has been the 'star' of genocide narratives, perhaps because of the sheer horror involved in her alleged actions, or perhaps as a trope for the terribleness of women offenders. It is for that reason that we explore the narratives surrounding the telling and retelling of Pauline Nyiramasuhuko's commission of genocide.

PAULINE NYIRAMASUHUKO

Pauline Nyiramasuhuko was born in 1946 in the commune of Ndora, Butare prefecture, Rwanda. Although she was born into a poor

GENDERED GENOCIDE 161

family, Nyiramasuhuko went to college. While she was in college, she met Agatha Habyaimana, who was married to then Hutu President Juvenal Habyarimana (and, some contend, later assassinated him). Nyiramasuhuko was only 22 years old when she obtained her first governmental post through Agathe, becoming National Inspector at the ministry. Peter Landesman describes Pauline Nyiramasuhuko's career as a social worker:

> Before becoming Rwanda's chief official for women's affairs, Pauline was a social worker ... offering lectures on female empowerment and instruction on child care and AIDS prevention. Her days as a minister were similarly devoted to improving the lives of women and children. (Landesman 2002a)

In her political career, Pauline Nyiramasuhuko was one of the leaders of the National Republican Movement for Democracy (the MRND, the party of President Habyarimana). In 1992, she was nominated to the position of Minister for the Family and the Advancement of Women, where she was to supervise government policy in the area of family and women's affairs. She was also a member of the Council of Ministers, a cabinet-like body, and therefore privy to most matters of national policy.

In her official capacity, Pauline Nyiramasuhuko has been accused of helping to plan and perpetrate the fastest and most effective genocide in human history. She 'had been open and frank at cabinet meetings, saying that she personally was in favor of getting rid of all Tutsi' (Melvern 2004: 229). Nyiramasuhuko argued that 'without the Tutsi, all Rwanda's problems would be over', and 'people listened to her' because she was an educated social worker and high-ranking government official. She also played an active role in the genocide. As Landesman writes:

> In his confession to genocide and crimes against humanity, former Hutu Prime Minister Jean Kambanda identifies members of his inner sanctum, where the blueprint of the genocide was first drawn up. The confession names only five names. Pauline Nyiramusuko's is one of them. (Landesman 2002b)

Narratives describe Nyiramasuhuko as an active participant in the genocide in the summer of 1994. According to Landesman, she was dispatched by the interim government to quell the revolt in Butare (2002a). She arrived in Butare and announced that the Red Cross was giving away food and supplies at a local sports stadium. Nyiramasuhuko's announcement, however, was a trap, and 'refugees were surrounded by ... thuggish Hutu mauraders' under her supervision. This is only one example of Nyiramasuhuko's alleged participation.

As Sperling explains, 'Pauline is accused of playing a leading role in the planning and implementation of the genocide' (2006: 646). In fact, a woman who knew Nyiramasuhuko through her work in the family planning department of the University Center for Public Health ranked her alongside the president and the Hutu prime minister, Jean Kambanda, as the person most responsible for the genocide in Rwanda (Sperling 2006: 646). Her role in the genocide made her the first woman ever to be charged with genocide and using rape as a crime against humanity in an international jurisdiction (Harman 2003; Obote-Odora 2005; Wood 2004). She was charged with genocidal rape because she commanded her Interahamwe:[6] 'before you kill the women, you need to rape them' (Landesman 2002a). This was a command that her soldiers took seriously and carried out. As Landesman describes, 'Tutsi women were then selected from the stadium crowd and dragged away to be raped' (2002a).

Nyiramasuhuko is accused of ordering the militia 'not to spare anyone, not even the fetus or the old' (Sperling 2006: 649). Her gender is key in many of the narratives about her, as is the position that she held in government. Landesman records that 'other survivors told me they heard the minister for women and family affairs spit invectives at Tutsi women, calling them cockroaches and dirt' (2002a). Nyiramasuhuko's interest in sex and rape is also emphasized; in Landesman's words, 'she advised the men to choose the young women for sex and kill off the old ... Pauline handed soldiers packets of condoms' (2002a). Several sources document Nyiramasuhuko's specific instructions to the Interahamwe about the methods that they should use to rape women. While there is substantial evidence that other leaders gave similar instructions, none is so publicly detailed as the instructions given by Pauline Nyiramasuhuko.

Elsewhere, Landesman has described Nyiramasuhuko as the

'minister of rape' (2002b), crediting a rivalry between women for her behaviour:

> The collective belief of Hutu women that Tutsi women were shamelessly trying to steal their husbands granted Hutu men permission to rape their supposed competitors out of existence. Seen through this warped lens, the men who raped were engaged not only in an act of sexual transgression but also in a purifying ritual. (Landesman 2002b)

Gendered descriptions of her existence and her crimes are commonplace. The most obvious is that, while her male colleagues and even her son are called by their full names, Pauline Nyiramasuhuko is almost universally referred to just by her first name, even in the same sentence. Second, the sexual nature of her alleged crimes has been emphasized, juxtaposed with reminders that she is indeed a woman. After recognizing that she was one of few women ever indicted for genocide, Russell-Brown makes a special note that 'allegations of rape, sexual assault, and other crimes of a sexual nature are part of the factual bases of the charge against Nyiramasuhuko for genocide' (Russell-Brown 2003).

Ansah also highlights the relationship between women as an explanatory factor, recounting that 'the soldiers, according to a witness, 'said that Pauline had given them permission to go after Tutsi girls, who were too proud of themselves ... she was the minister for women's affairs, so they said they were free to do it' (Ansah 2005: 199). A *gendered female* participant in a genocide which persecutes women is a puzzling phenomenon for the media to present. As Sperling documents, 'the genocide was not simply a campaign to kill all Tutsis, it was a campaign initially designed to kill Tutsi men and rape Tutsi women. The rape was as important as the killing, and during the genocide, rape was the rule and its absence the exception' (Sperling 2006: 644). The militia seemed particularly obsessed with what it did to women's bodies (644).

Nyiramasuhuko fled Rwanda in late summer 1994 when her party lost power. She was arrested in Kenya in 1997, indicted by the ICTR, and brought to trial. The arrest and prosecution of Nyiramasuhuko (whose trial has been going on for more than five years),[7] has largely been considered a victory for reconciliation in Rwanda specifically and for the status of wartime and genocidal rape in international law generally. As Balthazar documents:

> The ICTR established an incredible precedent by being the first tribunal ever to charge a woman with genocide and rape. Pauline Nyiramasuhuko, former minister for women's development and family welfare, was charged with two charges of rape: one as a crime against humanity and the other as a violation of the Geneva conventions on war crimes. Charging Nyiramasuhuko with rape committed by those under her command reinforces the principle that sexual violence of any kind committed by any person, male or female, should and will not be tolerated. Her trial is currently in progress at the Tribunal. (Balthazar 2003: 46–7)

While Balthazar sees Nyiramasuhuko's arrest as a gender equalizer, the press coverage hints that it is anything but. Gendered descriptions of Nyiramasuhuko and her role in the genocide permeate media and academic accounts of her case. Even Landesman's captivating narrative is littered with gendered language. As he describes her supervising the stadium massacre, he refers to the woman he insists on calling only 'Pauline' as 'a portly woman of medium height in a colorful African wrap and spectacles' (2002a).

Nyiramasuhuko's gender is also front and centre in descriptions of her trial. Landesman describes the 'new Pauline', whose 'appearance suggested a schoolteacher' because 'she favored plain high-necked dresses' (Landesman 2002a). Her appearance is also the subject of several other narratives. Danna Harman describes seeing Nyiramasuhuko at her trial:

> With her hair pulled neatly back, her heavy glasses beside her on the table, she looks more like someone's dear great aunt than what she is alleged to be: a high-level organizer of Rwanda's 1994 genocide who authorized the rape and murder of countless men and women. Wearing a green flowery dress one day, a pressed cream-colored skirt and blouse the next, the defendant listens stoically to the litany of accusations against her. ... Nyiramasuhuko adjusts one of the shoulder pads of her pretty dress and jots a note. (Harman 2003)

Sperling describes her as a 'broad-hipped, middle-aged woman in a Virgin Mary blue dress' (2006: 664). All of these articles spend more

GENDERED GENOCIDE

time discussing her appearance than the substance of the trial the day that they covered it.

Gender can be seen everywhere in news stories about and academic analyses of Pauline Nyiramasuhuko, but those are not the only places. Gender also plays a substantial role in what comments Nyiramasuhuko has made about her own situation. When asked about her actions during the war, Nyiramasuhuko characterized what she did as moving around the region to pacify (Landesman 2002a). When accused of murder, 'Pauline shot back: "I cannot even kill a chicken. If there is a person that says a woman – a mother – killed, then I'll confront that person"' (Landesman 2002a). She claims that women did not know how to massacre like the *actual* genocidaires did (Sperling 2006: 651). Friends and allies of Nyiramasuhuko corroborate her story about women's incapability to commit the crimes of which Nyiramasuhuko was accused. A number of articles point out that Nyiramasuhuko had four children, one of whom was also influential in the genocide (Miller 2003: 356). Her husband, Maurice Ntahobari,

> echoed Pauline's gender-based claims that women and mothers are incapable of committing murder. ... Ntahobari ... responded, 'she was committed to promoting equality between men and women. It is not culturally possible for a Rwandan woman to make her son rape other women. It just couldn't have taken place.' Pauline's mother gave a similar kind of response when asked about the allegations against her daughter. 'It is unimaginable that she did these things. She wouldn't order people to rape and kill. After all, Pauline is a mother.' (Sperling 2006: 651)

Nyiramasuhuko has also argued that sexism explains why she is being singled out for her conduct during the 1994 genocide. She contends that she was a 'target for prosecution precisely because she was an educated woman' (Sperling 2006: 650). Sperling believes that this framing is likely strategic on Nyiramasuhuko's part. She explains that 'Pauline either believes that by framing the issue around gender, she creates reasonable doubt about her capacity to commit the crimes for which she stands accused, or she shares the gender bias of her patriarchal culture, which incorrectly views women as incapable of heinous, violent acts' (650).

If there is any coverage about Pauline Nyiramasuhuko's case which eclipses the focus on her individual gender, it is the coverage that speculates about the implications of her case for women and gender more generally. In his evaluation, Landesman wrote that

> Pauline's case transcends jurisprudence. She presents to the world a new kind of criminal. There is a shared conception across cultures that women cannot do this kind of thing ... Society does not yet have a way to talk about it, because it violates our concepts of what women are. (2002a)

Landesman is admitting that gendered stereotypes about women frame them as incapable of the sort of violence that Nyiramasuhuko is alleged to have committed.

Others see additional symbolic value in Nyiramasuhuko's case. El Basri identifies her as 'not just any woman' but an educated woman whose position in government was taking care of other women, classifying Nyiramasuhuko as one of the 'Rwandan women rapists' who 'raise the problem of misogyny with a feminine name' and demonstrate that 'barbarity has no color and submits to no gender rule' (2004). Several sources identify Pauline Nyiramasuhuko's story as a counter-narrative to the story of women as victims (Drumbl 2005: 115).

Still other commentators critique the disproportionate publicity paid to Nyiramasuhuko's case, given the fact that several others were at least as responsible as she for the genocide. Wood explains:

> Nyiramasuhuko's role in inciting the sexual violence as a part of the genocide was not unique because other government officials also incited or sanctioned similar sexual violence; however, her case has received disproportionate media attention in comparison to her male counterparts. Presumably, rape warfare is not newsworthy in itself, but a female leader advocating violence against women is a less common occurrence. (Wood 2004, 288)

Michele Landsberg criticizes the *New York Times Magazine*, which published Landesman's article, for singling out Nyiramasuhuko, whose only fault was being as bad as men or even worse (Landsberg 2002a, 2002b; El Basri 2004). Still, Carrie Sperling contends that the publication of Nyiramasuhuko's case is important to counterbalance the myths of women's incapability and victimhood, because:

Pauline's case challenges the other side of the myth: that women, by their nature, are incapable of being warriors – somehow their roles as women and mothers prohibit them from planning or participating in depraved violence. Pauline's case says more about our continued resistance to view women as equals than it says about her uniqueness among her female peers. Because we continue to view women as less capable than men, as less worthy than men, and as confined to the roles of sexual objects or mothers. ... Pauline's case will hopefully prove to the world, once again, that women are equally human, even in their capacity for violence. (Sperling 2006: 638–9)

Sperling argues that those who view Nyiramasuhuko's actions as 'inexplicable because of her gender' perpetuate 'stereotypical thinking about the special victimization of women' (2006: 638). She contends that 'the gender-based fascination' with Nyiramasuhuko's role in the genocide underscores 'a sexist myth that women are, by their very nature, incapable of such atrocities' (638). The perpetuation of this stereotype has significance beyond marginalizing criminals' agency, Sperling argues. She contends that 'this arbitrary role of woman as the other, the pure, and the innocent, permits, if not perpetuates, the brutal and degrading treatment specifically forced on women in times of conflict' (658–9).

Nonetheless, in the same breath in which she argues for a logic of female genocidaires free of gender stereotypes, Sperling refers to Pauline Nyiramasuhuko as the 'mother of all atrocities', evoking the gendered images of the mother narrative (2006: 637). Others, concerned with Nyiramasuhuko's gender influencing the outcome of the trial, wonder if she will successfully *play to* stereotypes about women's innocence in order to secure her freedom. In other words, she may well take advantage of the gender-marginalizing perception that women are incapable of violence because the court is more likely to believe she is innocent if they believe that women are generally innocent. Miller explains:

> Without an enumerated charge of rape as genocide, the Tribunal may find it difficult to prosecute a woman for rape. Moreover, this sort of crime committed by a woman seems almost unfathomable because, historically, it is men who commit or instigate rape. The idea of finding a woman, the Minister of Family and Women's

Affairs no less, guilty of such atrocities performed on her own gender may prove to be too controversial for the tribunal. (Miller 2004: 373)

Another commentator actually blames feminism both for Pauline's crimes and for the likelihood that she will escape severe punishment (Rowles 2002). Rowles cites Pauline Nyiramasuhuko as an example of feminists' contempt for life (Rowles 2002), which can also be seen, he argues, in feminists' support for abortion.

MOTHER, MONSTER AND WHORE STORIES OF PAULINE NYIRAMASUHUKO

Several elements of the mother narrative are apparent in the stories of Pauline Nyiramasuhuko. Like the stories of Biljana Plavsic, many of the stories of Nyiramasuhuko emphasize the supporting role that she played: she was the bossy mother who, from the sidelines, told men to do terrible things. Many of the accounts portray her as a resourceful woman who solved the problems of male Interahamwe; for example, a story of her supplying gas for them to burn raped women when they had been injudicious with their supply.[8] She is described in maternal terms, by her first name when other perpetrators' full names are known, and as 'portly' and like a 'schoolteacher' (Landesman 2002a). A news article tells of her commanding her 'children', the Interahamwe, to commit atrocities.

A difference in the accounts of Pauline Nyiramasuhuko, however, is that the stories also portray her in her capacity as an *actual* mother. Most accounts of Pauline's conduct include the fact that her son, Shalom, was one of the men she commanded to commit rape and mass murder. The stories often explicitly state, and always imply, that Pauline's hand in killing and raping tens of thousands of people was worse because she employed her son to do substantial amounts of the 'dirty work' – *a real mother* would nurture her son, rather than exposing him to this kind of terrible violence. Further, the narratives always tell of Shalom *actually committing* the violence, but often relieve him of responsibility in whole or in part because his mother made him do it. Nyiramasuhuko's role as an *actual* mother, then, translates in the narrative into her role as a symbolic mother, placing culpability for the genocide generally on women (specifically, bad mothers) while leaving both the men who did the actual killing and 'real women' absolved of guilt.

Another element of the mother narrative in descriptions of the behaviour of Pauline Nyiramasuhuko is the emphasis on the political position she held in Rwanda. Nyiramasuhuko was the Minister of Women and Family Affairs in Rwanda. While this position had no formal description, Nyiramasuhuko's responsibilities included dealing with national policy on women's and family issues, publicizing available birth control, and educating women about sex, their bodies and their choices. Certainly, Pauline Nyiramasuhuko had more responsibility towards Rwandan women than someone who was not in public life, or even someone who was in public life in a position less visible for its apparent support of women's lives. Nevertheless, the mother narratives around Nyiramasuhuko's participation in the genocide tell the story as if she were Rwanda's, especially Butare's, potential saviour gone wrong. As previously established, Nyiramasuhuko was neither the only woman (mother) to participate in the genocide nor the only government official. However, the stories are told such that her refusal to live up to her perceived gender role (the pure mother) and instead to become a (vengeful mother) genocidaire was the linchpin of the atrocities in Rwanda, because when we lose the *mothers* to the dark side, all is lost. The characterization by Engle of Nyiramasuhuko as 'the mother of all atrocities' is demonstrative of this trend: her (bad) motherhood allowed evil to be 'born of' and incited by her; the woman, and specifically her motherhood, is responsible for both her violence and the genocide as a whole (2005).

The final element of the mother narrative can be found in Pauline Nyiramasuhuko's statements about her behaviour, and in the supporting statements made by her family and friends. Since, at the time of writing, her trial is ongoing, her punishment has yet to be set. Both to the court and to the court of public opinion, Nyiramasuhuko tells the story that *because she is a mother* she is incapable of the sort of violence of which she is accused. Using phrases like 'can't kill a chicken', she describes Rwandan women as essentially non-violent, both by nature and because they live in a patriarchal society where they cannot 'make' men do anything (Landesman 2002b). Whether this reflects her true belief in patriarchal society or is a calculated and strategic move may never be discernible, but the story has the effect that the mother narrative usually does: women, playing their role as mothers, even when it has gone awry, are not responsible for their 'maternal instincts', or for the violence that they cause because of them. Further, because of those maternal instincts, there is a limit both to the quality and to the quantity of violence that can be caused. Nyiramasuhuko contends that, as a mother, she was simply incapable of both the scale and type of violence she stands trial for.

The monster narrative is not primary in descriptions of Pauline Nyiramasuhuko's offences, but traces of it do appear in the discussion of her dress as 'wild' and the discussion of her desire for revenge against other (Tutsi) women. Local papers described her as a 'frenzied madwoman' who was out to kill her 'inner Tutsi'.[9] Such descriptions served to distance Nyiramasuhuko from 'real women' who do not commit crimes like those she is accused of.

Perhaps the most prominent narrative about Pauline Nyiramasuhuko is the whore narrative. This is present in several different descriptions of her actions. The first dimension is the emphasis on the sexual nature of Nyiramasuhuko's crimes. Although she seemed to have an equal hand in the killing of men and the raping and killing of women, her connection to the raping and killing of women plays a much more prominent role in most of the stories about her. As mentioned above, the specific tactics that she encouraged when commanding the Interahamwe to rape women are the subject of a substantial amount of the work that describes her. Additionally, in the midst of killing tens of thousands of people, offences like 'handing out condoms' and 'encouraging soldiers to use young women for sex' are prominently featured in several of the narratives (Landesman 2002b; Sperling 2006).

The whore narrative is also prominent in the discussion of Nyiramasuhuko's motivation in ensuring women were raped before they were killed, and prioritizing rape over killing. She is described as a part of a larger conflict between Hutu and Tutsi women, where Hutu women (like her) hate, despise and are jealous of the prettier Tutsi women (prettier because they are on average taller and more statuesque) because Tutsi women are perceived as trying to steal *their*

GENDERED GENOCIDE   171

Hutu men. Tutsi women, in this narrative, are already *sex objects* to Hutu women. Hutu women, then, like Nyiramasuhuko, encourage the rape of Tutsi women because it debased their sexuality and exacted revenge for their sexual prowess.

A third element of the whore narrative in descriptions of Pauline Nyiramasuhuko is the fascination that media and academic analysts have had with her appearance at her trial. She has been described as exotic and singled out for her 'wild' hairstyles and dresses. Several of her dresses have been described in detail, and some in explicitly sexual terms. One day she wore a 'green flowery' dress, and the next a 'pressed cream-colored' skirt (Sperling 2006). On another she wore 'Virgin Mary blue', but on a fourth day she wore a 'low-neck' dress which showed of the 'crucifix' that 'she wore between her breasts' (Harman 2003; Wood 2004). The sexualizing Pauline Nyiramasuhuko takes away the focus both from her crimes and from the possibility that she had agency in them.

GENDERED GENOCIDAIRES

Women who commit genocide are part of larger narratives about women's violence *and* about genocide. As we try to grapple with the horrors of genocide, finding sensationalized (and singular) women to blame seems to make the problem more possible to delineate and account for. Gendered metaphors, as discussed in Chapter 2, provide both content and cognizability to the genocides described in this chapter and their female perpetrators. Gendered lenses reveal, however, that there is more to the relationship between gender and genocide than finding and describing gendered genocidaires.

Charlotte Hooper points out a co-constitutive relationship between warfare and the expected gender roles of men and women (2001: 82). Expected gender roles of men and women are used to support and legitimize fighting, while they entrench war as a socially and politically masculine institution (Yudkin 1983: 263; Enloe 1990: 203). The expected gender role of women is as victims of the enemy's fighting; men can then fight wars to protect their women against the others' men. This is, however, not the only gendered construction which legitimates war *or* genocide. In the introduction, we identify genderings as diverse and hybridized, but sharing an element of subordination of women. In the genocides in this chapter, women do play the role of the victim that the war is *fought for*. They play other roles in the war narratives, however. In both the former Yugoslavia and Rwanda, women were seen as essential targets for the attainment of ethnic purity or the corruption of the purity of the opponents' ethnicity.

Characterizations of women warriors and genocidaires also played a key role in both war narratives. The patriarchal construction of Biljana Plavsic and Pauline Nyiramasuhuko as mother, monster and whore makes them invisible but central to genocide, because the deviant woman acts at once as men's shield from blame and as the explained-away exception to the rule of women's purity. Even when they are about violent women, specific gender-expected roles in warfare for men and women begin in and perpetuate the stereotype of women's weakness (Ruddick 1983: 219; Elshtain 1983). Judith Stiehm observes that 'for the most part, then, men [and masculinities] have forbidden women [and femininities] to act either as defenders or protectors' (1983: 367). When women act as attackers, they are discarded as freaks; mothers, monsters and whores who possess neither real femininity nor real humanity.

John Hoffman concludes that feminisms, and progress against gendered oppression, are 'weakened by "essentializing myths" whether these propagate or simply invert patriarchy' (2001: 123). Such essentializing myths include those that define what women *are* (pure, peaceful, etc.) but can also include those that define what women *cannot be* (perpetrators of genocide). Robin Schott explains that, in postmodern war, belligerent behaviour 'debunks myths of rigid gender patterns during wartime' but 'risks overlooking the way that gender may not be primarily fluid, but may be a predetermining factor in how war becomes carved on women's bodies' (Schott 1996: 21, 22). Descriptions of women who were victims of these conflicts often obscure their pain, but even descriptions of women as 'agents' are often very gendered, limiting their roles and obscuring their choices.

Cohn and Ruddick argue that war is dominated by men and masculinities; masculinities that perpetuate war are socially constructed as dominant, and the words and meanings that shape our thinking about war and provide metaphors for the assignment of hierarchical value come out of those masculinities (2002: 5). A similar argument might be made about the study of gender, genocide and gendered genocidaires. If men and masculinities dominate and narrate genocide, then the hybrid roles that women and femininity play need to be taken account of *through gendered lenses* which recognize both where women are and the role that a gendered global political and social context played in getting them there. Gendering women genocidaires is not about blaming their femininity or their womanhood for their actions, but about using gendered lenses to analyse not only female perpetrators but the genocidal war as a whole.

SEVEN

GENDERING PEOPLE'S VIOLENCE

As mentioned briefly in Chapter 6, feminist research in international relations is often concerned with searching for gendered silences in mainstream (malestream) international relations scholarship, which is largely dominated by male voices and/or masculine values while claiming gender-neutrality (Kronsell 2006: 109). The hegemony of values traditionally associated with masculinity[1] in popular culture naturalizes the gendered identities in everyday life (Peterson and True 1998: 21). In these terms, 'masculinity is not a gender, it is the norm' because (often unwittingly) gendered institutions, discourse and research present themselves as gender-neutral or gender-equal (Kronsell 2006: 109; Butler 1990: 19). In response, Kronsell takes Cynthia Enloe's challenge to 'use curiosity to ask challenging questions about what appear as normal, everyday banalities in order to try and understand and make visible' the hidden gendering of the practice and theorizing of international relations (2006, 110).

This curiosity, much like Charlesworth's searching for silences (1999), looks for masculine gender norms even where masculinity does not readily reveal itself. Feminists in international relations have long been directing such curiosity into deconstructing purportedly gender-neutral theories of international politics.[2] Feminists also engage the project of adding women's knowledge to institutions where masculine values are privileged. These feminists believe that 'the production of knowledge is deeply embedded in the gendered power structures of society and has excluded large segments of society from participating in the articulation of experiences as knowledge' (Kronsell 2006: 121). This exclusion is manifest in silences about gender. Charlesworth explains that 'all systems of knowledge depend on deeming certain issues irrelevant, therefore silences are as important as positive rules' (1999: 381). As a result, the absence of gender in analyses of political events and relations cannot be read simply as blind omission, but as (intentional or unintentional) bias.

Knowing that the most deeply gendered facets of the international political arena are those that do not acknowledge gender difference but present their theories and evidence within predominantly or exclusively masculine ontology, epistemology and method, feminists in international relations have learned to look for gender where gender is claimed as absent – in state governments and international institutions, for example. It is with this methodological disposition that we approach the question of theories of individual violence in global politics. In this chapter, we briefly introduce and use gendered lenses to critique various purportedly gender-neutral theories of people's violence. We then present a relational autonomy framework as a starting point for the redevelopment of a theory of individual violence that recognizes, takes account of, and is shaped around the socially constructed gender differences manifest in the four chapters leading up to this one. This chapter at once asks and debates the merits of the question, 'so why did they do it?'[3] while interrogating a field[4] which supplies only gendered answers to that question.

THEORIES OF INDIVIDUAL VIOLENCE IN GLOBAL POLITICS AND THEIR GENDERINGS

How do theories of individual violence accommodate violent women? We argue that, for the most part, they do not. Most theories used to describe the violence of the women in the preceding chapters, as we saw, dealt with their violence *as women* with theories tailored to expectations and assumptions about their gender. The first way that theories of individual violence fail to accommodate violent women, then, is that they are often not used to describe incidences of women's proscribed violence in practice. The practice of not applying these theories, we argue, is not anomalous, because most theories of individual violence either explicitly or implicitly exclude women. Those theories that are not explicitly *about men only* or gendered in their appraisal are still based on a male actor (as a man) as a stereotype and masculinized understandings of knowledge, values and actions. Many of the theories of individual violence were shaped by attention to men, and, when applied to women, therefore add women to an analysis, the terms of which have already been set by masculine discourses. Adding women to theories of individual (men's) violence shows *not only* that these theories omitted women, but that their genderings made them inadequate to explain *both* men's and women's violence. Below, we briefly discuss rational choice theory, psychoanalytic theory, social learning theory, frustration-aggression theory, relative deprivation theory, and narcissism theory as a sampling of theories of individual violence in global politics. These are not the only theories of individual violence, but they are among the most influential.[5] Further, these summaries are not intended to be comprehensive;[6] instead, they intend to serve as a preliminary introduction to the genderings of the theories specifically and their field generally, which suggest the need for feminist critique and reformulation of understandings of people's violence in global politics.

RATIONAL-CHOICE THEORY

Debra Friedman and Doug McAdam define rational-choice theory as 'the assumption that individuals have given goals, wants, tastes, or utilities' which direct their action (1992: 159). Because individuals do not have unlimited time, energy, or resources, they will have to choose between those goals). Decisions, then, are based on 'expected utility' where individuals 'select outcomes that bring the greatest expected benefits' (Walt 2000: 6). In a specific study of terrorism, terrorists are 'constrained in their operations by the lack of active mass support and by the superior power arrayed against them' by the state and international system (Crenshaw 1998: 11). Thus, terrorist groups have collective preferences or values and then select terrorism from a range of perceived alternatives (8). In this model, individuals choose proscribed violence because they see it as the best way to achieve their political goals.

The rational-actor model might appear appealing to authors who have expressed concern for the continued application of narratives which exclude the political from women's possible motivations to engage in proscribed violence and deny women agency in their choices. One reason it might be appealing is not least because it purportedly considers all individuals as political actors capable of making and acting on calculated decisions based on expected utility. The model is not the catch-all solution to the gendered nature of theories of individual violence that it appears to be, however.

First, rational-actor theory is rarely applied to an individual's political violence; instead, many scholars point to psychological factors.[7] Thus, it follows that it is often not applied to women's proscribed violence; indeed most researchers often seek psychological factors behind female terrorists' violence (see Crenshaw 2000: 408–9). Even when the rational-actor model is applied to individual violence, the individual is often (in body and in portrayal) gendered male. Second, just as the mother, monster and whore narratives ignore women's agency, the rational-actor model neglects the roles of emotion and interdependence in all decisions to commit proscribed violence. According to Hooper, rational-choice theory is 'physically disembodied and socially disembedded' from the gendered 'rational/emotional, mind/body, and reason/madness dichotomies of Western thought' (2001: 99). Despite claiming universal applicability, the rational-actor model is 'clearly grounded in highly individualistic and instrumental values' and 'cannot easily be divorced from the historically specific and highly gendered framework within which it was developed' (Hooper 2001: 100, 102). For example, the idea that men act only on the basis of some objective reason and duty is a partial view of global politics, whether in violence or any other political situation (Tickner 2001). Tickner explains:

> Feminists suggest that rational-choice theory is based on a partial representation of human behaviour that, since women in the West have historically been confined to reproductive activities, has been more typical of men.... Therefore, it tends to privilege certain types of behaviors over others.... This rational, disembodied

language precludes discussion of death and destruction, issues that can be spoken of only in emotional terms stereotypically associated with women. In other words, the limits on what can be said with the language of strategic discourse constrains our ability to think fully and well about ... security. (2001: 52–3)

In other words, gendered lenses are quick to point out the radical denial of individual politicization and agency present in the mother, monster and whore narratives of violent women in global politics. This does not, then, indicate a preference for a theory which ignores human emotion, incomplete autonomy, imperfect decision-making, or the constructed nature of the reason–emotion dichotomy in analysing individual violence. Such a theory is necessarily, as rational choice theory is, based on a partial view of the world that emphasizes men's experiences and the values associated with masculinities. Adding women to the 'subjects' of the study of people's violence helps us see that rational-choice theory, in its gendering, inaccurately represents men (as entirely rational) and women (as entirely emotional). Rational-choice theory is *gendered* both by omission (women) and by commission (the partiality of its theoretical insights).

PSYCHOANALYTIC THEORY

This is not to say that theories of individual violence which emphasize the emotional and psychological are more appropriate to the analysis of women's violence. Though it comes from the opposite side of the intellectual spectrum, psychoanalytic theory contains many of the same sort of genderings that rational-choice theory does. For example, the basis of psychoanalytic theories of individual violence is a fundamental difference between women and men. Freud, founder of the psychoanalytic tradition, argued that men 'are not gentle creatures'; they are 'creatures among whose instinctual endowments is to be reckoned a powerful share of aggressiveness' (Freud 1961: 58). According to Freud, men are instinctively violent creatures whose violence stems from the id, the unconscious part of humans' psychological make-up and the one responsible for instincts or 'drives'. Freud believed there is a death instinct, which cannot be proven to act internally, but does act externally and is seen as an instinct for aggression and destruction (Freud 1961: 66). Destruction provides, within certain boundaries, the ego, the mediator between the id and the superego (the conscience), a sense of 'control over nature' (68). It is the 'inclination to aggression' that prevents man from living in peace with his neighbours (59). In true dialectical fashion, Freud concludes that 'besides the instinct to preserve living substance and to join it into ever larger units', there is a contradictory instinct to 'dissolve those units and to bring them back to the primeval, inorganic state' (65–6). In other words, Freud argued that men are instinctively violent and women are instinctively non-violent.

Konrad Lorenz, the 'father of ethnology', agreed with Freud (Berkowitz 1991: 25). Aggressive or violent behaviour was seen as 'an impulse to action' (instinctive) and this drive (instinct) 'was independent of experience' (25). Thus, violence comes from a primitive place within a person and is not reliant upon cognitive processes. Lorenz's analysis of human behaviour and aggression was based on his observation of fighting birds and fish. This aggression in animals was seen as unlearned, and thus human aggression was similar in origin:

> Man has inherited instincts too ... and the instinct to aggress is not a reactive one, but is a spontaneous activity within ourselves.
> (Berkowitz 1990: 25)

A significant problem with the idea of the death or aggressive instinct 'is the assumption that all violent actions basically serve the same underlying purpose and are governed by the same biological mechanism – in other words, that there is one drive to aggression' (Berkowitz 1990: 27). This also indicates that there is no prescription for the violence – if it is instinctual, nothing influences it and nothing can be done about it. Therefore the psychoanalytic approach to individual violence has been widely dismissed. For the purposes here, the women in this study had a variety of reasons for their violence, some were blatant, others more nuanced. Freud and Lorenz do not take into account frustrations, social context or politics. There is no recognition for a person's participation in his or her decision to be violent.

Furthermore, Freud clearly wrote from a gendered agenda. It was men who were violent. They were the ones who had the 'death instinct', not women. In a personal letter to his fiancée, Freud demonstrated his gendered beliefs:

It seems a completely unrealistic notion to send women into the struggle for existence in the same way as men. Am I to think of my delicate sweet girl as a competitor? After all, the encounter could only end by my telling her, as I did 17 years ago, that I love her, and I will make every effort to get her out of the competitive role into the quiet undisturbed activity of my home. It is possible that a different education could suppress all women's delicate qualities – with the result that they could earn their living like men. It is also possible that in this case it would not be justifiable to deplore the disappearance of the most lovely thing the world has to offer us: our ideal of womanhood. But I believe that all reforming activity, legislation and education, will founder on the fact that before the age at which a profession can be established in our society, Nature will have appointed woman by her beauty, charm and goodness, to do something else.

... the position of woman cannot be other than what it is: to be an adored sweetheart in youth, and a beloved wife in maturity. (quoted in Buhle 1998, 53–4)

While Freud had welcomed women into the ranks of psychoanalysis, he clearly still saw them as wives and mothers, and viewed their drives in a gendered manner (Buhle 1998: 54). Indeed, many feminist scholars have critiqued psychoanalytic theory for its 'normative masculinity, masculine bias, [and] devaluation of women' (Chodorow 1994: 1). The Freudian interpretation of women's violence can be seen as a foundation for the monster narrative, arguing that, because women are not (like men) biologically predisposed to violence, a women who is violent is somehow biologically or psychobiologically flawed – less of a woman for her ability to commit violence. In psychoanalytic theory, the woman who commits violence is acting against her natural drives – maternity and peacefulness – which threatens her femininity.

SOCIAL LEARNING THEORY

Psychoanalytic theory is not the only gendered psychological theory of individual violence in global politics. Social learning theory differs from psychoanalytic theory by arguing that people's behaviours stem from observed and reinforced behaviours instead of from instinct. Learned behaviour happens when

People learn through their eyes and ears by noting the experiences of others and not merely from the outcomes they get directly for their own behaviour. Learning without direct reinforcement is sometimes called 'perceptual', sometimes 'cognitive', sometimes 'vicarious', and sometimes 'observational' or 'modeling'. (Mischel 1968: 150)

Studies have proven that 'many complex, verbal, emotional and motoric behaviours are learned, maintained, elicited, inhibited and modified, at least in part, by modelling cues' (Mischel 1968: 153). Reinforced behaviours are a result of conditioning. Classical conditioning is most often associated with Pavlov's dogs. In his study, Pavlov rang a bell every time the dogs were fed. After a while, the dogs would salivate when the bell rang – even when no food was present. The dogs, then, had been conditioned to associate two unrelated items: the sound of the bell with food. Observed behaviour and reinforced, conditioned behaviour contribute to social learning theory.

Social learning theory, however, has failed to contextualize both gender and learning (Miller 2001). Miller explains that this is a systemic problem in theories of crime, as

> Every theoretical perspective has within it both explicit and hidden assumptions about human nature and the individuals or groups in question. In criminology, assumptions about gender – about the 'nature' of males and females – have shaped the evolution of theories about women and crime. (Miller 2001: 219)

Miller explains that social learning theory, like many other theories of criminology, has 'either ignored women or ignored gender' by presenting a theory of male crime that does not account for women's crimes (2001: 219). In the context of individual violent crimes, social learning theory often blames video games or violent movies for individuals' violence, referring to the violence of men and ignoring the violence of women. Theories of why men commit crimes, or why men are more aggressive are precisely the fodder for gendered narratives of women's transgressions. If 'the theories' explain men's crimes but not women's, and women then commit crimes, their crimes are by definition outside of the realm of normative values and theory. Women, in fact, often do not 'learn' the same behaviours that allegedly encourage men's violence. This means that, while social learning theory could be seen to account for men's crimes, it does not account for women's. This then allows for the mother, monster and whore narratives to be applied to women's crimes as there has to be some other reason for them.

Some argue that social learning theory still explains men's violence but fails to explain women's violence. The real insight to be taken here, however, is that because it does not explain women's violence, the total explanatory power of social learning theory should be questioned. As Miller argues, there is insidiousness in

> Theories that are based on beliefs about fundamental differences between women and men. It is precisely women's greater emotionality, passivity, and weakness, according to these theories, that account for both their involvement in crimes and the nature of that involvement. (Miller 2001: 220)

So long as they are separate, theories of male crimes have been much more likely to take them as a part of a broader social world, like social learning theory does, while explanations of women's crimes are much more likely to consider them fantastic, abnormal, outside of the realm of theory, and fodder for gendered narratives.

FRUSTRATION-AGGRESSION THEORY

Dollard et al. take us to the other extreme by describing aggression as an emotional reaction to the frustration of an individual's goals and aspirations. John Dollard's theory of violence, in the famed work *Frustration and Aggression*, assumes 'aggression is always a consequence of frustration' (Dollard et al. 1944: 1). Aggression as the product of frustration can be directed at the source of frustration, displaced, or even directed at the self 'as in masochism, martyrdom and suicide' (Dollard et al. 1944: 7). Two types of frustration can lead to aggression. The first type of frustration is when an actor, on his way to a goal, is temporarily interrupted. This leads to aggression until the temporary interference ends. The second type is complete interference, which inspires more sustained aggression.

Frustration-aggression theory is not gender-neutral, however. Dollard argues that, from a psychological perspective, boys and girls are taught to deal with this aggression differently. Boys learn that aggression is an appropriate and necessary reaction to frustration for future manliness, while girls learn that aggression should be curtailed (Dollard et al. 1944: 49). Dollard suggests that men and women treat frustration differently because of different standards of social acceptability. Men learn aggression in response to frustration, while women learn stoicism or complacency.

While it is true that men and women are often exposed to different values, as discussed in Chapter 2, there is no universal experience of manhood or womanhood, masculinity or femininity. Certainly women's roles in conservative societies, such as the Middle East and Chechnya, do not encourage women's violence, yet women considered in this study acted aggressively. Likewise, many men who are taught that aggression is necessary for future manliness do not end up committing acts of proscribed violence. These inherited stereotypes are used in frustration-aggression theory to expand a theory of men's violence to account for women's supposed *non-violence*, not to produce a gender-sensitive theory of people's violence.

Further, the experience of gender subordination in the world proves frustration-aggression theory necessarily false and/or partial. If aggression were *any* individual's response to frustration, the frustration-aggression hypothesis predicts that women would be more violent than men, because they are more likely to be frustrated in their attempts to achieve individual goals than are men. Additionally, frustration-aggression theory acknowledges people's interdependence in descriptions of the genesis of frustration (people's goals are frustrated, and thus they are not entirely independent of each other), but then treats individuals as entirely autonomous for the purposes of aggression. This distinction is intellectually artificial and socially insidious. A feminist critique of frustration-aggression theory problematizes the exclusion of women from its explanations of violence, the stereotypical images of women it includes, the gendered nature of its understanding of frustration, and the gender bias in its understanding of interdependence and obligation.

RELATIVE DEPRIVATION THEORY

As one of the more influential relative deprivation theorists, Ted Gurr, in critiquing Dollard's theory, explicitly asks the question of why men are prone to violence. His answer is relative deprivation. Relative deprivation happens when '[p]eople feel unjustly treated or inadequately compensated when they compare themselves to some standard of reference' (Crosby 1976: 85). Crosby's study of egotistical relative deprivation engages the large field of relative deprivation theorists and synthesizes their work into a comprehensive model with five necessary preconditions for relative deprivation. A 'person who lacks X' must:

1. see that someone else (Other) possesses X,
2. want X,
3. feel entitled to X,
4. think it is feasible to obtain X, and
5. lack a sense of personal responsibility for not having X. (Crosby 1976: 90)

This theoretical approach reveals a number of genderings. First, as an approach specifically tailored to men's violence, it implicates a number of the problems discussed above about social learning theory's exclusion of women's violence. Second, though relative deprivation theory has been applied more broadly than only to men's violence since its inception, it remains based on the masculine ideal-type which is responsible for its establishment.[8]

Third, like frustration-aggression theory, the experience of gender subordination in the world is a problem for relative deprivation theory. Women are relatively deprived as compared to men by almost every indicator of social welfare (Inglehart and Norris 2003: 3). If relative deprivation inspired violence in any relatively deprived individuals, the relative deprivation hypothesis, like the frustration-aggression hypothesis, would predict that women would be more violent than men, since they are more likely to be relatively deprived. In reality, however, the relatively deprived in relative deprivation theory are gendered male, even in the study of gender violence. Schiffman and O'Toole use men's relative deprivation compared to each other to explain their violence against women:

> We can apply the concept of relative deprivation to the study of gender violence as well. When ideal masculinity involves possession of certain characteristics that are unevenly distributed (such

as 'Whiteness', success with women, athleticism, and money), men who are deficient in one or more of these central areas may become frustrated and angry. One way that men who experience relative deprivation compensate for real or perceived deficiencies is through the use of physical strength to gain power.... Relative deprivation ... cuts across race and class boundaries and is experienced by men in all sectors of U.S. society. (Schiffman and O'Toole 1997: 71)

While many scholars recognize that women *are* relatively deprived (e.g. Inglehart and Norris 2003), this realization does not translate into the prediction that relative deprivation causes women's violence. Instead, relative deprivation causes men's violence, not women's, because women's violence is seen as psychologically abnormal. Even before the relative deprivation hypothesis explicitly excludes women, it has a masculinized understanding of the violent individual. The relatively deprived individual in relative deprivation theory sees himself as both separate from the framework which deprives him and entitled to the things of which he is deprived (including, according to Schiffman and O'Toole, success with women). This individual perceives himself as living in a social anarchy and capable of obtaining whatever he needs through the exercise of individual power.

Feminists recognize that this is a partial understanding of the world. Most people, feminists note, and especially most women, neither see themselves as independent of the framework which oppresses them nor believe themselves entitled to everything it has to offer. Most people see themselves as constrained by the actions of and their interactions with others (Hirschmann 1989). The relative deprivation hypothesis not only omits the violence of actual women, it also omits the influences of interdependence, solidarity, uncertainty and communality.

NARCISSISM THEORY

Narcissism theory of participation in proscribed violence lays the blame for an individual's violent or terrorist act solely upon that individual's psychological make-up (Crayton 1983). Narcissism disorder develops due to wounds sustained during childhood. Often it is symptomatic of parental rejection or abandonment. This leads to the child 'defensively withdrawing' and believing one can only trust and 'therefore love' him- or herself (Emmons 1987: 11). Jerrold Post also believes that narcissistic personality traits 'are found with extremely high frequency in the population of terrorists' (Post 1998: 27). These traits include 'externalization' and 'splitting'. These happen because a damaged individual does not 'fully integrat[e] the good and bad parts of the self' (27). Thus, the self is '"split" into the "me" and the "not me"', which then leads to an individual idealizing 'his grandiose self and *splits out* and *projects* onto others all the hated and devalued weaknesses within' (27). Finding an exterior enemy allows the individual to use violence against them (28).

A number of critics argue that the credit given to narcissism in this theory is 'impressionistic, not empirical' (Victoroff 2005: 20). Martha Crenshaw highlights Silke's criticism of policymakers (and the academics who inform them) for 'diag[nosing] at a distance' in order to create personality profiles of terrorists (2000, 407). In this, there is too heavy a reliance upon narcissism and paranoia (Crenshaw 2000: 407). This is especially true of the studies conducted on female terrorists (408). All of this is problematic because 'most analysts of terrorism do not think that personality factors account for terrorist behaviour' (409).

Further, narcissism theory is based on the male ideal-type of the myth of Narcissus, who loved himself and his masculinity, and was scornful of all things feminine (Hamilton 1940: 88). Even though it is reliant on a gendered image of individual life and individual violence, narcissism theory has been employed to make sense of women's choice to engage in suicide terrorism. For example, Bloom and Victor assert that deep personal wounds, such as rape, divorce and the inability to have children, are reasons why women become violent (Victor 2003; Bloom 2005a, 2005b, 2005c, 2007). In its application, narcissism theory has some commonalities with the monster narratives which have been used to describe the women involved in proscribed violence examined in this book. Like the monster narrative, narcissism theory denies the possibility that individuals (especially women) act from political motivations. Several of the women in this book, including the Chechen 'black widows', Palestinian and al-Qaeda suicide terrorists, and Biljana Plavsic, have explicitly cited political motivations for their actions. Sufferers of the psychological damage of narcissistic injury can damage the self apolitically, either by suicide or by a non-terrorist attack on others, but do not have political motivations. Even if narcissism were a motivating factor in an individual's decision to engage in proscribed violence, many of the individuals discussed in this book show that it cannot be the only explanation for choosing political means to express their desire to do damage. Moreover, several of the women considered in this book who engaged in proscribed violence, and several other perpetrators of proscribed violence, damage others rather than themselves, making it impossible to consider narcissism fully explanatory.

Above and beyond the explanatory weakness that women's violence betrays in narcissism theory, it demonstrates the masculinized assumptions of not only the story of Narcissus but the theory derived from it. In the psychology literature, narcissism is strongly tied to the perception of self as a superior. According to Bushman et al., 'narcissists are strongly motivated to sustain their own and others' perception of them as superior beings' (2003: 1028). The perception of superiority can be linked to male privilege. Further, scholars often characterize narcissism as, like relative deprivation, something *women cause* in men rather than something that women have. In describing the narcissistic impulse to violence, Bushman et al. *assume* that a narcissist is male:

> There are multiple reasons for predicting that narcissists would be more likely than other men to engage in sexual coercion, in addition to their propensity for aggressive retaliation ... first, their inflated sense of entitlement may make them think that women owe them sexual favors. Second, their low empathy entails that they would not be deterred by concern over the victim's suffering ... Third, their tendency to maintain inflated views of self by means of cognitive distortions might help them rationalize away any borderline objectionable behaviors, such as if they could convince themselves that their coercion victims had really desired the sex. (Bushman et al. 2003: 1028)

When women are described as at all narcissistic, their narcissism is characterized as directed *internally* (to a vanity of person or dress), while men's narcissism is described as *outward* (aiming at the approval of others) (Marcus 1978). Female narcissism is also talked about as a 'castration complex' finding 'that women view themselves as inferior and their genitals as repugnant as understood in terms of their anxieties concerning fantasies of castration ... to compensate for their loss' she engages in obsession about appearance because 'it is the only socially condoned form of power openly afforded to her' (Young-Eisendrath and Wiedemann 1987: 18). In other words, while men's narcissism is framed as a public competition with other men, women's narcissism is characterized as based on women's inadequacy as compared to men. This is because narcissism theory, as applied to violence, is based on the masculine ideal of self-perceived and individual superiority.

GENDER-SPECIFIC THEORIES OF WOMEN'S VIOLENCE

Most of the psychological theories discussed above constitute, to a greater or lesser degree, gender-specific theories of men's violence. Many of the commentators cited in this book as a part of the mother, monster and whore narratives contain gender-specific theories of women's violence. The mother narrative insinuates that women's maternal instinct is a gender-specific explanation for women's violence. The monster narrative implies that the perversion of female psychology is a special, more terrible cause for violence than the perversion of male psychology. The whore narrative portrays gender-specific attributes of women's sexuality as culprits for women's violence. Several gender-specific theories of women's violence implicate one or more of these narratives. For example, in speculating as to why women engage in suicide bombings, Mia Bloom explains that 'motives vary: to avenge a personal loss, to redeem the family name, to escape a life of sheltered monotony and achieve fame. ... In many instances, women are seeking revenge', implicating the mother narrative (2007: 2). As discussed in Chapter 2, the monster and whore narratives also frequent the pages of scholarly work concerning women's violence.

There are two problems with theories of women's violence, as we see it. First, they are often fraught with gender stereotypes and negative sensationalisms of femininity. In other words, they are inaccurate and gender-subordinating as they apply to women's violence. Second is the separation of theories of women's violence and theories of men's violence. This is not to say that men *and* women do not commit their violence in a gendered world with a number of gendered influences and gendered implications. Instead, this book argues that separating theories of men's and women's violence cause those theories to miss agency in women's violence and relational autonomy in men's violence.

Because theories of individual violence often disaggregate motivations and responsibility for individual violence in global politics on the basis of perceived gender norms and gendered expectations of behaviour, they are not accurate explanations of the violent behaviour of either gender. When they do not explicitly gender individual violence in global politics, these theories often use maleness and the male experience to measure their understandings of individual psychology and politics, causing their explanatory power to be partial at best, even when explaining the violence of the men that they are analysing. Further, these theories are applied disproportionately on the basis of gender, with the bulk of male decisions to engage in proscribed violence explained either by rational choice or by relative deprivation (both theories of individual choice), and the bulk of female decisions being described in terms of theories which singularize violent women and detract from the possibility for individual choice.

These gendered disparities in theories of individual proscribed violence in global politics create space for and reify the mother, monster and whore narratives. The remainder of this chapter, while not claiming to be able to 'solve' the puzzle of individual motivations for proscribed violence, suggests a feminist theory of the contexts and constraints in which people's decisions to commit violence are made. Instead of trying to add or fit women to theories, the terms of which were set before women's violence was considered, the rest of this chapter reformulates a theory of people's violence *as if* women and gender mattered in theoretical formulation.

RELATIONAL AUTONOMY

Initially, a theory of political and moral agency seems to be a funny place to start a reformulation of theories of individual violence in global politics. But the narratives in this book are focused on the question of agency. Perhaps if we were trying to identify new and better answers to the question of why individuals commit violence, this would be a legitimate and important critique of relational autonomy as a starting point. Our goal is somewhat different, however, than the crafters of the theories enumerated upon above. We are interested less in the question of each individual's motivation than in the question of *how* individuals decide to participate in or lead proscribed violence.[9]

Feminists are interested in how much choice people (especially women) exercise in their decisions. The women in this book have often been described as having no agency in their choices whatsoever. The mother narrative characterizes women as having lost the will to live after losing their ability to have or raise children. The monster narrative portrays violent women as so insane that they have lost control of their faculties and decision-making power. The whore narrative tells of violent women as controlled either by their insatiable need for sex with men *or* by actual men. All of these narratives share one element: they characterize violent women as having been incapable of choosing their violence, and imply that, had they a choice, women would not have chosen the violence.

The mother, monster and whore narratives imply that when women choose, they choose within a specified spectrum of socially acceptable choices. When women behave outside of the realm of those choices, they have not chosen to do so. The theories presented at the beginning of this chapter, on the other hand, present their (male) subjects as individual decision-makers who are either rational or psychologically damaged but still operate with cognizable criteria in order to make their decisions (with the exception of psychoanalytic theory). These presentations imply that men who commit violence make autonomous decisions, while women who do so are controlled, coerced or insane.

Theories of individual violence, then, directly implicate the question: do women (or individuals more generally) choose? This question, then, asks for a theory of political and moral agency. Nancy Hirschmann's understanding, termed relational autonomy, allows insight into the subject position of individuals vis-à-vis their decisions in global politics. Most theories of individual behaviour in political situations begin with the assumption that individuals, through explicit consent or social contract, have accepted some limitations on their decision-making capacity in exchange for the right to live in a society which provides them with protection and easy access to a number of human necessities (Hirschmann 1989: 1228). This understanding of an individual's role in political decision-making, however, falls short in two important areas. First, consent is not always voluntary. Second, the process of consent, even when voluntary, is complicated by a number of mitigating factors.

The contention that consent is not always voluntary has been a tenet of feminist theory throughout its history (see MacKinnon 2001). There are many obligations that 'people do not choose, actively or passively' (Sjoberg 2006: 124). Gendered lenses see the incompleteness of choice because they recognize gender bias in the structure of political obligation and social agency (Hirschmann 1989: 1228–9). Women often are assigned obligations that they have not agreed to, implicitly or explicitly.

Pregnancy that is a product of rape is an example of a (gendered female) unassumed obligation. There is no part of such a pregnancy consented to by any woman individually or by women collectively. The woman did not consent to her rape, nor did women consent to pregnancy as a result of rape generally. Yet obligation exists. Some answer this problematic by pointing out that a woman pregnant from rape has the option to have an abortion. While there are a number of reasons (money, taboo, health conditions) why abortions are unavailable to most women in the world, even the complete and free availability of abortions would not 'solve' the problem of involuntary assumption of obligation. A woman would still be obligated both to make the choice between abortion and childbirth, and to follow through on either choice.

Further, non-voluntary obligation is assigned to human beings on gendered terms. Traditional understandings of political agency and responsibility emphasize freedom (Hirschmann 1989: 1233), while traditional understandings of femininity emphasize control (Tickner 2001). Hirschmann argues that freedoms perceived as natural are actually gender-biased. She argues:

> Psychoanalytically, the girl is more likely to learn sameness from mothers and the boy is more likely to learn difference, so the boy

develops conflictual tendencies and the girl peaceful ones. Boys' freedom is reactive autonomy; girls' is relational autonomy.... If the conception of freedom as negative is premised on the struggle for recognition, particularly on the ability to be recognized without reciprocation, if non-recognition is (as it is for the Oedipal boy and Hegel's master) a form of power and violence – freedom, too, must be at least in part an expression of that same power and violence. (1989: 1233)

In other words, obligatory relationships are always governed by gendered power. In describing what she calls the problem of 'oppressive socialization', Hirschmann explains that 'powers and freedoms are inevitably intertwined with, and even defined by limitations and structures' (2004: 204). These limitations differ based on social group membership, where oppressed social groups have less access to powers and freedoms (and thus to agency). Often, in social relationships, women are the obliged and men the obligor, meaning women must recognize men and men need not return the recognition (Hirschmann 1989: 1239). As a result, 'even acts of dissent are interpreted as acts of consent, and unfair bargaining positions belie the freedom implicit in free choice' (1239).

This brings us to the second shortcoming of the idea of consent: the many complexities surrounding it serve as mitigating factors. The first complexity, discussed above, is that people come to the 'consent table' with differential power, and thus have different capacities to choose and ignore obligations. The second complexity, as Hirschmann describes, has to do with the foundations of the choice that the consenting party makes. As she explains:

> Many theorists of freedom recognize that desires and preferences are always limited by contexts that determine the parameters of choice: if chocolate and vanilla are the only flavors available, I am not free to choose strawberry, but that does not alter the fact that I would have chosen strawberry if it were available. What is not addressed by most freedom theories, however, is the deeper, more important issue of how the choosing subject is herself constructed by such contexts: could the repeated absence of strawberry eventually change my tastes so that I lose desire for it? (Hirschmann 2004: ix)

In other words, consent is mitigated by the fact that the constant availability of limited choices narrows the spectrum of expected utility, giving people less incentive to want to choose some other option.[10]

Power and limited choices are not the only factors that limit consent, however. The lines between inside and outside of individual self are not impenetrable, but fluid and flexible. As Hirschmann argues:

> Freedom ... is centrally about choice, a claim with which many mainstream freedom theories would agree. But choice is constituted by a complex relationship between 'internal' factors of will and desire – impacting on the preferences and desires one has and how one makes choices – and factors 'outside' the self that may inhibit or enhance one's ability to pursue one's preferences, including the kind and number of choices available, the obstacles to making the preferred choice, and the variable power that different people have to make choices (Hirschmann 2004: ix).

Individual choice, then, is constrained by its (sometime) unavailability, individuals' (gendered) power differentials, limited choice, and the social construction of internal will and desire. Yet, within this complex maze of limits on human agency and the freedom of choice, individual identity remains (Sylvester 1990). Hirschmann argues that a feminist approach to the question of agency critiques understandings that all choices are made and responsibilities assumed fully freely. Instead, as we mentioned in the introduction, a relational autonomy approach sees responsibility as intersubjective. Responsibility is *responsive* and interactive, based on social and political interaction. If not all choices are made fully freely and not all obligations are assumed voluntarily, then obligation is relational.[11]

Christine Sylvester argues that feminists should embrace a notion of relational autonomy for actors in political relationships both because it more accurately describes the way that political relationships function and because it creates space for a feminist alternative understanding of power (1990). She argues that 'relational autonomy preserves identity independence for oneself while recognizing the interdependence of self and other and the political and social relationships one has with others' (Sylvester 2002: 119). Hirschmann describes a similar vision of contingent independence:

> Feminist freedom requires a double vision: while recognizing that social construction is a phenomenon or process that happens to and is participated in by everyone through language and discourse, social practices and customs, epistemological frameworks, knowledge claims, systems of ethics and moral beliefs, feminists concerned with freedom also want to acknowledge that some groups of people systematically and structurally have more power to participate in the constructing than do others. The fact that these practices, epistemologies, systems of knowledges, and discourses set the condition for everyone's ability to define themselves does not prevent us from seeing that it nevertheless is often more difficult for women to define themselves within a masculinist epistemology, language and discourse. (2004: 204)

In its simplest form, relational autonomy is the recognition that freedom of action is defined and limited by social relationships.[12] Political choice, then, is a question of both position and degree (Sjoberg 2006). The 'lived experiences of women … demonstrate that existing theories of freedom fail to challenge the duality of internal and external dimensions of freedom' (Hirschmann 2004: x).

In a world of relational autonomy, decisions can be made within constraints or with fellow constrainees, but are never entirely unavailable and never without any constraint. Accordingly, 'decisions are not made without others, but instead either with or around them' (Sjoberg 2006). Given this interdependence, actors can choose to use their limited autonomy to act against, around or with others.

The choice to act against others is often characterized in feminist analyses as the use of power-over (Allen 1998). Elshtain contends that this power is often conflated with 'the crude instrumentalism of violence' (1985: 51). In Allen's explanation, power-over is the 'ability of an actor or set of actors to constrain the choices available to another actor or set of actors in a non-trivial way' (1998: 33). People who act against others are concerned with 'the ability of A to get B to do something that B would not otherwise do' (Peterson and Runyan 1999: 69). Feminists argue that this understanding of action in a partly autonomous world 'privileges an androcentric definition of power – as power-over – and discriminates against women as political actors' (Peterson and Runyan 1999: 213).

The second option in a world of incomplete autonomy is acting *around* others insomuch as the choices available allow it. Amy Allen explains that power-to is 'the capacity of an agent to act in spite of or in response to power wielded over her by others' (1998: 34). Here, power is defined as action in opposition to power-over, as rebellion. In the view of people acting around restraints, power 'is procedural, circulating, and simultaneously restraining and producing new realities' (Dahl 2000; Bartky 1988).

A third option in a world of incomplete autonomy is acting with others. Amy Allen introduces the concept of power-with, or solidarity used to act in concert (1998: 35). Many feminists employ Hannah Arendt's understanding of power (Elshtain 1985, 1992; Tickner 1992). Arendt defines power as 'human ability to act in concert and begin anew' (Elshtain 1985: 51; Arendt 1970). John Hoffman explains that 'by emphasizing plurality and community, Arendt consciously seeks to distance power from *domination*' and to understand power collaboratively (Hoffman 2001: 151). Arendt's understanding makes power the true opposite of violence (Elshtain 1992a: 273). Power, here, can be seen as the *deconstruction* of force, rather than the use thereof. Allen contends that feminisms should look for an integrative approach to power, seeing it not as mutually exclusive ideal-types but as a complex web which we can understand and make choices about (1998: 26).

The options to act against, around or with others highlight potential *processes* of decision-making in a relationally autonomous world. In this interpretation, the existence and identity of the self and other are mutually dependent, mutually vulnerable, and mutually socially constructed. This mutual construction is not accomplished by harmony and cooperation, but by the ambivalence and conflict inherent in the environment. Hybridity is thus a complex sort of exchange, where issues of power, choice and consciousness are not clear. In traditional work on autonomy, the subordinate is silent and oppressed while the voice of the dominant is in control of the relationship. In a hybrid relationship much more is happening. The subordinate does have a voice and that voice does impact the dominant voice. While a power differential still exists, the world of the subordinate is a world of mimicry, counter-discourse and transculture. In other words, there is individual choice in individual political action for *each* individual, from the most to the least powerful. Those decisions are simply made dealing with the constraints of relational autonomy, which can be accommodated by acting against, around or with others.

RELATIONAL AUTONOMY, FEMINIST THEORY AND VIOLENCE IN GLOBAL POLITICS

One of the primary concerns of feminist theory is the reconciliation of women's lives and masculinist interpretation of key concepts like interpersonal relations, the state and the international system. The women in this book committed proscribed violence in international relations: torture, terrorism and genocide. There are, as we discovered earlier in this chapter, well-developed theories about how and why individuals come to commit proscribed violence. Just as the feminists ask international relations where the women are, gendered lenses look for explanations of the systematic exclusion of women from theories of individual proscribed violence. Where are the women in rational-choice theory? In relative deprivation theory? Women are not usually present in these theories, and when they are, one of two discursively exclusive moves are made. In some cases, women are included in a theory that defines individual violence in reference to masculine standards of individual conduct. More often, though, women are included *but gender differentiated* in these theories of individual violence.

A relational autonomy framework provides a basis for us to move beyond these problems. According to a feminist understanding of relational autonomy, human choice is never entirely free, but it is also never entirely constrained. Thus the radical denial of agency in the mother, monster and whore narratives is both gendered and unwarranted, but the (masculine) rational-choice theory (or psychoanalytic or frustration-aggression theory) at the other end of the spectrum is also an incomplete explanation.

Any move towards a gender-conscious theory of individual violence in global politics would need to account at once for political and social motivations, gendered context and individuality. Including previously hidden gender inequalities in the analysis of individual violence in global politics 'allows us to see how many of the insecurities affecting us all, women and men alike, are gendered in their historical origins, their conventional definitions, and their contemporary manifestations' (Tickner 1992: 129). Recognizing that women sometimes commit proscribed violence ('adding women') is insufficient.

Even though scholarly analyses and the political arena at large have recognized that women can and do participate in proscribed violence, they have done so on very gendered terms. These gendered terms still valorize masculinity and subordinate femininities. They still describe women's choices as narrow and men's as expansive, a problem which will not be fixed until we reach a point where both the people and values associated with femininity are 'more universally valued in public life' and women's agency in their decisions is as recognized as men's agency in theirs' (Tickner 1992: 141). The beginning of this re-visioning is gendered lenses' recognition of human interdependence and relational autonomy, which shows that all decisions are contextual and contingent, not only women's, and that all decisions are made, not only men's.

Feminist theory provides a way forward for the creation of such an understanding of individual violence in global politics. Kathy Ferguson explains that 'praxis feminisms focus on affirmative intersubjective connections between persons rather than on autonomous or combative selves', which would cause them to suggest that individual violence be discussed in relational, rather than abstract, terms (1993: 69). An intersubjective theory of individual violence in global politics would account for both context and individual choice, both personal and political.

As mentioned in Chapter 2, women's positions in international relations are improving – at least, that is, on the surface. It should be celebrated that international organizations, such as the United Nations Security Council, the European Union, the International Monetary Fund and the World Bank are concerning themselves with gender in their official policy; and that the 1995 Fourth World Conference on Women was a success. Yet, one has to ask what this all means when women begin to hold positions of power while their agency as individuals is still often denied. It is a milestone that women and gender have gained some prominence in international politics, but this does not necessarily promote the agency of all women in every place.

Hirschmann, as mentioned earlier, is concerned that the oppressed have less access to powers, freedoms and agency. Women are finally being allowed into positions of power; women's freedoms are finally being promoted globally, with the growing acceptance of rape as a war crime and a part of genocide. Thus, in some cases, women are being granted more agency. Yet this is really just an allowance – men still hold the primary roots of power – and this book highlights an additional problem with agency.

This book examines the problematic language used to describe how and answer why women chose to use proscribed violence. It does not say their violence is acceptable; after all we refer to it as 'proscribed' for a reason. However, the narratives remove not only agency but personhood. Moser and Clark wrote that essentializing the genders (through the equation of woman = peace and man = war, which we extend to the narratives) 'treats men and women as "objects"' (2001: 5). When people, men and women, are objectified, agency is removed, but so is personhood. Thus the women implicated in the narratives cease to be women and instead become a mother, a monster or a whore, something other than a person.

EIGHT

CONCLUSION:
LET US NOW SEE 'BAD' WOMEN

The personal is international ... the international is personal.
(Enloe 1990: 196)

In 2001, *International Security* published an article by Daniel Byman and Kenneth Pollack entitled 'Let Us Now Praise Great Men: Bringing the Statesman Back In'.[1] The article tells exciting stories of men[2] who have played a great role in crucial moments of world politics. Byman and Pollack claim that it would have been impossible to explain the events of the twentieth century without reference to Adolf Hitler, Josef Stalin, Vladimir Lenin, Franklin Roosevelt, Winston Churchill, Mahatma Gandhi, or Mao Zedong (2001: 108). In referencing these men's roles in shaping international history, Byman and Pollack instruct that 'giants still walk the earth' who, individually, can influence global politics (2001: 145). Therefore, they advocate that scholars study Waltz's 'first image', individual behaviour, with more attention and rigor in the future (Byman and Pollack 2001: 146; Waltz 1959).

While Byman and Pollack are right to 'bring in' people to the study of global politics, they do so in a way which is gendered on a number of levels. They look only at the individual with elite power to explain international relations, and even then they look only at the male individual with elite power. While this perspective 'widens' the international relations spectrum to include individuals, the narrowness of the group that it includes limits its effectiveness as an interpretive framework and reproduces the gender, class and race biases in system-level international relations scholarship. Further, while 'individuals' matter to Byman and Pollack, their interdependence and their relationships do not – they appear to act alone, without reliance on each other, and with a complete set of choices. This is unlike the behaviour of most people in the real world – who act in a world of relational, rather than reactive, autonomy.

Feminists have critiqued this narrow understanding of the role of specific individuals and people generally in international politics, arguing that international politics is inscribed on women's lives, and women's lives are international politics. Cynthia Enloe transforms the popular feminist phrase 'the personal is political' into 'the personal is international' (Enloe 1990: 195; Hooper 2001: 93). Enloe explains that, 'to make sense of international politics we also have to read power backwards and forwards. Power relations between countries and their governments involve more than gunboat maneuvers and diplomatic telegrams' (1990: 196). Instead, international relations is about everything from a Campbell's soup can to a nuclear bomb. Enloe describes the relationship between public and private (and personal and international) as hybridized and complex. Gillian Youngs concludes that feminisms need 'multi-locational perspectives on patriarchal forces in terms of state and market, to recognize that the public/private social and spatial constructions are, in certain senses, mobilized and reconfigured in this globalizing world' (2000: 56). Gendered lenses see 'people as actors, the system as multiple hierarchies, and as characterized by multiple relations' (Goldstein 2001: 53). In other words, it is not only 'great men' who matter in international politics, or to whom international politics matters. It is, as feminists have explained, Korean prostitutes (Moon 1997), foreign domestic servants (Chin 1998), and, yes, even violent women. Further, the 'individuals' of global politics do not work alone, live alone or politic alone – they do so in interdependent relationships with others, maintaining a sense of individualized identity while being inseparable from political and social context.

THE INTERNATIONAL RELATIONS OF WOMEN'S LIVES

The international is personal. As Katharine Moon comments, 'we have a tendency to understand foreign relations as sets of policies that are formulated and executed by an elite group of men in dark suits, as abstracted from individual lives, especially the lowest reaches of society' (Moon 1997: 2). Moon, in her book, *Sex among Allies*, demonstrates the crucial role that Korean camp prostitutes, both actually and as an ideal-type, played in relationships between the United States and South Korea in the 1970s. Much like the violent women in this book, these women 'have experienced the pain of contempt and stigma ... treated as trash ... branded as doubly "impure"' and characterized as 'fallen women' (Moon 1997: 3). The invisibility of these women's real stories beneath insidious characterizations is, according to Moon, because 'to question their role in U.S. camptown life would have been to raise questions about the need for and the role of U.S. troops and bases in the two countries' bilateral relations' (10). Moon and Enloe agree that military prostitution generally and the lives of military prostitutes *individually* are 'not simply a women's issue, sociological problem, or target of disease control' but 'a matter of international politics and national security' (Moon 1997, 11; Enloe 1990). Moon argues that camptown women are not only a part of international relations but '*personify and define*, not only underlie, relations between governments' (12). Moon credits South Korea's 'priorities for state-building, national security, and economic development, over any concern for the social welfare of women and/or the moral order of society' with determining that prostitution would be a state-sponsored industry there (41).

National security is a privileged category both in international 'high' politics and in the study of international relations (Tickner 2001: 37). In the late 1930s, Virginia Woolf challenged the notion that states function to preserve the interests of their people. Instead, Woolf and many feminist scholars following her have understood that states function to preserve only the interests of some people. Several important scholarly works have drawn attention to individual non-elite men and women as the 'subjects' of international security

(Buzan 1991; Tickner 2001). These works recognize individuals as needing security. Terms like 'common security' (Walker 1990), 'human security' (Axworthy 2001), and 'structural violence' (Galtung 1971) have been used to describe the ways that international 'high' politics affects and is inscribed on the lives of people, even at the margins of global politics. As Tickner explains, many of the proponents of critical security 'argue for a broader definition of security, linked to justice and emancipation; a concept of security that starts with the individual allows for a global definition of security that moves beyond hierarchical binary distinctions between order and anarchy and inside and outside' (2001: 47–8). In arguing for a broader definition of security, many feminists and other critical security scholars are trying to expand the group of actors whom global politics considers worthy of security, protecting not only states but the people within them from the threats of international insecurity.

Even a critical understanding of security, however, betrays elements of masculinity as the dominant ethos in global politics. Discourse of human security can quickly become a protection racket, where states speak of protecting their most vulnerable citizens while actually putting them at risk (Tickner 2001: 49; Stanley 1996). In this sense, the discourse of national security is a gendered discourse, a 'parable of man's amoral, self-interested behaviour in the state of nature' which is a partial representation of human behaviour (Tickner 2001: 51). Instead, many feminists argue, gender-sensitive and relational understandings and women's needs should be included in the 'security' discourse, rather than only the idea of women's protected bodies.

THE WOMEN'S LIVES OF GLOBAL POLITICS

Even including women and other marginalized individuals in the group of actors with a recognized right to security is only part of the battle. This move only catches half of Enloe's phrase: the international is personal. Enloe's other observation, and the one more crucial for this book, is that *the personal is international*. People, even those at the margins of global politics, play significant roles in the construction of the meaning of international relations and international security, individually and as members of social and political groups.

Historical tales of international security revolve around women's lives without acknowledging their gendering. The Greeks' largest war was described as being over the romantic affections of Helen of Troy. The United States' war effort in Afghanistan was justified, at least in part, by the idea of saving Afghan women from the misogynist governance of some Afghan men, the Taliban. The United States and South Korea held high-level security talks about women's (actual or potential) venereal diseases (Moon 1997). Henry VIII's dissatisfaction with his wife is credited with the beginning of the Anglican Church. These women's lives were not only *affected by* international politics, they *were* international politics.

Moon contends that we need to begin by 'viewing even the most dispossessed women as 'players' in world politics' and instructs that, 'without jumping back from two opposite poles of self-agency and victim-hood, a middle ground must be found' (1997: 52). Agents have traditionally been understood as actors capable of making decisions in global politics; as people or political entities that make a difference in how politics develops. While structural realist accounts of international politics deny that the international system has room for agency, many other approaches disagree (Wendt 1999; Byman and Pollack 2001). While Byman and Pollack characterize important individuals as agents in global politics, Wendt sees states as agents (1999). Wendt sees state agency as reliant on the context of the interstate system, but still existent:

> The distinction between individuality per se and its social terms allow us to see how the relationship between the agents and structure can at once be dependent and independent, causal and constitutive, we can have both dualism and duality. This distinction resolves the apparent paradox by showing that two kinds of properties are involved in constituting agents, self-organizing properties and social properties. (Wendt 1999: 183–4)

Wendt's description of agency has touched on two important dimensions of people as actors in global politics. First, actors do not act in a world of fully independent choice. As we described in Chapter 7, actors act in a world of relational autonomy where choice exists but is dependent on social context. Second, it is not only actors and their choices that matter in global politics, but the ways that those actors' choices are socially portrayed in global politics.

Some of the women in this book are international actors in the traditional sense. For example, Bijana Plavsic was the president of the Bosnian Serb Republic; this is a role that even Byman and Pollack would recognize as influential, if they saw women. Other women in this book, however, are not political leaders or influential in the traditional sense of the word. The fact that these women are not 'great men' (or the like), however, does not make their lives less consequential for global politics, either in their living or in the stylized narratives told of their lives. Instead, like scholarship on the international system, scholarship on people as agents in global politics is deeply gendered.

Jacqui True challenges that 'relationships between domestic and international, masculine and feminine agents are mystified by the levels-of-analysis schema that separates the individual, the state, and the international system' (1996: 227). She laments the dominance of this trichotomous lens that takes 'specifically masculine ways of being and knowing in the world as universal' (227). She hypothesizes that 'feminist alternatives to the levels of analysis in international relations do not promote more universal abstractions, but demand greater context in order to map more adequately the complexity and indeterminacy of agent and structure' (229).

A feminist understanding of women's lives *as* international politics, then, has several dimensions. First, women's choices matter in global politics. For example, the choice that Wada Idris made to become the first Palestinian woman suicide bomber had great ramifications not only for the relative status of organizations within the Palestinian territories, but also for gender roles within Palestinian society, for the relationship between Israel and the armed Palestinian resistance, and for the roles that women had in resistance and terrorist organizations more generally.

Second, governmental and media portrayals of women's choices have implications beyond the gender subordination inherent in the mother, monster and whore narratives. While those characterizations *do* serve the function of maintaining gender subordination in local and global politics, that function is inadequate in explaining their nuances

CONCLUSION

and variations. States just looking to continue gender subordination in their characterizations of women's violence might not need even one narrative, much less three. The narratives also serve a function in global politics *in addition to* gender subordination – the portrayal of the state or political organization making the characterizations in a certain light. An example of the monster narrative *as* international relations can be seen in the Chechen case, where the Russian government used the monstrousness of the *shakhidka* as a mandate to continue the war effort. Likewise, discursive competition between the West and Palestinian resistance organizations over whether or not women's participation in suicide bombing is gender-emancipatory is a competition for cultural superiority and moral worth reliant on the presence of women's dead bodies. Competing narratives about these women's violence constitute an international conflict.

Finally, if women's lives and the stylized narratives thereof *are* international relations, an understanding of global politics which neglects them is necessarily incomplete. The narratives about the violent women in this book and their influence in international politics demonstrates that a theory of international politics must take account of gender, of gendered stories, and of the interaction between actual and sensationalized stories of gender to create the dominant narratives of international politics. As Moon argues, the 'key is to pinpoint which women at what time in what gendered way are identified with the politics of a foreign policy issue' (1997: 56). This chapter takes on that mission with regard to the lives of the women that the empirical chapters of this book have featured.

THE INTERNATIONAL POLITICS OF ABU GHRAIB

International relations influenced the lives of the women who participated in the Abu Ghraib prison scandal. International relations is a competitive system which prizes military strength, so it created and sustained the military system that these women joined. The United States' post-9/11 insecurity inspired both the war in Afghanistan, which drained the United States' troop readiness, and the war in Iraq, for which the government then had to call on the reserves, of which all three of these women were a part. The international community's lack of support for the war effort in Iraq meant that prison specialists from around the world were not forthcoming, and that the United States would have to supply its own. Short of prison specialists, the military put together a number of incomplete Military Police Brigades with officers of questionable experience and integrity (for example, Charles Graner, who had been disciplined within the military structure on several occasions). The story could go on, but this much of it seems sufficient to make the point that global politics influenced these particular women's lives.

The ways that these women's personal lives *are* international relations have not been as thoroughly explored. This section explores two dimensions of the lives of the women at Abu Ghraib as global politics: the prominence of their participation as a part of a victory narrative for American masculinities over Iraqi masculinities and the mother, monster and whore narratives of the women's involvement as a shield to hide the misogyny of American empire-building.

The women who committed prisoner abuses at Abu Ghraib did so in the context of a very gendered relationship between the United States and Iraq (Sjoberg 2007). The relationship between the United States and Iraq had been framed as a competition between masculinities for more than a decade; each government told stories of emasculation of the other (Elshtain 1992b). Each government held standards of masculinity which the other did not meet. The United States relied on 'the contrast between the tough but tender and technologically sophisticated Western man and the hypermacho Arab villain from an inferior civilization' (Niva 1998: 119), while the Iraqi government challenged the virility of this new, tender American masculinity. When masculinities compete, a hegemonic masculinity dominates subordinated masculinities (Connell 1995).

The prominence of the stories about the female abusers at Abu Ghraib can be explained by viewing the relationship between the United States and Iraq as a competition between masculinities. While the United States likely did not plan the publicity of the Abu Ghraib prison scandal as a part of the gendered narrative of state relations, emphasizing the women whose participation serves an important function as a victory narrative for American masculinities. After all, 'nothing feminizes masculinity like being *beat by a girl*, as the old playground adage explains. The images of the prisoner abuse at Abu Ghraib silently tell a story of the ultimate humiliation of Iraqi masculinity because Iraqi men were deprived of their manliness by American women' (Sjoberg 2007).

The use of the mother, monster and whore narratives to describe the women at Abu Ghraib can be seen as a shield to disguise the gendered nature of American empire-building. American empire-building relies at once on the perceived equality of American women and on the purity of American femininity. The prominent featuring of the women who committed war crimes at Abu Ghraib, coupled with descriptions that characterize their specific choices as an aberration to American femininity, accomplish this task in international politics. The attention given to the female perpetrators communicates the message that 'male or female can be a masculinized commander, or imperial collaborator while white women look like masculinist empire builders and brown men look like women and homos' (Eisenstein 2004). By their very presence in the abuse narratives, these women 'create confusion by participating in the very sexual humiliation that their gender is usually victim to. This gender swapping and switching leaves masculinist/racialized gender in place' (Eisenstein 2004). In other words, women abusing men obscures the gendered nature of the abuse and the empire-building that it perpetuates. As Eisenstein explains:

> Females are present to cover over the misogyny of building empire. So I think that there is little if anything to consider feminist here. Most women are in the military because of globalization, the restructuring of the labor force in the U.S., and their desire to get an education, and/or a job.... Women are used in the Abu Ghraib pictorial narrative to protect a heterosexist normativity. We see women abusing men which protects sexual hierarchy and opposition. (2004)

Covering up the misogyny of the process of empire-building, however, is only half of the task of the narratives about the women at Abu Ghraib. The other half of the tale, as related above, is their ability to serve as decoys for misogyny *while maintaining* the purist stereotype of American women, which is a linchpin of American soft power.

Accounts of women and femininity as *responsible* for the horrors at Abu Ghraib needed to be juxtaposed with images of American women as fair, humane and emancipated (see, for example, Elshtain 2003). This dual move is made by combining substantial attention to the women's conduct and the mother, monster and whore narratives which distance these women specifically and femininity more generally from responsibility, preserving the purist image of the rising tide of gender equality as a result of Pax Americana (Inglehart and Norris 2003).

THE INTERNATIONAL POLITICS OF THE *SHAKHIDKI*

The lives of women in Chechnya tell a poignant story of how the international is personal. Descriptions of life in Chechnya, from Amnesty International to the Russian government, tell a story of chaos and fighting that continued for months then years, without any real end in sight or hope of international intervention. Human rights advocates' accounts of the situation in Chechnya describe it as horrendous, and describe that horrendousness as gendered to disproportionately affect women (No Borders 2004). The terrible and terrifying abuses endured by the women in Chechnya resonate from a conflict over Russian identity and authority, Russia's position in the post-Cold War world, and Chechen–Russian relations (Kramer 2005). These state power and identity conflicts are daily inscriptions on Chechen women's lives.

Chechen women, however, are not only the victims of an international conflict that affects their daily lives. They are also actors in that conflict. Many Chechen women were integral in the cross-national alliance of mothers which ultimately made the first Chechen conflict unpopular in Russia (Eichler 2006). Other Chechen women protest during the conflict or participate in peace-making movements. The *shakhidki*, featured in Chapter 4 of this book, also constitute international politics, not only through the implications of the mother, monster and whore narratives through which they are described, but also in a more direct way.

As explained in Chapter 4, women actually constitute a majority of Chechen suicide bombers. Chechen suicide bombers are key to the morale of Chechen communities seeking independence. The narratives that states and media outlets publicize about Chechen women also make their lives international politics. Chechen *shakhidki* lives (or dead bodies) are narrated outside of Chechnya in several ways that justify and prop up the Russian war effort in Chechnya. First, the 'black widow' narratives villify (allegedly) deranged, wild and irrational Chechen femininity and valorize ordered, militarized Russian masculinity. Feminist international relations theorists have described state legitimacy as reliant on hegemonic masculinities, which are the ideal of citizenship and serve to 'support male power and female subordination' (Tickner 2001: 15). State power is located in idealized manhood which mystifies the incoherence of the state. In order to be powerful, then, a state must have a strong idealized manhood (True 1996). Ideal-types of masculinity almost always rely on a feminized, enemy other (Huston 1983) for their strength and coherence. The lives of Chechen *shakhidki* fill that gap for Russian masculinities, which were lost when they lost the enemy of American masculinity.

Second, because it presents Chechen femininity specifically and Chechen society generally as dangerous, the black widow narratives garner public support among Russians for the continuation of the conflict in Chechnya. Kramer explains that Russia takes its licence for broad counterinsurgency from the suicide attacks of Chechen women (2005) because the involvement of women in suicide attacks underscores, in Russian narratives, the desperation of Chechen society and the impossiblility of a negotiated settlement. That *women* are involved is used in Russian government rhetoric to characterize the conflict as one that cannot possibly be solved diplomatically. Involving women makes Chechens uncivilized. This conclusion legitimates the continued use of force in Chechnya, even after more than a decade of unsuccessful fighting.

Third, as discussed in the introductory section to Chapter 4, the successful association of Chechen women and terrorism breaks up a powerful coalition of Russian and Chechen women who opposed the Russian effort to maintain control over Chechnya by force. Cynthia Enloe (2000: 257–8) explains that: 'the regime of Boris Yeltsin and his military commanders had to contend not only with stubborn male Chechen fighters, who were rapidly militarizing the meaning of Chechen masculinity, but also with bold ethnic Russian mothers-of-soldiers', who, according to Eichler (2006), teamed up with Chechen mothers to critique the Russian military intervention in the Chechen separatist movement. The successful association of Chechen women with the 'black widows' and the employment of the mother, monster and whore narratives which sustained that connection broke up the alliance of women from both sides of the conflict, which had been influential in ending the fighting in 1996 (Eichler 2006). Stylized narratives of women's suicide attacks cleared the roadblock of a women's peace movement from Russia's path towards enforcing Chechen compliance.

Fourth, the association of Chechen women suicide bombers and Palestinian women suicide bombers successfully places Chechen women outside the realm of political legitimacy within Russia: they are other (Palestinian), not Russian or even Chechen. Anthias explains that a substantial part of group formation has to do with narratives of group belonging and group exclusion (2002: 277). Citizenship is a narrative of belonging. Functionally, 'narratives of belonging also relationally construct difference and otherness and there has been an explosion of interest in this issue' (277). In dichotomous terms, narratives of group belonging construct an 'inside' and an 'outside', and assign membership relationally. Excluding a person or group of persons from citizenship, then, is a powerful discursive move which allows a different sort of treatment of those actors. Membership then has meaning for the political relationships between those 'inside' and 'outside' or a group, or between groups, in 'peace' or in conflict. Because the Russian government uses racialized elements of the monster and whore narratives to compare the 'black widows' to the Palestinian suicide bombers, it is able to exclude them from belonging to the group of Russian citizens. Once they are excluded from belonging to the group of Russian citizens, Chechen *shakhidki* specifically and women generally can be treated less humanely because they are 'them' rather than 'us' in Russian discourses.

Finally, this same metaphorical association between the *shakhidki* and Palestinian women bombers permits Russia to talk about the conflict in Chechnya not as a civil war in Russia but as a part of the global war on terror, which gives the war effort legitimacy as well as national and international support. The global war on terror is by definition good in the eyes of Russia's peers and allies. By participating in the global war on terror against Chechen-come-Palestinian women, then, Russia is not only protecting its security but also contributing to the betterment of the world.

All of these appropriations of the lives of *shakhidki* demonstrates that, not only is the international personal, but the personal lives of individual women are *international relations* in the Russian–Chechen conflict.

THE INTERNATIONAL RELATIONS OF MIDDLE EASTERN WOMEN SUICIDE BOMBERS

The conflict between Israelis and Palestinians is now more than five decades old, and the lives of men and women in Israel and Palestine have been dominated by the conflict for generations. If the international conflict in Israel and Palestine is *personal* to Israelis and Palestinians, Israelis' and Palestinians' personal choices are also international relations. Such is the case with Palestinian women who choose suicide terrorism. Several aspects of these women's lives (and deaths) are international relations. These include the cultural war over the meaning of women's participation and the key role that narratives of gendered suicide bombers play in defining the security situation between Israel and Palestine.

First, there is the cultural war over the meaning of women's (dead) bodies for gender emancipation and competition between masculinities. As mentioned in Chapter 5, Palestinian resistance groups often characterize women's participation in martyrdom attacks as a sign that women are equal in their groups and would be equal in their societies, if those groups were allowed political control of Palestine. Like Palestinians, al-Qaeda has presented, through *Al Khansa*, a discourse of women's liberation through the service of jihad. These discourses claim that, since women are now allowed to engage in the ultimate political sacrifice, women are equal both in theory and in practice in their societies.

Counternarratives emphasize women's lack of agency in their suicide attacks. In Western and Israeli responses to these discourses of gender emancipation through political violence, the argument that Middle Eastern women's participation in suicide bombing is a continuation of their traditional, subordinated role in society is featured prominently. Even though the very existence of women's agency is questioned, directly or through the use of the mother, monster and whore narratives, the blame for the conflict and death in Palestine is placed squarely on the shoulders of femininity. This cultural conflict over whether or not women are liberated by their participation in self-martyrdom takes women suicide bombers' lives into the international arena in several ways. This conflict makes women's liberation important not because gender subordination matters, but because a masculinized competition between cultures to assert (real or apparent) gender emancipation has trumped any real discourse on the subject. Also, dead women are not experiencing any liberation or subordination. The focus on what their attack meant when the women were alive focuses attention away from the fact that they are dead, and that each death is only one of many in an intransigent conflict. Finally, the discourses that deny women's agency in their suicide attacks can be used to both sexualize and demonize Palestinian culture, a move that distances the actors from peace rather than bringing them closer to that goal.

Second, gendered narratives of women attackers play an important part in the gendered presentation of the conflict between Israel and Palestine. As in the Chechen conflict, much was made of the cross-conflict solidarity of Israeli 'women in black' and Palestinian women peace protesters (Pettman 1996; Sharoni 1995) in the 1990s. Women have been described as influential to the successes that the peace process has had (Peterson and Runyan 1999). Even though women are praised for the successes of Israeli–Palestinian negotiations, women suicide bombers are chided for the reversal of that success. The characterizations of Palestinian women as mothers, monsters and whores frame Palestinians as a group which has lost all sense of normalcy and all rationality in negotiations. Female monstrosity, then, is at fault for the continued militarization of the conflict between Israel and Palestine.

THE INTERNATIONAL RELATIONS OF GENDERED PERPETRATORS OF GENOCIDE

Both the lives of and the narratives of Biljana Plavsic and Pauline Nyiramasuhuko constitute international relations. As mentioned earlier in this chapter, these women are those most likely to be considered international actors by traditional international relations scholars. Plavsic, a president, and Nyiramasuhuko, a cabinet minister, held positions traditionally defined as powerful within states. Their lives are international relations in the traditional sense, then: both likely affected interstate relations *directly* by their participation in interstate negotiation and dialogue. Gendered lenses reveal that these women's lives are international relations in several other, more nuanced, ways as well.

The first way in which these women's lives are international relations is the fact that they serve the purpose of those who would claim international relations are degendered because women are leading states in non-feminine ways. R.W. Connell clarifies that the masculinity of the state is more complicated than being governed by those who are identified as men and masculine. He explains that 'this is not to imply that the personalities of the top male office-holders somehow seep through and stain the institutions. It is to say something much stronger: the state organizational practices are structured in relation to the reproductive arena' (Connell 1995: 73). Connell is not denying that most people in power are men; he is simply arguing that men being in power is a circular result of the function of a masculine institution. Most people in power 'are men because there is a gender configuring of recruitment and promotion, a gender configuring of the internal division of labor and systems of control, a gender configuring of policymaking, of practical routines, and ways of mobilizing pleasure and consent' (73).

It is not only women's exclusion from the highest levels of political office that is problematic, but the gendering of those highest levels of politics, whether the offices are filled by women or men. This is not to argue political organization itself is *necessarily* gendered, but instead that current institutional structures manifest gender subordination (Connell 1990; Pringle and Watson 1992).[3] Discourses about women leaders like Plavsic and Nyiramasuhuko, however, are used to reject uncritically the feminist argument that states are gendered. This rejection usually contends that women placed in the same position as men are 'as bad as' men, so the state is not gendered in its policies or actions. Instead, we should take men's and women's gendered behaviour as a sign of the continuing salience of gender in global politics.

The second way that female perpetrators of genocide are international relations is the interaction between the sexualized discourses of their behaviours and the sexualized discourses of ethnonationalist conflict. Jill Steans explains that 'the rhetoric of ethnonationalism is heavily sexualized and gendered', which results in genderings in its manifestations. As sexualized stories of perpetrators of genocide reduce them to sexual objects, the discourses that their movements perpetrate are sexualized and gender-subordinating, gendering the opponents and 'their women'. In addition to this correlation, a nationalist ethos often causes women to be treated as biological reproducers of group members needed for defence, signifiers of group identities, agents in political identity struggles, and members of sexist and heterosexist national groups (Peterson 1999: 44–52).

In addition to generally gendered discourses which incorporate the lives of gendered perpetrators of genocide into the public domain of international relations, specific discourses surrounding Pauline Nyiramasuhukp and Biljana Plavsic reflect a similar move. Specifically, the whore narrative can be seen as operative in implying that these women were responsible for the abuse and subordination of other women within their ethnic conflicts. Characterizations of Plavsic as praising rapists, kissing and sleeping with warlords, and sexualizing ethnic difference in Bosnia imply that the sexual crimes of the war fall on her shoulders. Likewise, constant reminders that Nyiramasuhuko was the Minister for Women and Family Affairs in Rwanda are often juxtaposed with the sexual nature of her crimes. These narratives at once emphasize her maternal role (as the caretaker of women and children) and her violation of that role through sexual crimes (invoking the whore narrative), implying once again that deviant women are responsible for normal women's suffering. These narratives' ability to place blame on deviant women for 'real' women's pain at once other the deviant women and maintain a false image that the societies that normal women live in are not thoroughly misogynistic. Abuse of women *caused by* other women is not seen as a gender problem. The gendered international arena, then, appears gender-neutral through these constructed narratives of gendered perpetrators of genocide. Their lives are incorporated into the macronarrative of international politics for states' purposes of legitimation and continuation of their current gendered structures and governance.

THE INTERNATIONAL RELATIONS OF VIOLENT WOMEN'S LIVES

The study of violent women's lives as international relations is certainly a far cry from the study of 'great men' (Byman and Pollack 2001) or even camp women in Korea. While it reinforces some of the same points, it also adds to these analyses. Actors in international relations are not limited to the international system or even to states (Byman and Pollack 2001), and sometimes actors in international politics need to be sought and found in locations not traditionally considered bastions of power (Moon 1997).

The study of violent women in global politics shows that the term 'actor' for the purpose of analysing individual influence in international relations needs to be deconstructed. In each of these cases, the women's lives *were* international relations, but so were stylized narratives about those women's lives produced outside of their knowledge and consent. The role of the women's lives and the narratives that are inscribed in them in international politics is a critique of the story of international politics as the realm of great men. After telling the stories of great male warriors, Byman and Pollack (2001) set forth several (gendered) hypotheses about the role of individuals in international politics. Among them are that (1) 'individuals set the ultimate and secondary intentions of the state', and that (2) 'individuals can be an important component of a state's diplomatic influence and military power' (134).

Gendered lenses focused on gendered narratives of women's violence see that these hypotheses are a starting point, but that gender, relational autonomy and political marginality are missing. As Moon mentioned, people can be actors in world politics with or without influencing the ultimate or secondary intentions of the state (1997). Further, people as a component of diplomatic influence or military power can volunteer for that role (as do the men that Byman and Pollack discuss) or be conscripted into it (like the women that Moon focuses on). Byman and Pollack's hypotheses do not cover the role of people in global politics, not to mention their contingencies, relationships and relational behaviour. Instead, a theory that accounts for the meaning of personal life in global politics must account at once for peoples' *impact* on global politics and for the impact of narratives others construct for and about them.

The women in this book matter in global politics, but how they matter is often defined by the mother, monster and whore narratives which confine them to vengeance, insanity and sexuality and deny the possibility that they could by choosing their actions impact on global politics. Cynthia Enloe has been insistent that 'seemingly private conduct, such as sexual relations between men and women, are intimately related to international politics through their organization and institutionalization by public authorities' (Moon 1997: 11; Enloe 1993). The seemingly private decisions of individual women to engage in proscribed violence is intimately related to international politics not only on its face, but also through the gendered characterizations of these women's violence by gendered states in gendered conflicts.

Women's seemingly private conduct in the area of proscribed violence matters in international politics *because it matters*, first and foremost. This is not simply a truism; it is intended only to point out the obvious – a number of the women in this book tried to affect the relationships between states. This is not the whole story, though. The women's conduct matters, but the part of these women which is most influential in global politics is the appropriated and stylized narratives about their choices and their behaviours. These stylized narratives are used in and compared to stories of ethnonationalistic pride, national virility and war. Lynddie England changed international relations posing for photographs with abused Iraqi prisoners. But stylized narratives about her sex life, her lack of femininity, and her lack of agency also changed international relations. The mother, monster and whore narratives show that the role of the individual in international relations is both complex and hybrid.

Wendt tries to confine the individual to a causal, but not constitutive, role in international relations by arguing that 'individuals must be constitutionally independent' (1999: 169). He thereby singularizes the individual, failing to recognize that the individual exists relationally to other individuals, social groups, and political entities. As an implication of that argument, 'any would-be individualist theory of how agents are constructed, individuals, and thus culture, (which is carried by them), can play only a causal but not constitutive role' (169). Gendered lenses rebut this argument. As discussed in the last chapter, relational autonomy means that social constitution reaches not only *behaviour* but also *being*:

> This construction of social behaviors and rules comes to constitute not only what women are allowed to do, however, but also what they are allowed to *be*: how women are able to think and conceive of themselves, what they can and should desire, what their preferences are, their epistemology and language. (Hirschmann 2004: 11)

People, then, are relationally autonomous, and play both causal and constitutive roles. If people can constitute international structure, and international structure can constitute individuals, however, this is not to say that every individual, from 'mean girls' like Lynndie England to 'great men' like Adolf Hitler and Saddam Hussein, have either quantitatively or qualitatively the same power to define and steer global politics.

Instead, power plays a role in the size and type of influence a person has in international relations and the impact that international relations has on an individual's life. The political universe is much as Foucault described – where power is everywhere inscribed and produced. Peterson and Runyan explain that 'ideologies are reconfigured to suit the changing interests of those in power, not those whose lives are controlled by them' (1999: 42). This power-rule is inescapable so long as power is seen as power-over, feminisms contend. In order to understand this constancy, one must see political and social relations as existent in a Foucauldian universe: a world in which power is everywhere inscribed and produced. Gendered lenses are interested in exploring power in order to see domination, empowerment, and power relations within feminist movements (Allen 1998: 32).

Given these observations about a gendered international arena and gendered actors within it, we derive several propositions concerning the role of gendered people in global politics. These propositions below provide a preliminary framework feminist theory of the role of people in global politics:

1. People's actions and relationships influence international politics.
2. The mode of influence of those actions can be causal, constitutive or symbolic but is always relationally autonomous.
3. People's influence, regardless of the gender of the individual, occurs in an international system gendered masculine.
4. The degree and type of people's influence will rely heavily on the people's place in the gendered power structure of global politics and their relationships with others.
5. The symbolic appropriation of people's behaviour by the powerful is key to maintaining race, gender and class distinctions in global politics.
6. Neither constitutive nor symbolic influence can be value-neutral.

First, people's actions, even when not performed from a place of traditionally understood power or strength, are capable of influencing the relationships between states and the atmosphere of global politics more generally. The young, working-class women in Chapter 3 and the virtually unknown faces of the Moscow Theatre occupation in Chapter 4 demonstrate this point. Second, the mode of influence of those actions can be causal, constitutive, symbolic, or all of the above. Causal influence is where a person's behaviour provokes a response from other actors in global politics; or where a person's actions influence others in an interdependent world. An example of causal influence in this book was the contemporaneous Bosnian leadership's reaction to Biljana's Plavsic's 2001 Guilty plea to crimes against humanity with a call for reconciliation in Bosnia and Herzegovina, which is said to have positively affected the healing process in the area. Constitutive influence happens when an individual's behaviour changes the meaning of a concept or relationship in international relations. For example, Wafa Idris's suicide attack changed the meaning of 'martyr' in the context of the Palestinian resistance movement. Symbolic influence is where a stylized appropriation of individuals' behaviour is used by other political actors in the furtherance of their political interest or goals. An illustration of symbolic influence is the use of the whore narrative about the sale and control of women's bodies in Chechen suicide attacks to vilify Chechen men. These paths of influence do not only go one way. Women's violence influences global politics causally, constitutively and symbolically; global politics also influences women's violence causally, constitutively and symbolically. Women who commit acts of violence live in a relationally autonomous world, interdependent with the political atmospheres in which they live.

Our third proposition is that the influence of people, men or women, occurs in an international political system gendered masculine. Feminists contend that the current dominant notion of the international system assumes a sovereignty contract between citizen and state, a masculine myth of history (True 1996). It depends on an assumption of female inferiority; a woman's need for a man/state to protect her through marriage, laws, and military force (235). Thus the malignant construction of the state fosters a malignant construction of the international system, in the image of and with the values of the state. National and international security are self-reproducing threat-concepts which are 'profoundly endangering to human survival and sustainable communities' (235). A female suicide bomber, then, does not bomb in a world which is automatically gender neutral for her gender equality (if her equality even exists). Instead she, relationally autonomously, performs a gendered act in a gendered conflict in a gendered global political arena. An example of the gendered context of women's violence is the debate surrounding whether Palestinian women are allowed to participate (and therefore be liberated) by their suicide terrorist attacks, or are used (and therefore subordinated) by organizations which make their decisions for them. This debate takes place within the competition between Western and Islamic masculinities, and the Israeli and Palestinian nationalist movements. Each of these gendered contexts influences the gendering of violent women's impact on global politics and global politics' impact on women's violence.

The fourth proposition is that the degree and type of people's influence will rely heavily on that person's perceived place in the gendered power structure of global politics. 'Great men' like those on the pages of Byman and Pollack's article, who have substantial amounts of power-over – the currency of international politics – will have more influence in global politics. That influence is more likely to be causal or constitutive rather than symbolic. 'Regular' or even violent women, on the other hand, are less likely to have as much influence, and their influence is more likely to be symbolic (i.e. filtered through the interpretation of the powerful). Persons further from the loci of power are less likely to be able to control either how their story is related or who they are in it. As an extension, the powerful write the stories of their influence, while those with less power often have their stories written for them. Therefore, the fifth proposition is that the symbolic appropriation of people's behaviour by the powerful is key to maintaining race, gender and class distinctions in global politics. Stylizing images of the Other is key to empire-building (Eisenstein 2004).

Finally, causal, constitutive and symbolic influence cannot be value-neutral. Interpretation of meaning and appropriation of behaviour into *stories* of people's actions is filtered through the lenses of the teller and the gazer. It is these filters which show the gender subordination inherent in the mother, monster and whore narratives of violent women in global politics.

WOMEN'S VIOLENCE, GENDER EQUALITY AND FEMINIST INTERNATIONAL RELATIONS THEORY

Each manifestation of the mother, monster and whore narratives in this book tells a story of women's violence that denies their capacity to have made an independent, interdependent or even rational choice to commit violence, even when descriptions of violent men almost always characterize their choices as autonomous. When popular wisdom had it that women could not work like men, women worked like men until men believed they could. When popular wisdom had it that women could not vote like men, women campaigned until men believed they could. When popular wisdom had it that women were

CONCLUSION

not as intellectually capable as men, women competed in classrooms and workplaces until men believed they belonged there. When popular wisdom had it women had no place in the text of international human rights declarations or war crimes tribunal, women advocated until men listened. Now, popular wisdom says women are not capable of violence like men.

We are not advocating that women commit proscribed violence (war crimes, terrorism and genocide) until men notice they are capable. We are also not arguing that men and women are fundamentally the same. Nor have we endorsed any of the alleged criminal behaviour of the women discussed in this book. Still, it is important to notice when common knowledge says that there is something women cannot do, even among the supposed leaders in gender equality (see Inglehart and Norris 2003). Male and female have classically been presented on a polarized spectrum. What man is (or supposed to be) woman cannot be, and what woman is (or supposed to be) man cannot be. As those who study gender have concerned themselves with defeating the essentialized arguments that men make wars and women are the ones who are fought for, these objectifications are diminishing. As gender equality has been fought for, the spectrum's polarity which defines and limits women's capabilities as compared to men's has weakened, perhaps even so much that those who are not looking closely can no longer tell that it exists. Yet, the continuous denial of women's agency in violence and denial of the womanhood of violent women via the mother, monster and whore narratives demonstrates that the spectrum which limits women's capabilities both persists and remains vigilant in its existence.

So long as a spectrum which limits women's capabilities exists, then women (and traits associated with femininity) will be less than men in society, even were they to achieve actual (rather than rising) equality in political, social and economic indicators. This is precisely why this sort of discursive subordination is so dangerous: those who are not looking closely might miss it. In fact, some feminists, whose intellectual mission is looking for gender subordination in global politics, are not eager to discover the gender subordination of violent women. Many feminists, Morrissey argues, are as uncomfortable with the idea of women's violence as many conservatives, because the women's liberation movement is for women's rights as citizens, not to create space for women criminals (2003).

That the mother, monster and whore narratives marginalize violent women is part of the problem. That they marginalize all women, however, is our primary concern. These narratives define what violent women are (less than women; less than human; crazy, sexualized or controlled) but they also define what all women are (peaceful, incapable of violence, and in the personal rather than the political sphere). By setting up another polarity, this time between 'violent' women and 'normal' women, the narratives singularize violent women who do not fit the mould of idealized femininity. This leaves the image of idealized femininity intact and does not challenge idealized masculinity. Both of these polarities do a disservice to both genders by objectifying their idealized types.

This is not to say that we dream of a world where all women are allowed to engage in suicide bombings and incite genocide; we dream of a world where no one does those things. Until that happens, however, idealized notions of femininity which trap (any) women into an idealized role based on gender are a threat to, if not a reversal of, the 'rising tide' of gender equality.

The impact of gender-subordinating discourses on gender equality is twofold. First, as discussed above, these manifest discourses are marginalizing both to the women who are featured in them and to all women everywhere. Second, this discursive subordination *is* material in women's lives around the world. Subjectivity is lived and performed in people's discursive and material relationships. If subjectivity is performative, talk and performance in political and social (and international) relations is material (Weber 1998: 77). In this interpretation, sex and gender are both discursive constructs (79).

Anne Phillips notes that the integration of women into society has left in place the discursive structures of gender oppression, because integrationists have not been cognizant of the discursive and performative nature of gender dichotomies (1987: 5; Hooper 2001: 31). The mother, monster and whore narratives are an example of the continued salience of discursive and performative gender dichotomies in global politics. Perhaps these narratives are even more insidious because they appear to be supporting narratives of gender liberation.

If we do not look closely enough, it appears that the trend of blaming women for men's political errors is lifting, and that the global political discourses vilifying women are disappearing. After all, rather than hunt down violent women for witch trials, all the international community is doing is estranging violent women, agency and femininity. Not only are these discourses gender subordination, then; they are gender subordination which can be disguised as gender liberation. This suggests a new, under-the-radar sort of gender subordination which has adapted to women's advocacy for their own recognition to find alternative pathways to maintain gender dichotomies.

WHY NARRATIVES OF VIOLENT WOMEN NEED FEMINISM NOW MORE THAN EVER

As we explore in Chapter 7, there are certainly gendered aspects of women's violence. Those gendered elements, however, cannot be dealt with until we deconstruct the stylized narratives about women's violence that are discussed throughout this book. These gender-subordinating discourses are a part of two separate metanarratives: one of women's innocence and another of gendered war stories between masculine states.

Within the discipline of international relations, the study of these narratives betrays that scholars and members of society reproduce gender and race stereotypes without conscious intent through the othering and/or sexualization of violent women. In order to embrace women's agency and move towards a more gender-equal international society, we, as scholars and political actors, must be willing to embrace and study the agency of not only the best of women but also the worst of women. In order to do so, scholars must come to terms with our own implicitly racialized and sexualized discourse in order to transform the (increasingly subtle) discursive structures of gender subordination.

Feminist international relations theory is uniquely poised to add to international relations' understanding of the scope of the role of *people* (and stories told about them) in global politics. If the international is personal, gender lenses focused on women's violence can show the violent women of international relations and the international relations of violent women. The way that international relations have shaped women's agency is personal to all women everywhere. The narratives about women's proscribed violence in global politics tells us what 'normal' women look like. It also tells us who the acceptable perpetrators of unacceptable violence are – and women are not part of it. But feminists have asked, repeatedly, (1) where are the women, and (2) what is their agency? If those same questions are applied to these narratives, the women are not there, and thus they have no agency. When women are there, their choices are trivialized by the mother, monster and whore narratives, which describe them as incapable of decision-making. By contrast, men's violence is often characterized as rationally chosen. Neither is accurate – both men and women live in a world where their violence is relationally autonomous. Actors have agency and choice in their actions, but they live in a world of interdependence and interhuman relationship.

If we could possibly remove the manifest discourse and examine the latent discourse, the women are there and they are perpetrating violence. The 'whys' and 'hows' are the next questions to be answered in relation to the gendering of each woman and her participation in her context – but each story of why and how will battle inherited ideal-types of violent women as mothers, monsters and whores, and of real women as peaceful and caring.

The prevalence of theses discourses even among the 'leaders' in gender equality betrays an international political atmosphere entrenching a changed, and perhaps more lasting, form of gendering global politics. As studies reveal additional layers of complexity in the gendering of international relations, feminist international relations inherits yet another group of gendered narratives to deconstruct, destabilize and engender. Contrary to Barbara Ehrenreich's claim, women's violence does not demonstrate the end of the need for feminism; stories about women's violence show the continuing urgency of the feminist cause. Feminists look for *women* (female bodies), *gender* (characterizations of traits assigned on the basis of perceived membership in sex groups) and *genderings* (application of perceived gender tropes to social and political analyses) in stories about women's violence and in global politics more generally. The stories that have been told throughout this book are about gendering gendered women who commit violence. This book has argued that a feminist approach to women's participation, agency and emancipation is the only tool to combat the mother, monster and whore narratives. Only through gendered lenses may we come to see and deconstruct the increasingly subtle, complex and disguised ways in which gender pervades international relations and global politics.

NOTES

ONE

1. This is not to say that all feminists believe that women are non-violent. Quite the contrary, most of the feminists that we have talked to about this project, upon reflection, accept the contention that women are capable of violence. Still, before these conversations take place, the implicit assumption that violence is a man's domain does pepper some feminist scholarship. These tropes are not meant to be generalizations, but to show a commonality between many understandings of gender.
2. Butler (1990) calls these ideal-typical understandings the 'heterosexual matrix', which Richter-Montpetit (2007) characterizes as implicated in the discussion of women's violence and gender equality, specifically in the United States surrounding the abuse at Abu Ghraib.
3. See, for example, Sjoberg 2006; Connell 2003; Tickner 2001; and Enloe 2004.
4. Enloe uses 'womenandchildren' in one word to demonstrate the tendency of leaders, militaries and activist groups alike to conflate women, children and women with children as a group of people generally without agency in war, as the 'victims' to be protected or to be discarded, rather than as participants whose voices require consideration. Womenandchildren is a stereotype that denies women's full personhood; but the grouping has another insidious implication. When belligerents claim that they have to fight for their womenandchildren, they are doubly passivizing women: taking away their agency and using their helplessness to justify violence.
5. For example, see the reports on the status of women in war coming from the Red Cross (2005), UNIFEM (Rehn and Sirleaf 2003) and several scholars (Kumar 2001; Matthews 2003). Advocacy groups have led the charge, but governments have picked up the discourse of gender equality as well.

6. Violent women are often characterized as lacking humanity or sanity, due to denial of women's agency in violence. Feminist criminologists point out that there is no evidence that women's capacity for violence is any less than, or different to, men's. See Keitner 2002. When we presented the introduction to this book at the 2007 Annual Meeting of the International Studies Association and gave a brief overview of the empirical chapters, our discussant (a psychologist) answered our presentation with the contention that women fit into theories of individual violence crafted around men and masculinities. We contend that, while there may not be a *fundamental* difference between women's and men's violence, gender lenses identify both the gendered nature of theories of 'individual' violence and the gendered factors that contribute to individuals' violent actions. Chapter 7 discusses theories of individual proscribed violence in international politics which are purportedly 'gender neutral', exploring their marginalization and omission of women and the violence that they commit. It shows that even 'ungendered' theories gender both by commission and omission.

7. We do not use the word 'terrorism' lightly, and try not to use it very often. This is, at least in part, because we give substantial credit to several critiques of the employment of the word 'terrorist' and the connotations that it holds. First, we recognize the often-repeated (if gendered) cliché that 'one man's terrorist is another man's freedom fighter', which has been enough to cause some major media sources to reject the use of terrorism discourse. This cliché also explains why there is no agreed-upon definition for terrorism, and the USA alone has multiple operating definitions that change from agency to agency and department to department to fit their particular jurisdictions. According to Howard Kurtz, Stephen Jukes, Reuters' head of news, would not use the word 'terrorist' to describe the 9/11 attacks on the United States, explaining that 'We all know that one man's terrorist is another man's freedom fighter and that Reuters upholds the principle that we do not use the word terrorist.... To be frank, it adds little to call the attack on the World Trade Center a terrorist attack' (Kurtz 2001: C01). Noam Chomsky explored the implications of this argument in a 2001 interview published by ZNet, where he explained that 'alongside the literal meaning of the term, as just quoted from US official documents, there is also a propagandistic usage, which unfortunately is the standard one: the term "terrorism" is used to refer to terrorist acts committed by enemies against us or our allies. Political scientist Michael Stohl is quite correct when he writes that "we must recognize that by convention – and it must be emphasized only by convention – great power use and the threat of the use of force is normally described as coercive diplomacy and not as a form of terrorism", though it commonly involves "the threat and often the use of violence for what would be described as terroristic purposes were it not great powers who were pursuing the very same tactic." This propagandistic use is virtually universal. Everyone "condemns terrorism", in this sense of the term ... Given these conventions, even the very same people and actions can quickly shift from "terrorists" to "freedom fighters" and back again' (Chomsky 2001). These critiques being recognized, however, we do employ

the word 'terrorism' intermittently to keep this debate at the surface level and recognize some self-identification within terrorism and even terrorism studies. It instead attempts to refer to the actors in the terms by which they refer to themselves. Still, this book does not mean to imply approval or endorsement of state-authorized violence or universalistic judgement of 'terrorist' violence.

8. See Intersex Society of North America, www.isna.org/faq/hermaphrodite (accessed 23 August 2006). From the Survivor Project,(www.survivorproject.org), intersex people naturally (that is, without any medical intervention) develop primary or secondary sex characteristics that do not fit neatly into society's definitions of male or female. Many visibly intersex people are mutilated in infancy and early childhood by doctors to make their sex characteristics conform to their idea of what normal bodies should look like. Intersex people are relatively common, although the society's denial of their existence has allowed very little room for intersexuality to be discussed publicly. Trans people break away from one or more of the society's expectations around sex and gender. These expectations include that everyone is either a man or a woman, that one's gender is fixed, that gender is rooted in their physiological sex, and that our behaviours are linked to our gender. Survivor Project uses 'trans' as a very broad umbrella term. Transsexual people perceive themselves as members of a gender or sex that is different from the one they were assigned at birth. Many transsexual people pursue hormone and/or surgical interventions to make it easier to live as members of the gender or sex they identify as. The term 'transgender' is used in so many different ways that it is almost impossible to define it. Some use it to refer to people whose behaviour and expressions do not match with their gender. Some use it to describe a gender outside of the man/woman binary. Some use it to describe the condition of having no gender or multiple genders. Other possibilities include people who perform genders or deliberately play with/on gender as well as being gender-deviant in other ways.

9. For example, homosexual or transsexual men, perceived as less masculine by the standards of hegemonic masculinity (see Connell 1995), are often the subjects of hate crimes committed by other men who see their existence as a challenge to masculinity generally and their masculinity specifically. As a pedagogical tool, Sjoberg often uses the story of Brandon Teena and the movie *Boys Don't Cry* to illustrate this point to students who have difficulty conceptualizing competitions between different masculinities.

10. This distinction is important because women's violence that is 'protected' by the justificatory narrative of the state is, while not 'mainstreamed', often not the subject of the intense scrutiny that women who commit violence outside of that framework are. Perhaps this is because women who commit state-sanctioned violence can still be seen in a subordinate position, as following the will of their state, while being women who defy their state's expected gender boundaries.

11. Even when analyses object to or do not approve of the reasons that men commit war crimes, engage in suicide bombing, perform anti-state political

violence, or engage in genocide, most of these analyses, as we see in Chapter 8, recognize that *men have reasons* for choosing these behaviours and that these reasons can be rational, and based in the political realm. Women, on the other hand, are characterized as motivated by personal reasons, if they are characterized as having a motivation at all.

12. In addition to scholarship of women who commit proscribed violence specifically (including Morgan 1989; D'Amico 1998; D'Amico and Beckman 1995; Beckman and D'Amico 1994; D'Amico and Weinstein 1999; Moser and Clark 2001; and Cockburn 2001a), there is a literature on women's participation in revolutionary movements which has its origins more than two decades ago, and is a growing research programme in feminist political science. To take one example, there is substantial and growing work on women in the Palestinian resistance movement, including works referred to in Chapter 5, as well as work by Antonius (1979), Sayeh (1986), Hammami (1990), Abdo (1991), Kanaana (1993), Dajani (1994). Still, the majority of this literature focuses more on why and how women come to be involved in these movements than on the content and meaning of gender-differential participation narratives.

13. Lizzie Borden was a New England woman accused of the 1892 brutal double murder of her mother and her stepfather with an axe. Though she was acquitted of the murders when tried, they were never solved, and popular lore has it that Borden was the murderer. The tale was as infamous then as it is more than one hundred years later: Borden is sensationalized as the United States' first public female murderer (Brown 1991). We see the Lizzie Borden hype, and the narratives about her (including sordid tales about her sexuality and her monstrousness) as foreshadowing the mother, monster and whore narratives which greet women's violence in the twenty-first century.

14. By masculine violence, we don't mean men's violence. We mean, instead, violence inspired by the privileging of values (toughness, etc.) associated with hegemonic masculinities (Connell 1995; Tickner and Sjoberg 2006). R.W. Connell explains a number of different hegemonic and subordinated masculinities in relation to each other (1995). A hegemonic masculinity is dominant, but not stable – instead, different hegemonic masculinities are articulated in different ways in different times, but are always concerned with the subordination of other masculinities and femininities (which will be addressed later). Differences between hegemonic masculinities and subordinated masculinities play a role in the ordering of the social process of gendered power (Hooper 2001: 70). For example, heterosexual (hegemonic) masculinities must subordinate homosexual masculinity to maintain identity for the masculine ideal (Hooper 2001: 55; Connell 1995: 99). This is self-sustaining; Hooper explains that 'as long as masculinity is perceived as a relatively unitary, stable and coherent phenomenon that corresponds to the experiences of all men, dichotomous thinking remains either obviously or secretly at the core of these solutions, compromising their radical potential' (Hooper 2001: 48) – in other words, failure to see gender as a multiple, constitutive social power process would be damning to the feminist project of emancipation.

TWO

1. Baudrillard takes the implications of this argument further: if people 'choose' 'the truth' from competing narratives, instead of being certain of what is 'true' or 'real', inquiry into reality forms a discourse with itself. This circular discourse of inquiry into the real in turn creates discourses, languages and activities; 'realness' becomes less discernable in the dialogue. This creates a state of hyperreality in social and political life. Hyperreality is the penetration of fantasy into the real. This penetration is complete when 'unreality no longer resides in dream or fantasy, or in the beyond, but in the *real's hallucinatory resemblance to itself* and 'reality loops around itself in pure repetition' (Baudrillard 1983: 127). In other words, reality has become fictionalized by the separation of sign and referent. What Baudrillard is saying is that words, discourses and dispositives have lost their tie to material meaning, but are used by people unaware of this 'fictionalization' (2001: 96). These representations, then, compete in a world where there is no clear relationship between representation and referent. Their competition happens through discursive seduction. This contention will be picked up again in the conclusion to this book, but, for now, serves to demonstrate the potential that the narratives about women's violence related in the empirical chapters *could be* radically disconnected from reality, if reality is discernible at all.
2. Feminisms see theory as explanation, as critique and as practice (Zalewski 1996; Tickner 2001). Theory-as-practice means both that theory in itself is an activism and that theory and political action are interconnected. June Lennie describes feminisms as 'critical, emancipatory, and action-oriented' (1999: 246). J.K. Gibson-Graham agrees, explaining that research projects can be used to create new political space (1994: 214). Jane Flax clarifies that both theory and action are necessary to clear political space: each is alone insufficient (Flax 1987: 623).
3. Edith Hamilton relies upon Euripides' account of Medea and Jason. Ovid also relayed the story of Medea and Jason in *Metamorphoses*.
4. One woman said, 'My movement is restricted [by] the checkpoints and my human basic right to move freely around my territory has been denied. ... I have younger brothers and sisters who have never seen a park, never visited the sea' (Jaber 2003: 2).
5. Saradzhyan 2004; Groskop 2004a; Agence France Presse 2004; Myers 2003: 2; Franchetti 2003: 20.
6. *Attack of the 50 Foot Woman* was a movie made in 1958, and remade in 1993. The main character, Nancy, is jaded by her husband and abducted by aliens. Contact with one of the aliens causes her to grow to a monstrous 50 foot tall. The 50 Foot Woman wreaks havoc on all who have wronged her, walking over the city, picking them up, and killing them.
7. Boudica or Boudicca is the current and modern spelling; the more familiar Boadicea was a mistranslation from the Latin.
8. Interestingly enough, Boudica's image was used in the Victorian era as a representation of the British Empire. As an empire under the rule of a woman, Boudica's image was revived to demonstrate the strength and virtue of a woman who had defended her country and her people. As such, Alfred,

Lord Tennyson, like William Cowper before him, wrote poems to portray a positive and virtuous image of Boudica. Even now, Boudica's image is being buffed and polished and used as a comparison for Queens Victoria and Elizabeth as well as Princess Diana (Harbison 2006: 82).

9. In the Bible this does not necessarily imply sexual behaviour but can indicate anything to do with the selling of oneself, such as to idols and false gods.
10. The account of Theseus and Hippolyta is also quite interesting. Ubiquitous Greek hero Theseus, son of Athenian King Aegeus, loved 'danger for the sake of danger'. This love led him to the Amazons and he took away their queen, Hippolyta (also sometimes referred to as Antiope), as his wife. After she gave birth to Hippolytus, the Amazons invaded Attica and made their way to Athens. They were defeated. No mention is made of whether they were able to rescue their queen (Hamilton 1940: 154). It is interesting that many of the Greek wars were fought for the love of a woman; mostly it was described as two men warring for the affection of one woman. In the Amazon myth, it is a tribe of woman fighting a man for their queen. Of course, in this myth told by those socialized by the patriarchy, the women were unsuccessful.
11. One of the earliest articles on female terrorists blames the problem of female terrorism on 'erotomania' (Top Security Project 1976).
12. An example of this is the feminization of the victims at Abu Ghraib, who were described as robbed of their masculinity in the most humiliating possible way by women (see Sjoberg 2007).
13. The flip side of that coin, however, is that, if discourses matter, this book and discussions of it can serve as a counterhegemonic discourse of women's violence in global politics. This will be taken up again as the book concludes.

THREE

1. There are some who say that there were as many as several hundred photos on a number of different cameras, including those of Charles Graner and Sabrina Harman (see aclu.org, for example). Other reports say that there were fewer than two dozen pictures, more than half of which have been publicly released (Karpinski 2006). The dispute about how many pictures there are is only one complication in the battle for their release.
2. Some photos depicted sexual interactions between United States military personnel (Karpinski 2006).
3. The ACLU has filed a Freedom of Information Act lawsuit for the release of the remaining photos taken at Abu Ghraib. On 7 October 2003, the ACLU filed a FOIA request for videotapes, photographs and other records of abuse from the Defense Department. After months went by without a response, the ACLU filed suit. The government cited a number of FOIA exemptions when it refused to release the photos and videos: Exemption 6, which provides that 'personnel and medical files and similar files the disclosure of which would constitute a clearly unwarranted invasion of personal privacy' are exempt

from disclosure, and Exemption 7(C), which exempts records compiled for law enforcement purposes that 'could reasonably be expected to constitute an unwarranted invasion of personal privacy'. The Defense Department also argued that releasing the photographs would conflict with US treaty obligations under the Geneva Convention, which provide that a detaining power must protect a prisoner of war, 'particularly against acts of violence or intimidation and against insults and public curiosity'. The government argued that the release of the photographs could cause the subjects to 'suffer humiliation and indignity against which the Geneva Conventions were intended to protect.' *Am. Civil Liberties Union v. U.S. Dep't of Def.*, 389 F. Supp. 2d 547, 550 (S.D.N.Y. 2005). We are of the opinion that the indignity which the government is claiming would be suffered would be the exposure of female victims of the sex abuse at Abu Ghraib. This hunch is strengthened by Karpinski's descriptions of photos with female victims (Karpinski and Strasser 2005; Karpinski 2006).
4. Torture scandals are the norm and not the exception in war (for example, the reputed torture at Guantánamo of Afghan prisoners. While military torture is condemned, it is not seen as especially novel. Stylized accounts of warriors experiencing torture are all popular culture (for example, movies like *Three Kings* and *True Lies*). Abu Ghraib received the attention that it did, we argue, because women were involved in torture, which is a man's game.
5. While the definition of a war crime is controversial in the United States, and there is no official tally of American soldiers implicated in or convicted of war crimes, the image of a war criminal is always male, be it depictions of 'enemy' war criminals or examples in instructional material.
6. A list of these websites is available upon request from the authors, but is not being published in the book because of the nature of the content.
7. Citations and website content available on request.
8. Dr Sjoberg asked Megan Ambuhl for an interview to discuss the accuracy of our perceptions of the narratives told about her as compared to her perception of herself. She returned an email objecting to participating in a project where the other women she has been grouped with would also have the opportunity to speak, should they so desire. She wrote, in part, 'I am still working on my husband's appeals and clemency. Those take precedence over anything in the immediate future. I do appreciate the idea of getting the truth out. However there are many people involved in this case (women included) that continue to perpetuate lies about their responsibility, the case in general, my husband and overall events as they took place. These people having a say in any project I would be involved with dilutes the truth and what I have to say.'
9. Of the women who are featured in this book, Karpinski stands out in our analysis because, from the evidence we have collected, it is fairly obvious that she actually did not have any role in proscribed violence, as a leader, a witness or a participant. Instead, her failure was a failure to know that such violence was going on. While this failure itself is complicity (and Karpinski will admit that), it is different than the sort of complicity that comes from being in the photographs or operating the camera. This is not

to say that the stylized narratives of *actually* violent women are any more true or representative or any less gender subordinating than the invented narratives about *allegedly but not actually* violent women, which is why we chose to include a discussion of Karpinski, even after it became obvious that she had no direct role in proscribed violence.

10. In a personal interview with Karpinski, one of the things that we found most interesting was Karpinski's knowledge that the prison scandal at Abu Ghraib was whatever the dominant and gendered stylized narrative portrayed. In discussions with Karpinski, she showed a keen awareness for the gendering of military discourse. She emails: 'I think the male military officers of today, who made their careers on guns and weapons and combat operations are really in fear of the future, and the prospect of their skills becoming obsolete. They lack people/compassion skills and often lack cultural awareness, made more obvious in wars of occupation in the international arena. They must exhibit the macho coldness of traditional warriors. Women, of course, tend to excel in these areas so their place and value to the military would increase and become substantially more significant as warfare shifts to more dialogue and understanding and less bombing and direct combat. ... Men often devise ways to exploit "traditional" weaknesses of women and show examples of how they are not suited to combat operations or higher military assignments. ... It remains a very firmly entrenched "man's world" and "good old boys" network.'

11. These results questioning Karpinski's sexuality number around 500, from various sources from the Free Republic to individual blogs. None of them has any real evidence behind them, but they share intense sexualization in descriptions of Karpinski's alleged conduct.

12. Google orders a search by frequency of visits to the site by clicking on the site as a result of a Google search. In other words, were you to search for this book's title, and click on the 300th link several million times (or fewer – we are flattering ourselves), it would become the first link. As Google explains, 'Google runs on a unique combination of advanced hardware and software. The heart of our software is PageRank a system for ranking web pages developed by our founders Larry Page and Sergey Brin at Stanford University. ... PageRank relies on the uniquely democratic nature of the web by using its vast link structure as an indicator of an individual page's value. In essence, Google interprets a link from page A to page B as a vote, by page A, for page B. But, Google looks at more than the sheer volume of votes, or links a page receives; it also analyses the page that casts the vote. Votes cast by pages that are themselves "important" weigh more heavily and help to make other pages "important." Important, high-quality sites receive a higher PageRank, which Google remembers each time it conducts a search. Of course, important pages mean nothing to you if they don't match your query. So, Google combines PageRank with sophisticated text-matching techniques to find pages that are both important and relevant to your search. Google goes far beyond the number of times a term appears on a page and examines all aspects of the page's content (and the content of the pages linking to it) to determine if it's a good match for your query. Google's complex, automated

methods make human tampering with our results extremely difficult. And though we do run relevant ads above and next to our results, Google does not sell placement within the results themselves (i.e., no one can buy a higher PageRank). A Google search is an easy, honest and objective way to find high-quality websites with information relevant to your search' (www.google.com/technology/index.html). This means that the prominence of these sexualized characterizations high in the ranking of a Google search about Karpinski demonstrates that the content is frequently viewed and referenced.

13. Citations available upon request.
14. This is another result which peppers Google searches and Internet blogs for 'Janis Karpinski.'
15. Citations available upon request.
16. Citations available upon request.
17. Not only were the stories that the military and the media told about Jessica Lynch false, the same stories were *truer* of women who fit the idealized 'woman soldier' trope less tightly. Another member of Lynch's company, Shoshana Johnson, was one of the four other prisoners of war that the Iraqi military captured on the same day, but did not make the headlines. Johnson was an African-American. She was also a single mother, who had two children. While Jessica Lynch was injured in a car accident, Shoshana Johnson was shot in the confrontation with the Iraqi military (Douglas 2003). While Lynch was kept in a hospital and attended to, Johnson was kept in a prison and denied medical care (Douglas 2003). While Lynch's story was on the front page of every newspaper, Shoshana Johnson's story is still all but unknown. William Douglas wonders if Shoshana Johnson's relative obscurity is because she did not have the right face to serve as the heroine for a new militarized femininity (2003). A false story about Lynch's capture overshadowed the true stories of others' tragedies in the interest of mainstreaming a certain image of the militarized woman and her role in the fighting.

FOUR

1. Also known as 'Chechenization', which *The Economist* refers to as 'the practice [of] putting the republic in the hands of a favored local strongman' (*Economist* 2004).
2. Russia's Freedom House score for 2005 is an average of 5.6 (the lowest being 7) (freedomhouse.org 2006).
3. Chechens may be the most threatening to Russia, but have not proven themselves to be the most dangerous to the rest of the world.
4. 'Wahhabite' is an outsider's term for Salafism. Those who practise this form of Islam refer to themselves as Salafists (Valiyev 2005: 6).
5. Eke 2003; Mainville 2003: A15; Stephen 2003: 11; Walsh 2003: 15; Weir 2003: 1.
6. Russia has refused to name the gas that it used. This cost 127 hostages their lives because the hospitals were unable to treat them effectively. It is believed that the Russian Alpha force used BZ (Agent Buzz), a 'colorless,

NOTES

odorless, incapacitant with hallucinogenic properties' (Rawstorne and Benson 2002: 4).

7. It is not clear, as will be discussed further in the chapter, if she backed out or if the bomb failed to detonate. The bomb eventually detonated as it was being dismantled, killing the officer working on it.
8. The other hijacker, Satsita Dzhebirkhanova, also apparently lost a brother (Kalman 2004: 8). Myers, of the *New York Times*, adds that all three women were divorced and unable to have children (2004: 1).
9. Walsh 2005: 6; Kalman 2004: 8; Arvedlund and Kishkovsky 2004; *Statesman* 2004.
10. There are other articles which offer an excellent contrast to the avenging monster narrative and present a factual account and more nuanced understanding of the Chechen situation. These depictions tend to present the women as related to those killed by Russian forces without using the language of vengeance. For example, 'black widow' is 'the media term for Muslim women whose husbands have been killed by government troops' (Vinogradova 2003: 4); for 'Chechen women who have lost family members in the conflict' (*Economist* 2004); and '[m]any of the women bombers are relatives of Chechens killed by the Russian bombers' (Zakaria 2003, 57). Others place the women's actions within the historical and cultural context of *adat* (Bruce 2003: 8) or in seeking justice (Kowalski 2004: 82).
11. Saradzhyan 2004; Groskop 2004a; Agence France Presse 2004; Myers 2003: 2; Franchetti 2003: 20
12. All Palestinian martyrs' families are given monthly allowances following the operation. Saddam Hussein infamously paid $25,000 to each Palestinian family when he was still in power.
13. Speckhard and Akhmedova found that her two sisters willingly participated in the Moscow crisis and that the family was split between the mother, who encouraged engagement in proscribed violence, and the father, who was vehemently opposed to it (2006: 70).
14. One article says Zarema was 'held as a 'virtual slave' by [Chechen] rebels' after her husband's death (Beeston 2004: 4).
15. Yet, supposedly the leader of the group disapproved of her choice because she was killing herself for money 'rather than religious principles' (Ward 2004: A6). There is also an element of the whore narrative, Muzikhoyeva also purportedly slept with the male leader (Vinogradova 2003: 4).
16. See also Baker 2004: A12.
17. Of course, the Chechens have not helped their cause. Their actions have cost them the international support they once enjoyed, in the 1990s. With the hospital hostage-taking scenarios of the late 1990s, the Moscow hostage crisis in 2002 and the Beslan elementary school hostage-takaing in 2004, when approximately 350 children died, the Chechen nationalists moved from what might have been seen as supportable actions to insufferable ones.

FIVE

1. Much like Enloe's stories of women soldiers, this shows the rising salience of the concept of femininity (1993). Attention to women suicide bombers

as women is a sign not of gender emancipation, but of gender subordination in the public eye.
2. Indeed, this plays into the subjective nature of the term 'terrorist', which automatically connotes illegitimate violence and deflects from the Palestinians' belief that they are fighting for a just cause in the only way they feel is available to them.
3. The first two female suicide bombers (non-al-Qaeda) in Iraq happened just after the Coalition forces invaded on 29 March 2003 (Bloom 2005a: 60).
4. 'Successful' refers to the woman detonating herself at the desired place and time or upon approach of the security forces.
5. While this is not the place to get into the debate about whether or not Middle Eastern women are uniquely subordinated, we find it important to note the hybrid nature of the question (Gole 2000), the impossibility of making a determination of the answer to the question (Yuval-Davis 1997), the inappropriateness of our asking the question as Western women gazing 'in' (Mohanty 1991), and the fundamental irrelevance of the question for the analysis of assigning agency and capability (Spivak 1988).
6. There are some accounts, like those at the end of the chapter, of women choosing suicide terrorism to demonstrate and gain agency – i.e. not for their particular cause but for that of women's liberation. While we have seen no evidence of this in our research, it would be an interesting question to explore.
7. The use of child soldiers has been universally condemned as abhorrent and unacceptable. Yet over the last ten years hundreds of thousands of children have fought and died in conflicts around the world, including in Sri Lanka, Uganda, Sierra Leone, the Palestinian Territories, etc. Children involved in armed conflict are frequently killed or injured during combat or while carrying out other tasks. They are forced to engage in hazardous activities such as laying mines or explosives, as well as using weapons. Child soldiers are usually forced to live under harsh conditions with insufficient food and little or no access to health care. They are usually treated brutally, subjected to beatings and humiliating treatment. Punishments for mistakes or desertion are often very severe. Girl soldiers are particularly at risk of rape, sexual harassment and abuse as well as being involved in combat and other tasks. The conflation of women soldiers and child soldiers has been the source of some controversy, however (Mitchell 2006; Cheney 2005; Rosen 2005).
8. Al-Aqsa is the 'striking arm of Yassir Arafat's Fatah organization'. It was founded by radicals in Nablus, many of whom were inspired by the first Intifada. They are extensively involved in the second Intifada (often referred to as the Al Aqsa Intifada) and have committed as many as 2,000 car-bombings, shootings, kidnappings and knife attacks. It is a secular nationalist group, as opposed to an Islamic group (www.ict.org/il 2006).
9. More specifically known as Fateh Tanzim, it is the armed wing of the PLO. Fateh Tanzim 'acts as [a secular] paramilitary counter-balance to the military wings of ... Hamas and the Palestinian Islamic Jihad' (www.ict.org/il 2006). They have played a leading role in the second Intifada (www.ict.org/il 2006)

NOTES

10. Palestinian Islamic Jihad was founded in 1979/80 by Palestinian students who split from Egypt's Muslim Brotherhood. They were influenced by the Iranian Revolution and the radical mobilization of the Egyptians. They were one of the first Palestinian groups to use suicide bombings in the time between the two Intifadas (www.ict.org/il, 2006)
11. Hamas (an Arabic acronym for the Islamic Resistance Movement, which also means 'zeal') is a radical Islamic group which came into force during the first Intifada. It operates primarily in Gaza but also in the West Bank. In the 2006 elections it won a majority of the seats in the Palestinian parliament (www.ict.org/il 2006; see also Hoffman 2006).
12. Her name was Reem Saleh al-Riyashi; she is described in more detail further on in the chapter.
13. Atzlan.net 2007; Al-Mughrabi 2006; Farrell 2006; *Washington Post* 2006; Katz 2006; Xinhua General News Service 2006; Brunner 2005; Toles Parkin 2004; Fisher 2004; Victor 2003; Walker and Beeston 2002; Usher 2002a, 2002b.
14. Brunner also examines the use of maternal language, among other topics, in her article (2005).
15. *Shahida* is Arabic for 'martyr'.
16. Al-Qaeda is the organization that has set the definition for 'global terrorism'. It recruits, spreads information, and fundraises globally through the use of the Internet (Gunaratna 2005: 32). Al-Qaeda as one enormous entity is a misconception. Instead al-Qaeda can be broken down into four parts: (1) al-Qaeda central, which was weakened by the war in Afghanistan; (2) al-Qaeda affiliates and associates, groups that have been assisted by al-Qaeda central, such as Zarqawi's al-Qaeda in Iraq; (3) al-Qaeda locals which are groups and individuals 'who have had some direct connection with al Qaeda [central] – however tenuous or evanescent' ; and finally, (4) the al-Qaeda network, which refers to 'home-grown Islamic radicals', either from Muslim communities or converts who have no direct contact with al-Qaeda (Hoffman 2005: 6–7).
17. This specific mention of 'stages' is something either ignored or unknown in the 'black widow' accounts covered in Chapter 4.
18. The Battle of Al Qadisiyyah was the decisive engagement between the Arab Muslim army and the Sasanian Persian army during the first period of Muslim expansion which resulted in the Islamic conquest of Persia. Although there is little doubt that this battle occurred, scholarship suggests that its legend has grown many fold and a whole mythological literature (full of *topoi*) has developed around it. In particular, uncertainty with respect to the date of the battle (variously given anywhere between 634 and 640 CE, most likely to have been around 636 CE) and the size of the forces, and the fact of scarce mention in non-Muslim annals, suggest that the current perception of Al Qadisiyyah differs starkly from the original event. However, this scholarship in no way demeans or marginalizes the role of the battle in the perception of Muslims today. Rather, it highlights the significant function of history and memory in the modern Middle East; Saddam Hussein's evocation of this battle during the Iran–Iraq War exemplifies the emotive power of this ancient engagement (Wikipedia 2007).

19. On 25 February 2007, the worst attack on a Baghdad university took place. A woman detonated herself outside the Mustansiriya University's college of economics and management. She killed at least 42 people and wounded 55 others (CNN.com 2007; BBC 2007). It is likely she was part of the general insurgency and not affiliated with al-Qaeda (tkb.org 2007).
20. Victor 2003; Bloom 2005a, 2005b and 2005c; Jaber 2003; Dickey 2005; Ward 2004.
21. The public–private divide marginalizes the interests of the private sphere. Some rights and privileges do not receive recognition because they are part of the 'private' sphere (Okin 1998: 39). This is troubling and Okin contends that feminists should examine this critically and find alternatives. Several feminists go on to do just this. Spike Peterson finds that the 'private' is always public: because 'personal gender identities constitute a "core" sense of "self", they fundamentally condition our self-esteem and psychological security' (1999: 37). Gillian Youngs documents that the politics of the public realm works through a 'patriarchal prism' which prioritizes 'public sphere activities over the private realm on the basis of a power relationship between the two' (Youngs 2000: 45). These feminist critiques of the public–private division draws attention to the spatial separateness of oppression, and this is vital to understanding the dynamics of gendered and other subordinations (Youngs 2000: 48).
22. Men's actions are accepted as politically driven statements. Women's actions are not and are seen rather as due to some biological or mental instability.
23. Toles Parkin also points out this problem (2004: 85–6).
24. Dickey 2005; Jaber 2003: 1–2; Ragavan 2003a: 33; McLaughlin 2003: 10; Jacinto 2003: 1–3; Campbel 2003: 2.
25. 'Suicide terrorism' as opposed to 'suicide bombing' because some missions may not involve the person killing him- or herself but going into a mission with no plan for escape (Pape 2005: 10).
26. The title refers to the speech Yasser Arafat gave welcoming women's equal participation in the Palestinian struggle. The speech took place on the same day, 27 January 2002, that Wafa Idris committed the first female suicide attack.
27. There are those who contend that non-feminist studies of gender are adequate to include gender in global politics (Carpenter 2002). In fact, Charli Carpenter contends that non-feminists who study gender would undertake insightful studies that feminists would eschew based on their epistemological break with orthodox methodology. Carpenter's assumption is wrong, however: it is not her methods that feminist international relations scholarship problematizes; it is the incompleteness of non-feminist substantive analysis. It is not *gender as a variable* that feminist work critiques; it is an insufficient understanding of that variable. The use of the mother, monster and whore narratives about violent women *means something* about gender; it means more than that there is no man in the picture. It means that women are not dealt with as political actors; it means that their gender is at once blamed for and cast as innocent in their actions. Without the tools of feminist analysis, however, it is impossible to explain either the causes or the effects of this gendered

discourse. Where a non-feminist analysis sees the neglect of studies of masculinity, feminists see that history is the study of masculinity in global politics. The gender essentialism in descriptions of violent women *reflects* gender essentialism inherent in millennia of war narratives and *continues* the gender subordination perpetrated by those gendered narratives.
28. Here we are thinking of the emphasis placed on the virgins waiting in heaven for male suicide bombers' actions; even when a man commits proscribed violence in global politics, his transgression can be traced back to and blamed on (even innocent and pure) femininity.

SIX

1. Rubinstein 2004; Straus 2001; Fein 1990.
2. We bring this up here, and go into it in a little more detail below, because we are interested not only in the historical evolution (or lack of evolution, as the case may be) of narrative about women's violence generally and women's participation in genocide specifically, but also in how the analyses that we have done concerning narratives employed in the (near and distant) past apply to the production of knowledge on the subject today.
3. Others are free to come to their own conclusions, but we understand feminism this way: feminism is interested in women's emancipation. Feminists are, fundamentally, *for women*. We consider ourselves feminists. In order to be an effective feminist, then, we cannot just be *for* good women's freedom, but for *all* women's freedom. Until society recognizes a woman's capacity to commit genocide (and condemns it universally rather than on the basis of gender-based logic), we are also not truly free, because there are limits on the things that society views women as capable of, against unlimited masculinities.
4. For example, see Marysia Zalewski's (1995) article, 'Well, What is the Feminist Perspective on Bosnia?' which details both the treatment of women and the gendering of the conflict. A number of accounts also describe in detail the gendered impacts of the conflict (Hansen 2001; Stiglmayer and Faber 1994; Olujic 1998).
5. In fact, the only indication I have that she is married is the 'Mrs' used in most of the seventy-five articles I read about her; a husband or children are never mentioned, and a Google search finds no evidence that she has either.
6. The Interahamwe (a word that means 'standing together') was the largest of the militias formed by the Hutu, led by Robert Kajuga. Not officially disbanded, members still take part in border raids, such as those that led to the wars in the Congo.
7. On her initial court appearance on 3 September 1997, Nyiramasuhuko pleaded Not Guilty to the five charges with which she was indicted, based on an initial indictment. After modification of the indictment, reflecting a decision dated 10 August 1999 to include rape as a crime against humanity and which brought the number of charges up to eleven, Pauline Nyiramasuhuko again pleaded Not Guilty on 12 August 1999. On 6 October 1999,

the ICTR, on the request of the prosecutor, ordered a combined trial for Nyiramasuhuko and five other persons accused of crimes committed in the Butare prefecture of Rwanda in 1994. The five co-accused (see related cases) are: her son, Arsène Shalom Ntahobali (leader of a militia group), Joseph Kanyabashi (mayor of Ngoma), Sylvain Nsabimana (prefect of Butare) and Elie Ndayambaje (mayor of Muganza). Pauline Nyiramasuhuko was accused of 'conspiracy to commit genocide', 'genocide', or alternatively 'complicity in genocide', as well as 'public and direct incitement to commit genocide', 'murder as a crime against humanity', 'extermination as a crime against humanity', 'rape as a crime against humanity', 'persecutions on political, racial and religious grounds as a crime against humanity', 'inhumane acts as a crime against humanity' and various war crimes. Her trial, referred to as 'the collective trial of the Butare group', commenced on 12 June 2001 before the Second Trial Chamber of the ICTR. At the time of writing, the trial was still under way.

8. Shortly afterwards, according to another witness, Nyiramasuhuko arrived at a compound where a group of Interahamwe was guarding seventy Tutsi women and girls. One Interahamwe, a young man named Emmanuel Nsabimana, told me through a translator that Nyiramasuhuko ordered him and the others to burn the women. Nsabimana recalled that one Interahamwe complained that they lacked sufficient gasoline. "Pauline said, "Don't worry, I have jerrycans of gasoline in my car"', Nsabimana recalled. 'She said, "Go take that gasoline and kill them." I went to the car and took the jerrycans. Then Pauline said, "Why don't you rape them before you kill them?" But we had been killing all day, and we were tired. We just put the gasoline in bottles and scattered it among the women, then started burning' (Landesman 2002a).

9. Nyiramasuhuko's mother has revealed that Pauline's grandfather was 'demoted' from Tutsi to Hutu when he became poor. Since ethnic group membership in Rwanda is patrilineal, that means that Nyiramasuhuko is a Tutsi as well. Her mother also told Peter Landesman that Nyiramasuhuko knew that she was part Tutsi, and that that discovery was a crucial turning point in her hatred of Tutsis (Landesman 2002a).

SEVEN

1. See Chapter 1, n12.
2. Ann Tickner's 1992 book on *Gender in International Relations* has been presented as a good example of such deconstruction: it reveals what she considers to be the gendered underpinnings of the field. This 'deconstruction makes gender relations visible by overturning the oppositional logic that mystifies categories like woman/man, domestic/international, and peace/war' (Kronsell 2006: 110).
3. While the main focus of this book *is not* the question of why women commit proscribed violence (war crimes, terrorist attacks and genocide), substantial time and energy have been spent critiquing gendered narratives which address that question. We originally were not interested in contributing

NOTES

to the debate about why women do the things that we have recounted in this book; we still have very little interest in that discussion. The reason we find that an uninteresting question is because the accounts which do take note of gender almost exclusively do so by entrenching rather than interrogating gender stereotypes. Much like our critique of Robert Pape's book *Dying to Win* (2005) in Chapter 5, this chapter argues that, *in their gender blindness*, theories of individual violence in global politics are gendered.

4. The field from which most of the analyses in this chapter are drawn is Terrorism Studies, which is the source of most scholarly approaches to individual proscribed violence in global politics.
5. Certainly Jeff Victoroff's 2005 article, 'The Mind of the Terrorist', was influential. But these theories have also been debated by such Terrorism Studies scholars as Martha Crenshaw, Jerrold Post, and E. Sprizak, especially the chapters in Walter Reich's edited volume (1998).
6. In fact, they intentionally leave out the controversy and debate within criminology and Terrorism Studies about each position, largely because those debates have yet to touch on gender questions with any sort of consistency. These brief introductions, for reasons of space, also do not cover the extent of possible gender critiques. They intend, instead, to show gendered assumptions on the surface level of these theories, and to demonstrate the need for the proposal of an alternative modality to deal with the genderings of individual violence in global politics.
7. There are exceptions, such as Crenshaw, but also Robert Pape (2005), who, in studying suicide terrorism, understands all suicide terrorists, male and female, as rational actors acting on expected utility.
8. An important exception to this is Crosby's 1982 study.
9. Perhaps a bolder way to state this is that our interest lies primarily in the question of how much of an individual's decision to participate in proscribed violence is his/her own, and what influences that part that is not his/her own.
10. A classic example of this dilemma is the question of whether you would rather be slapped or shot. Of course, the answer is a third one, outside of the realm of choices presented: we would all prefer to be neither slapped nor shot. But if being slapped or shot are the only choices, than we do *have a preference* – we would rather be slapped. It is not that all choice goes away when the ideal choice is taken off the table. We can, and do, also choose the lesser of evils. This choice is not completely free (because we would have chosen another option if our choice had been completely free), but neither is it completely constrained (because we have more than one substantially different option). Instead, we are acting *relationally autonomous*, with both individuality and a choice, but without radical detachment from any constraint.
11. By relational here, we mean reliant on relationships (both in the active and passive sense) with others.
12. Hirschmann 1989; Sjoberg 2006; McKenzie and Stolgar 2000; Sylvester 2002, 1994, 1990.

EIGHT

1. Byman and Pollack's title is itself taken from James Agee and Walker Evans's seminal work *Let Us Now Praise Famous Men*.
2. In fact, the only woman that we can find in the article is Czarina Elizabeth, whose death was the 'miracle' that Fredrick the Great needed in order to keep Prussia intact in 1762, when he was facing losing the war to the combined strength of Russia, Austria and France (Byman and Pollack 2001: 107).
3. To see the state as *not necessarily* but *currently* patriarchal is to see the state as an ongoing social construction process. Jill Steans explains that feminisms can see statehood 'as a *process*. That is, the state is not seen as a "thing", an entity with independent existence, but actually a dynamic entity which is constantly being made and remade' (1998: 13). She explains that a static understanding of the state is reductionist, reifying, methodologically individualist, and fails to recognize the union of theory and practice. Instead, the state can move from *patriarchal* to *non-patriarchal* or along a continuum of patriarchy.

REFERENCES

Abdo, N. (1991) 'Women and the Intifada: Gender, Class, and National Liberation', *Race and Class*, vol. 32, no. 4.
Abedin, M. (2005) 'New Security Realities and al-Qaeda's Changing Tactics: An Interview with Saad al-Faqih', *Spotlight on Terror*, vol. 3, no. 3, 15 December. www.jamestown.org/terrorism/news/article.php?articleid=2369847 (accessed 4 August 2006).
Africa Rights (1995) *Not So Innocent: When Women Become Killers*, African Rights, London.
Agence France Presse (2004a) 'Airline Bombings and Moscow Subway Attack Revives Spectre of Chechen "Black Widows"', 1 September, http://web.lexis-nexis.com/universe (accessed 8 June 2006).
Agence France Presse (2004b) 'Chechen Female Would-be Suicide Bomber Gets 20 Years', 8 April, http://web.lexis-nexis.com (accessed 8 June 2006).
Agence France Presse (2004c) 'Chechen Women Tell of Fear and Loathing After Russia Attacks', 6 September, http://web.lexis-nexis.com (accessed 8 June 2006).
Ahmed, L. (1992) *Women and Gender in Islam*, Yale University Press, New Haven CT.
Ali, F. (2005) 'Muslim Female Fighters: An Emerging Trend', *Jameston Global Terrorism Analysis*, vol. 3, no. 21, 3 November, www.jamestown.org/terrorism/news/article.php?articleid=2369824 (accessed 6 December 2006).
Aliev, T. (2003) 'Chechen Women Arrested after Recent Explosions', *Prague Watchdog*, 19 May, www.watchdog.cz (accessed 31 March 2006).
Alison, M. (2007) *Women and Political Violence: Female Combatants in Ethno-National Conflict*, Routledge, London.
Alison, M. (2004) 'Women as Agents of Political Violence: Gendering Security', *Security Dialogue*, vol. 35, no. 4.

Allen, A. (1998) 'Rethinking Power', *Hypatia*, vol. 13, no. 1.
Allen, B. (1996) *Rape Warfare: The Hidden Genocide in Bosnia-Herzegovina and Croatia*, University of Minnesota Press, Minneapolis.
Almond, M. (2004) 'Savages Who'd Think Nothing of Butchering Innocent Youngersters', *Daily Mail*, 2 September.
Al-Mughrabi, N. (2006) 'Palestinian Leaders Hold Talks on New Government', www.swissinfo.com (accessed 17 November 2006).
Al-Shishani, M.B., and C. Moore (2005) 'From Egyptian Islamic Jihad to Chechnya: A Portrait of Mahmoud Hannawi', *Terrorism Monitor*, vol. 3, no. 13, 1 July.
Amal, K. (1993) 'National Mobilization, War Conditions, and Gender Consciousness', *Arab Studies Quarterly*, vol. 15, no. 2, Spring.
Ambuhl, M. (2006) 'Former Abu Ghraib Guard Speaks Out: Wife of Jailed Soldier Charles Graner Says Pattern of Abuse Was Well Established', *Washington Post*, 23 January, www.washingtonpost.com/wp-dyn/content/discussion/2006/01/23/DI2006012300493_pf.html (accessed 1 January 2007).
Amnesty International (2004) *Sudan: Darfur: Rape as a Weapon of War: Sexual Violence and Its Consequences*, AFR 54/076/2004, 19 July.
Ansah, T. (2005) 'Genocide and the Eroticization of Death: Law, Violence, and Moral Purity', *Southern California Interdisciplinary Law Journal* 14.
Anthias, F. (2002) 'Beyond Feminism and Multiculturalism: Locating Difference and the Politics of Location', *Women's Studies International Forum*, vol. 25, no. 3.
Antonius, S. (1979) 'Fighting on Two Fronts: Conversations with Palestinian Women', *Journal of Palestine Studies* 31.
APS Diplomat News Service (2004) 'Bin Laden is Recruiting Female/Child Terrorists for Jihad on Both Sides of Suez', 20 September, http://web.lexis-nexis.com/universe (accessed 1 September 2006).
Apter, E. (2006) 'On Oneworldness, or Paranoia as a World System', *Journal of American Literary History*, vol. 18, no. 2.
Arendt, H. (1940) *On Violence*, Harvest Books, New York.
Argumenty y Fakty (2003) 'How Many More Suicide Bombers?', 9–16 July, *What the Papers Say*, http://web.lexis-nexis.com/universe (accessed 8 June 2006).
Arvedlund, E.A., and S. Kishkovsky (2004) 'After a Spate of Bombings, Moscow's Full of Forboding', *New York Times*, 2 September, www.nytimes.com/2004/09/02/international/europe/02moscow.html (accessed 2 September 2004).
Askin, K.D. (1999) 'Sexual Violence in Decisions and Indictments of the Yugoslav and Rwandan Tribunals: Current Status', *American Journal of International Law* 93.
Askin, K.D. (2003) 'The Quest for Post-Conflict Gender Justice', *Columbia Journal of Transnational Law* 41.
Associated Press (2004) 'Female Suicide Bomber Fulfills Grim Wish, Killing 4', 15 January, http://web.lexis-nexis.com/universe (accessed 9 May 2006).
Atkinson, J. (2006) 'Jezebel', *The Latter Rain Page*, http://latter-rain.com/eschae/jezebel.htm (accessed 28 June 2006).
Atlanta Journal–Constitution (2004) 'Supervisor: Suspect in Iraq Abuse Unruly',

Atlanta Journal–Constitution, 5 August, p. A5.
Axworthy, L. (2001) 'Human Security and Global Governance: Putting People First'. *Global Governance*, vol. 7, no. 1.
Ayers, B. (2001) *Fugitive Days: A Memoir*, Beacon Press, Boston MA.
Badger, T.A. (2005a) 'Lynndie England to Plead Guilty to Abu Ghraib Abuses', *Pittsburgh Post Gazette*, 30 April.
Badger, T.A. (2005b) 'England Sentenced to Three Years in Prisoner Abuse Case', *Philadelphia Inquirer*, 28 September.
Bagnall, J. (2005) 'What Motivates Suicide Bombers is a Mystery', *The Gazette*, 22 July.
Baker, P. (2004) '"New Stage" of Fear for Chechen Women', *Washington Post*, 19 October, www.washingtonpost.com/ac2/wp-dyn/A43296–2004Oct18?language=printer (accessed 31 March 2006).
Baker, P. (2004) 'Chechnya: Now They Are Taking Over Our Women', *Toronto Star*, 24 October.
Balburov, D. (2003) '"Black Widows" Takes a Heavy Toll', *Moscow News*, 11 June, http://web.lexis-nexis.com (accessed 8 June 2006).
Baldick, R. (1965) *The Duel: A History of Dueling*, Chapman & Hall, New York.
Ballinger, A. (1996) 'The Guilt of the Innocent and the Innocence of the Guilty: The Cases of Marie Fahmy and Ruth Ellis', in A. Myers and M. Wight (eds), *No Angels: Women Who Commit Violence*, Pandora, London and San Francisco.
Balthazar, S. (2001) 'Fulfilling the Legacy: International Justice 60 Years after Nuremberg', *Gonzaga Journal of International Law* 10.
Bandura, A. (1998) 'Mechanisms of Moral Disengagement', in W. Reich (ed.), *Origins of Terrorism: Psychologies, Ideologies, Theologies, States of Mind*, Woodrow Wilson Center Press, Washington DC.
Banerjee, S. (2005) *Make Me a Man: Masculinity, Hinduism, and Nationalism*, SUNY Press, Albany NY.
Barnett, M. (2002) *Eyewitness to Genocide: The United Nations and Rwanda*, Cornell University Press, Ithaca NY.
Barron, A. (2002) 'The Palestinian Women's Movement: Agent of Democracy in a Future State?', *Critique: Critical Middle Eastern Studies*, vol. 11, no. 1.
Bartky, S.L. (1988) 'Foucault, Femininity, and the Modernization of Patriarchal Power', in I. Diamond and L. Quimby (eds), *Feminism and Foucault*, Northeastern University Press, Boston MA.
Bartz, D. (2006) 'Rumsfeld Okayed Abuses Says Former US General', Reuters, 25 November, http://today.reuters.com/news (accessed 25 November 2006).
Basel, S. (2005) 'Palestinian Suicide Attacks Revisited', *Peace Magazine*, vol. 21, no. 2, 1 April, http://web.lexis-nexis.com/universe (accessed 5 September 2006).
Baudrillard, J. (2001) *Selected Writings*, ed. M. Poster, Stanford University Press, Stanford CA.
Baudrillard, J. (1983) 'De la croissance a l'excroissance', *Debat*, vol. 23, no. 2.
Baudrillard, J. (1979) *De la séduction*, Éditions Galilée, Paris.
Baudrillard, J. (1976) *L'Echange symbolique et la mort*, Gallimard, Paris.

BBC News (2003) 'Biljana Plavsic: Serbian Iron Lady', 27 February, http://news. bbc.co.uk/go/pr/fr/-/1/hi/world/europe/1108604.stm (accessed 1 January 2007).
BBC (2007) 'Baghdad College Bomber Was Female', 26 February. http://news. bbc.co.uk/1/hi/world/middle_east/6396301.stm (accessed 4 March 2007).
Beaumont, P. (2002) 'Woman Suicide Bomber Strikes', *Guardian*, 28 January.
Beckman, P., and F.J. D'Amico (1994) *Women, Gender, and World Politics*, Greenwood, Westport CT.
Beeston, R. (2004) 'Black Widow Suicide Bombers Are Extremists' Worst Weapon', *The Times*, 3 September.
Bell, D. (2004) *Silent Covenants: Brown v. Board of Education and the Unfulfilled Hopes for Racial Reform*, Oxford University Press, Oxford.
Bell, S. (2003) 'Al-Qaeda Forms Brigade of Female Suicide Bombers', *Ottawa Citizen*, A7, http://web.lexis-nexis.com/universe (accessed 8 June 2006).
Bennett, A. (2002a) 'The Reintegration of Child Ex-combatants in Sierra Leone with a Particular Focus on the Needs of Females', MA thesis, University of East London.
Bennett, J. (2002b) 'Mideast Turmoil; Rash of New Suicide Bombers Exhibit No Patterns or Ties', *New York Times*, 21 June.
Beres, L.D. (1999) 'The Reemergence of the Suicide Bomber, Gamla.org, www. gamla.org.il/english/beres/46.htm (accessed 1 January 2007).
Berkowitz, L. (1990) 'Biological Roots: Are Humans Inherently Violent?', in B. Glad (ed.), *Psychological Dimensions of War*, Sage, Newbury Park CA.
Bernstein, N., A. Elliot and W.K. Rashbaum (2005) 'Girl Called Would-be Bomber Was Drawn to Islam', *New York Times*, 8 April.
Berrington, E., and P. Honkatukia (2002) 'An Evil Monster and a Poor Thing: Female Violence in the Media', *Journal of Scandinavian Studies in Criminology and Crime Prevention*, vol. 3, no. 1.
Blanchard, E. (2003) 'Gender, International Relations, and the Development of Feminist Security Theory', *Signs: Journal of Women in Culture and Society*, vol. 28, no. 4.
Blandy, C.W. (2003) 'Military Aspects of the Two Russo-Chechen Conflicts in Recent Times', *Central Asian Survey*, vol. 22, no. 4.
Blanton, D., and L. Cook (2002) *They Fought Like Demons: Women Soldiers in the American Civil War*, Louisiana State University Press, Baton Rouge.
Bloom, M. (2007) 'Female Suicide Bombers: A Global Trend', *Daedalus*, Winter.
Bloom, M. (2005a) *Dying to Kill: The Allure of Suicide Terror*, Columbia University Press, New York.
Bloom, M. (2005b) 'Mother. Daughter. Sister. Bomber', *Bulletin of the Atomic Scientists*, November/December.
Bloom, M. (2005c) 'Terror's Deadly New Stealth Weapon: Women', *Guelph Mercury*, 2 December.
Bourdieu, P. (1991) *Language and Symbolic Power*, ed. J.B. Thompson, trans. A. Raymond and M. Adamson, Harvard University Press, Cambridge MA.
Boswell, R. (2003) 'Black Widows Put Moscow under Siege', *Ottawa Citizen*, 11 July.
Bouchard-Kerr, J. (2003) 'The Texas Cadet Murder Case', *CourtTV Crime Library*:

Criminal Minds and Methods, www.crimelibrary.com/notorious_murders/young/zamora/1.html (accessed 3 September 2007).

Bourke, J. (1999) *An Intimate History of Killing: Face-to-Face Killing in Twentieth Century Warfare*, Basic Books, New York.

Boussy, Second Lieutenant L. (1996) 'No Women in Ground Combat', *United States Naval Institute Proceedings*.

Bowers, S.R., A.A. Derrick and M.A. Olimov (2004) 'Suicide Terrorism in the Former USSR', *Journal of Social, Political and Economic Studies*, vol. 29, no. 3.

Bragg, R. (2003) *I Am a Soldier Too: The Jessica Lynch Story*, Knopf, New York.

Braendle, C., and M. Felix (2006) 'Sexual Determination: Ways to Evolve a Hermaphrodite', *Current Biology*, vol. 16, no. 12.

Brennan, Major T.P. (1994) 'Putting Politics before Military Readiness', *Marine Corps Gazette*, vol. 78, no. 12.

Bretherton, C. (2001) 'Gender Mainstreaming and EU Enlargement: Swimming Against the Tide?', *Journal of European Public Policy*, vol. 8, no. 1.

Brown, A.R. (1991) *Lizzie Borden: Legend, the Truth, and the Final Chapter*, Rutledge Hill, Nashville TN.

Brown, D.P. (2002) *The Camp Women: The SS Auxiliarie Who Assisted the SS in Running the Nazi Concentration Camp System*, Schiffer, London.

Brown, S. (2003) 'Russia's 'Black Widows'', 25 July, www.frontpagemagazine.com (accessed 31 March 2006).

Browne, A. (2005a) 'Western White Woman in Suicide Bomber', *Times Online*, www.timesonline.com (accessed 4 August 2006).

Brown, M. (2006) 'A Woman in the Army is Still a Woman: Recruitment of Women into an All-Volunteer Force', paper presented at the annual meeting of the International Studies Association, San Diego CA.

Brownmiller, S. (1975) *Against Our Will: Men, Women, and Rape*, Simon & Schuster, New York.

Bruce, I. (2004) 'Special Force Has Unenviable Record', *Herald*, 3 September.

Bruce, I. (2003) 'Attacks Blamed on Black Widows', *Herald*, 7 July.

Brunner, C. (2005) 'Female Suicide Bombers – Male Suicide Bombing? Looking for Gender in Reporting the Suicide Bombings of the Israeli–Palestinian Conflict', *Global Society*, vol. 19, no. 1.

Buchanan, D. (2002) 'Gendercide and Human Rights', *Journal of Genocide Research*, vol. 4, no. 1.

Buhle, M.J. (1998) *Feminism and Its Discontents: A Century of Struggle with Psychoanalysis*, Harvard University Press, Cambridge MA.

Burelli, D. (1998) *Women in the Armed Forces*, Congressional Research Service, 18 November.

Burke, A.R. (2004) 'Sabrina Harman and Her Corpse', *Counterpunch.org*, www.counterpunch.og/burke05222004.html (accessed 1 January 2007).

Bushman, B.J., A. Bonacci, M. Van Dijk and R. Baumeister (2003) 'Narcissism, Sexual Refusal, and Aggression: Testing a Narcissistic Resistance Theory of Sexual Coercion', *Journal of Personality and Social Psychology*, vol. 84, no. 5.

Butler, J. (2004) *Undoing Gender*, Routledge, London.

Butler, J. (1993) *Bodies that Matter: On the Discursive Limits of Sex*, Routledge, New York.

Butler, J. (1990) *Gender Trouble: Feminism and the Subversion of Identity*, Routledge, New York.
Buzan, B. (1991) *People, States, and Fear: An Agenda for International Security Studies in the Post-Cold War Era*, Lynne Rienner, Boulder CO.
Byman, D., and K. Pollack (2001) 'Let Us Now Praise Great Men: Bringing the Statesman Back In', *International Security*, vol. 25, no. 4.
Campanaro, J. (2001) 'Women, War and International Law: The Historical Treatment of Gender-Based War Crimes', *Georgia Law Journal* 89.
Campbell, M. (2003) 'Black Widows of Chechnya Take another Deadly Revenge', *Sunday Times*, 6 July.
Card, C. (2003) 'Genocide and Social Death', *Hypatia*, vol. 18, no. 1.
Card, C. (1996) 'Rape as a Weapon of War', *Hypatia*, vol. 11, no. 4.
Carpenter, R.C. (2003a) '"Women and Children First": Gender, Norms, and Humanitarian Evacuation in the Balkans 1991–95', *International Organization*, vol. 57, no. 4.
Carpenter, R.C. (2002) 'Gender Theory in World Politics: Contributions of a Non-Feminist Standpoint', *International Studies Review*, vol. 4, no. 3.
Carter, B. (1997) 'A Real Life Drama', *New York Times*, 5 February.
Carver, T. (2004) 'Men and Masculinities in Gender/Genocide', in A. Jones (ed.), *Gender and Genocide*, Vanderbilt University Press, Nashville TN.
Caryl, C., and A. Nivat (1999) 'We Will Not Yield an Inch', *US News and World Report*, vol. 127, no. 23, 13 December.
CBS News (2004) 'She's No Stranger to Grizly Images', 10 May, www.cbsnews.com/stories/2004/05/10/iraq/main616584.shtml (accessed 1 June 2006).
CBS News (2003) 'FBI Warns of Al Qaeda Women', www.cbsnews.com/stories/2003/04/01/terror/main547237.shtml (accessed 4 August 2006).
Cecil, C. (2003) 'Suicide Bombers' Trainer "Killed by Russian Military"', *The Times*, 14 July.
Chang, I. (1997) *The Rape of Nanking: The Forgotten Holocaust of World War II*, Penguin, New York.
Charlesworth, H. (1999) 'Feminist Methods in International Law', *American Journal of International Law*, vol. 93, no. 2.
Cheney, K.E. (2005) '"Our Children Have Only Known War": Children's Experiences and the Uses of Childhood in Northern Uganda', *Children's Geographies*, vol. 3, no. 1.
Chesler, P. (2004) 'Feminism's Deafening Silence', *Frontpagemagazine.com*, www.frontpagemagazine.com (accessed 26 July 2006).
Childs, S. (2006) 'The Complicated Relationship between Sex, Gender, and the Substantive Representation of Women', *European Journal of Women's Studies*, vol. 13, no. 1.
Childs, S., and M.L. Krook. (2006) 'Gender and Politics: State of the Art?' *Politics*, vol. 26, no. 1.
Chin, C. (1998) *In Service and Servitude: Foreign Female Domestic Workers and the Malaysian 'Modernity' Project*, Columbia University Press, New York.
Chodorow, N. (1994) *Femininities, Masculinities, Sexualities: Freud and Beyond*, University Press of Kentucky, Lexington.
Chomsky, N. (2001) 'Chomsky Interview 5', *ZMag*, www.zmag.org/chomsky_

interview_5.htm (accessed 3 September 2007).
Christenson, S. (2005) 'Abu Ghraib Inmate Describes Torment; Insurgent from Syria Details Humiliation, Laughter', *San Antonio Express-News*.
Christie, A. (2006) 'Guarding the Truth', *Washington Post*, 26 February.
Clinton, H.R. (2000) '"The Century of the Woman" Talk It Over', 7 June. http://clinton3.nara.gov/WH/EOP/First_Lady/html/columns/2000/hrc06072000.html (accessed 1 June 2006).
CNN.com (2004) 'Ex-chief of Iraqi Prisons Baffled by Suspension', 23 May, http://ww.cnn.com/2004/WORLD/meast/05/26/iraq.abuse/index.html.
CNN.com (2007) 'Female Suicide Bomber Kills 40 at University', 26 February, www.cnn.com/2007/world/meast/02/25/iraq.main/index.html?eref=rss_topstories (accessed 4 March 2007).
Cockburn, C. (2001a) 'Gender, Armed Conflict, and Peace Processes', *Cyprus Review*, vol. 13, no. 1.
Cockburn, C. (2001b) 'The Gender Dynamics of Armed Conflict and Political Violence', in C. Moser and F. Clark (eds), *Victims, Perpetrators or Actors? Gender, Armed Conflict and Political Violence*, Zed Books, London.
Cockburn, C. (1991) *In the Way of Women: Men's Resistance to Sex Equality in Organizations*, Zed Books, London.
Cockburn, C., and D. Zarkov (eds) (2002) *The Post-War Moment: Militaries, Masculinities, and International Peacekeeping*, Zed Books, London.
Cohler, D. (2006) 'Keeping the Home Front Burning: Renegotiating Gender and Sexuality in United States Mass Media after September 11', *Feminist Media Studies*, vol. 6, no. 3.
Cohn, C., and S. Ruddick (2002) 'A Feminist Ethical Perspective on Weapons of Mass Destruction', in S. Lee and S. Hashmi (eds), *Ethics and Weapons of Mass Destruction*, Princeton University Press, Princeton NJ.
Coman, J., and C. Freeman (2004) 'U.S. Soldiers Seen Raping Women in New Jail Photos', *Telegraph*, 5 September.
Combs, N.A. (2003) 'Prosecutor v. Plavsic. Case No. IT-00-39&40/1-S', *American Journal of International Law*, vol. 97, no. 4.
Conley, B. (2004) 'For the Women of Chechnya, Hope Dies Last', *Journal of Human Rights*, vol. 3, no. 3.
Connell, R.W. (2003) 'Globalisation and the Future of Gender', in D. Bird, W.W. and T. White (eds), *Future Imaginings: Sexualities and Genders in the New Millennium*, University of Western Australia Press, Perth.
Connell, R.W. (1995) *Masculinities*, University of California Press, Berkeley.
Connell, R.W. (1990) 'The State, Gender, and Sexual Politics: Theory and Appraisal', *Theory and Society* 41.
Constable, B. (2006) 'Why Hasn't the U.S. Joined Chile, Liberia in the 21st Century?', *Chicago Daily Herald*, 14 March.
Cooper, H.H.A. (1979) 'Woman as Terrorist', in F. Adler and R.J. Simon (eds), *The Criminology of Deviant Women*, Houghton Mifflin, Boston MA.
Copeland, L. (2002) 'Female Suicide Bombers: The New Factor in the Mideast's Deadly Equation', *Washington Post*, 27 April.
Copelon, R. (1999) 'Surfacing Gender: Reengraving Crimes against Women in Humanitarian Law', in N.A. Dombrowski (ed.), *Women and War in the Twentieth*

Century: *Enlisted with or without Consent*, Garland, New York.
Coughlin, K.M. (2000) 'Women, War, and the Veil: Muslim Women in Resistance and Combat', in G.J. De Groot and C. Penniston-Bird (eds), *A Soldier and a Woman: Sexual Integration in the Military*, Pearson, New York.
Cox, R. (1986) 'Social Forces, States, and World Orders: Beyond International Relations Theory', in R.O. Keohane (ed.), *Neorealism and Its Critics*, Columbia University Press, New York.
Crayton, J.W. (1983) 'Terrorism and the Psychology of the Self', in L.Z. Freedman and Y. Alexader (eds), *Perspectives on Terrorism*, Scholarly Resources, Wilmington DE.
Crenshaw, M. (2000) 'The Psychology of Terrorism: An Agenda for the 21st Century', *Political Psychology*, vol. 21, no. 2.
Crenshaw, M. (1998) 'The Logic of Terrorism: Terrorist Behavior as a Product of Strategic Choice', in W. Reich (ed.), *Origins of Terrorism: Psychologies, Ideologies, Theologies, States of Mind*, Woodrow Wilson Center Press, Washington DC.
Crim, B. (2000) 'Silent Partners: Women and Warfare in Early Modern Europe', in G.J. De Groot and C. Penniston-Bird (eds), *A Soldier and a Woman: Sexual Integration in the Military*, Pearson, New York.
Croft, W., and D.A. Cruse (2004) *Cognitive Linguistics*, Cambridge University Press, Cambridge.
Crosby, F. (1982) *Relative Deprivation and Working Women*, Oxford University Press, New York.
Crosby, F. (1976) 'A Model of Egoistical Relative Deprivation', *Psychological Review* 83.
Cunningham, K.J. (2003) 'Cross-Regional Trends in Female Terrorism', *Studies in Conflict and Terrorism*, vol. 26, no. 3.
Cuomo, C.J. (1996) 'War is Not Just an Event: Reflections on the Significance of Everyday Violence', *Hypatia*, vol. 11, no. 4.
Curphy, S. (2003) '1 in 7 US Military Personnel in Iraq is Female', *Women's ENews*, www.womensenews.org/article.cfm/dyn/aid/1265/context/cover/ (accessed 1 June 2006).
D'Amico, F. (1998) 'Feminist Perspectives on Women Warriors', in L.A. Lorentzen and J. Turpin (eds), *The Women and War Reader*, New York University Press, New York.
D'Amico, F. (1990) 'Women at Arms: The Combat Controversy', *Minerva Quarterly Report on Women in the Military*, vol. 8, no. 2.
D'Amico, F., and L. Weinstein (eds) (1999) *Gender Camouflage: Women and the U.S. Military*, New York University Press, New York.
D'Amico, F., and P.R. Beckman (1995) *Women in World Politics: An Introduction*, Bergin & Garvey, Westport CT.
Dahl, H.M. (2000) 'A Perceptive or Reflective State?', *European Journal of Women's Studies*, vol. 7, no. 4.
Dajani, S. (1994) 'Between National and Social Liberation: The Palestinian Women's Movement in the Israeli Occupied West Bank and the Gaza Strip', in T. Mayer (ed.), *Women and the Israeli Occupation: The Politics of Change*, Routledge, New York.
Dallaire, R., and B. Beardsley (2003) *Shake Hands with the Devil: The Failure of*

Humanity in Rwanda, Random House, Toronto.
Davies, M.L., and C. Hughes (2004) 'Inside the Gym: First Harrowing Pictures', *Mirror*, 8 September.
De Groot, G.J. (2001) 'A Few Good Women: Gender Stereotypes, the Military, and Peacekeeping', *International Peacekeeping*.
De Groot, G.J. (2000a) 'Arms and the Woman', in G.J. De Groot and C. Peniston-Bird (eds), *A Soldier and a Woman: Sexual Integration in the Military*, Pearson, New York.
De Groot, G.J. (2000b) 'Lipstick on Her Nipples, Cordite in Her Hair: Sex and Romance among British Servicewomen during the Second World War', in G.J. De Groot and C. Peniston-Bird (eds), *A Soldier and a Woman: Sexual Integration in the Military*, Pearson, New York.
Debatin, B. (1995) *Die Rationalitat der Metapher*, De Gruyter, Berlin.
Delahoussaye, M. (2005) 'US Soldier Gets Six Months in Jail for Iraqi Abuse', *Middle East Online*, 18 May.
Deleuze, G., and F. Guattari (1987) *A Thousand Plateaus: Capitalism and Schizophrenia*, trans. B. Massumi, University of Minnesota Press, Minneapolis.
Demichele, M.T. (2004) 'Men and Masculinities: Key Themes and New Directions', *Journal of Men's Studies*, vol. 12, no. 1.
Dickey, C. (2005) 'Women of Al Qaeda', *Newsweek*, December, www.msnbc.msn.com/id/10315095/site/newsweek/ (accessed 5 December 2005).
Dietz, E. (1996) 'Violence against Women in the United States: An International Solution', *Arizona Journal of International and Comparative Law* 13.
Dimen, M., and V. Goldner (eds) (2002) *Gender in Psychoanalytic Space*, Other Press, New York.
Dougherty, J. (2003) 'Chechnya's "Black Widow" Bombers', 11 July, www.cnn.com/2003/world/europe/07/11/russia.black.widows/ (accessed 31 March 2006).
Douglas, W. (2003) 'A Case of Race? One POW Acclaimed and Another Ignored', *Seattle Times*, 29 November.
Dollard, J., N.E. Miller, L.M. Doob, O.H. Merver, R.R. Sears (1944) *Frustration and Aggression*, Kegan Paul, London.
Donsbach, M. (2004) 'Celtic Queen Who Challenged Rome', *Military History*, vol. 21, no. 1.
Dow, J. (2007) Personal correspondence, 13 March.
Dowler, L. (1998) '"And They Think I'm Just a Nice Old Lady": Women and War in Belfast, Northern Ireland', *Gender, Place and Culture – A Journal of Feminist Geography*, vol. 5, no. 2.
Drumbl, M.A. (2005) 'The ICTR and Justice for Rwandan Women', *New England Journal of International and Comparative Law* 12.
Drumbl, M.A. (2004) 'Rights, Culture, and Crime: The Role of Rule of Law for the Women of Afghanistan', *Columbia Journal of Transnational Law* 42.
Duncan, G. (2004) 'Women of the Third Reich', http://members.iinet.net.au/~gduncan/women.html (accessed 3 September 2007).
Dworkin, A. (1986) 'Pornography is a Civil Rights Issue', in A. Dworkin (ed.), *Letters from a War Zone*, Lawrence Hill Books, Brooklyn.
The Economist (2004) 'Victims of a Conflict Without End', 6 September, www.

economist.com/agenda/displayStory.cfm?story_id=3170269 (accessed 4 April 2006).

The Economist (2004) 'Shireen and Others Like Her', 22 May.

The Economist (2003) 'The Black Widow's Revenge', 10 July, http://economist.com/PrinterFriendly.cfm?Story_ID=1914363 (accessed 4 April 2006).

Edgar, Spc. L.B. (2005) 'Harman Found Guilty for Abu Ghraib', *Army Public Affairs Record*.

Ehrenrich, B. (2005) *Abu Ghraib: The Politics of Torture*, North Atlantic Books, Berkeley CA.

Ehrenrich, B. (2004) 'Prison Abuse: Feminism's Assumptions Upended: A Uterus is Not a Substitute for a Conscience', *Los Angeles Times*, 16 May.

Eichler, M. (2006) 'A Gendered Analysis of the Chechen Wars', *International Feminist Journal of Politics*, vol. 8, no. 4.

Eisenstein, Z. (2004) 'Sexual Humiliation, Gender Confusion and the Horrors at Abu Ghraib', *ZNet*, www.zmag.org/content/showarticle.cfm?ItemID=5751 (accessed 1 January 2007).

Eke, S. (2003) 'Chechnya's Female Bombers', 7 July, www.news.bbc.co.uk/2/hi/europe/3052934.stm (accessed 31 March 2006).

El Basri, A. (2004) 'Not So Innocent', *Liberation Daily*, 19 January, www.voices-unabridged.org/article2.php?is_ss_article=196&id_rub=1&sous_rub=violence&numero=1 (accessed 1 January 2007).

El-Bushra (2000) 'Transformed Conflict: Some Thoughts on a Gendered Understanding of Conflict Process, in S. Jacobs, R. Jacobson and J. Marchbank (eds), *States of Conflict: Gender, Violence, and Resistance*, Zed Books, London.

Ellingwood, K., and S. Simon (2003) 'War with Iraq: Hope and Despair for POWs' Families', *Los Angeles Times*, 25 March.

Elshtain, J.B. (2003) *Just War against Terror: The Burden of American Power in a Violent World*, Basic Books, New York.

Elshtain, J.B. (ed.) (1992a) *Just War Theory*, New York University Press, New York.

Elshtain, J.B. (1992b) 'Just War as Politics: What the Gulf War Told Us about Contemporary American Life', in D.E. Decosse (ed.), *But Was It Just? Reflections on the Morality of the Persian Gulf War*, Doubleday, New York.

Elshtain, J.B. (1987a) *Women and War*, New York University Press, New York.

Elshtain, J.B. (1987b) 'Against Androgeny', in A. Phillips (ed.), *Feminism and Equality*, New York University Press, New York.

Elshtain, J.B. (1985) 'Reflections on War and Political Discourse: Realism, Just War, and Feminism in a Nuclear Age', *Political Theory*, vol. 13, no. 1.

Elshtain, J.B. (1983) 'On Beautiful Souls, Just Warriors, and Feminist Consciousness', in J. Stiehm (ed.), *Women and Men's Wars*, Pergamon Press, Oxford.

Elshtain, J.B. (1981) *Public Man, Private Woman: Women in Social and Political Thought*, Princeton University Press, Princeton NJ.

Emmons, R.A. (1987) 'Narcissism: Theory and Measurement', *Journal of Personality and Social Psychology*, vol. 52, no. 1.

Engle, K. (2003) 'Feminism and Its (Dis)contents: Criminalizing Wartime Rape in Bosnia and Herzegovina', *American Journal of International Law* 99.

Enloe, C. (2000) *Maneuvers: The International Politics of Militarizing Women's Lives*, University of California Press, Berkeley.
Enloe, C. (1993) *The Morning After: Sexual Politics at the End of the Cold War*, University of California Press, Berkeley.
Enloe, C. (1990) 'Womenandchildren: Making Feminist Sense of the Persian Gulf War', *Village Voice*, 25 September.
Enloe, C. (2004) *The Curious Feminist: Searching for Women in a New Age of Empire*, University of California Press, Berkeley.
Enloe, C. (1983) *Does Khaki Become You? The Militarization of Women's Lives*, Pluto Press, London.
Eremitcheva, G., and E. Zdravomyslova (2001) 'Die Bewgung der Soldatenmutter-eine zivilgellschaftliche initiative: der fall St. Petersburg', in M. Ritter (ed.), *Ziviligesellschaf und Gender-Politik in RuBland*, Campus Verlag, Frankfurt.
Express (2004) 'Fanatical Sisters of Suicide' 3 September, http://web.lexis-nexis.com/universe (accessed 8 June 2006).
Farrell, S. (2006) 'Grandmother Blows Herself Up in Gaza', *The Times Online*, 24 November, www.timesonline.co.uk/article/0,,3-2469119,00.htm (accessed 1 January 2007).
Fattah, H.M. (2005) 'Jordan Arrests Iraqi Woman in Hotel Blasts', *New York Times*, 14 November.
Fanon, F. (1965) *The Wretched of the Earth*, Grove Press, New York.
Fausto-Sterling, A. (2005) 'Bare Bones of Sex: Part I, Sex and Gender', *Signs: A Journal of Women in Culture and Society*, vol. 20, no. 2.
Fausto-Sterling, A. (2000) S*exing the Body: Gender Politics and the Construction of Sexuality*, Basic Books, New York.
Fay, Maj. Gen. G. (2004) 'AR 15-6 Investigation of the Abu Ghraib Detention Facility and the 205th Military Intelligence Division', declassified document.
Fein, H. (1990) 'Genocide: A Sociological Perspective', *Current Sociology*, vol. 38, no. 1.
Ferguson, K.E. (1993) *The Man Question: Visions of Subjectivity in Feminist Theory*, University of California Press, Berkeley.
Festic, F. (2003) 'Antigone in (Post-) Modern Palestine', *Hecate*, 1 October.
Fisher, M. (2004) 'Bomber Kills 2 Israeli Police', *The Gazette*, 23 September, http://web.lexis-nexis.com/universe (accessed 31 March 2006).
Fitzpatrick, J. (1994) 'The Use of International Human Rights Norms to Combat Violence against Women', in R.J. Cook (ed.), *Human Rights of Women: National and International Perspectives*, University of Pennsylvania Press, Philadelphia.
Fitzpatrick, P. (2000) 'It Isn't Easy Being Biljana', *Central Europe Review*, vol. 22, no. 2.
Flax, J. (1987) 'Postmodernism and Gender Relations in Feminist Theory', *Signs: Journal of Women in Culture and Society*, vol. 12, no. 4.
Foster, M.D., and K. Matheson (1995) 'Double Relative Deprivation: Combining the Personal and Political', *Personality and Social Psychology Bulletin*, vol. 21, no. 11.

Franchetti, M. (2003) '"Wish Me Luck", Said the Suicide Widow Waiting to Kill Russians', *Sunday Times*, 17 August.
Freud, S. (1961) *Civilizations and Its Discontents*, trans. and ed. J. Strachey, W.W. Norton, New York.
Friedman, D., and D. McAdam (1992) 'Collective Identity and Activism: Networks, Choices and the Life of a Social Movement', in A. Morris and C.M. Mueller (eds), *Frontiers in Social Movement Theory*, Yale University Press, New Haven CT.
Galtung, J. (1971) 'A Structural Theory of Imperialism' *Journal of Peace Research*, vol. 8, no. 2.
Gardam, J.G. (1993a) 'Proportionality and Force in International Law', *American Journal of International Law*, vol. 87, no. 3.
Gardam, J.G. (1993b) 'Gender and Non-combatant Immunity', *Transnational Law and Contemporary Problems*, vol. 3, no. 345.
Gentry, C. (2006) 'Overcoming Biological Determinism: Seeing the Female Terrorist for Who She Is', Paper Presented at the Annual Meeting of the International Studies Association, San Diego, California.
Gentry, C. (2004) 'The Relationship Between New Social Movement Theory and Terrorism Studies: The Role of Leadership, Membership, Ideology and Gender', *Terrorism and Political Violence*, vol. 16, no. 2, Summer.
Gentry, C., and L. Sjoberg (2007) 'Reduced to Bad Sex: Narratives of Violent Women from the Bible to the War on Terror', *International Relations*.
Geringer, J. (2002) 'Recipe for Death', *CourtTV Crime Library*, www.crimelibrary.com.
Giacaman, R., and P. Johnson (1989) 'Palestinian Women: Building Barricades and Breaking Barriers', in Z. Lockman, Z. and J. Beinin (eds), *Intifada: The Palestinian Uprising Against Israeli Occupation*, MERIP, Washington DC.
Gibbs, N. (2003) 'The Private Jessica Lynch', *Time*, 17 November, www.time.com/time/magazine/article/0,9171,1006147,00.html (accessed 1 January 2007).
Gibson-Graham, J.K. (1994) '"Stuffed if I Know!": Reflections on Post-modern Feminist Social Research', *Gender, Place, and Culture*, vol. 1, no. 2.
Gilbert, P.R. (2002) 'Discourses of Female Violence and Societal Gender Stereotypes', *Violence against Women*, vol. 8, no. 11.
Goering, D., and W. Woo (1997) 'Comparison of Service Populations of the Vietnam Conflict and the Persian Gulf War', *DMDC Data Request Archive*, www.dmdc.osd.mil/ids/archive/vietnam/body.htm.
Gogola, T. (2006) 'Chris Shays: Porn Loser', *New Haven Advocate*, 19 October, www.ctnow.com/custom/nmm/newhavenadvocate/hce-nha-1019–nh43votingrites43.artoct19,0,577106.story (accessed 1 January 2007).
Goldstein, J.S. (2001) *War and Gender: How Gender Shapes the War System and Vice Versa*, Cambridge University Press, Cambridge.
Gole, N. (2000) 'Snapshots of Islamic Modernities', *Daedalus*, vol. 129, no. 1.
Goodman, J. (1986) *The Moors Murders: The Trial of Myra Hindley and Ian Brady*, David & Charles, London.
Gourevitch, P. (1998) *We Wish to Inform You That Tomorrow We Will Be Killed With Our Families: Stories from Rwanda*, Picador, New York.
Groskop, V. (2004a) 'Women at the Heart of the Terror Cells', *Guardian*, 5 Sep-

tember, www.guardian.co.uk/chechnya/Story/0,,1297692,00.html (accessed 31 March 2006).

Groskop, V. (2004b) 'Chechnya's Deadly Black Widows', *New Statesman*, 6 September, http://web.lexis-nexis.com/universe (accessed 8 June 2006).

Gubar, S. (1977) 'The Female Monster in Augustan Satire', *Signs: Journal of Women in Culture and Society*, vol. 3, no. 2.

Gunaratna, R. (2005) 'The Prospects of Global Terrorism', *Society*, vol. 42, no. 6, September/October.

Gurr, T.R. (1970) *Why Men Rebel*, Princeton University Press, Princeton NJ.

Hafner-Burton, E., and M. Pollack (2002) 'Mainstreaming Gender in Global Governance', *European Journal of International Relations*, vol. 8, no. 3.

Hall, J. (2004) 'Black Widows and Bombs – The Hell of School's Hostages', *The Scotsman*, 8 September.

Hall, J.R. (1999) *Cultures of Inquiry: From Epistemology to Discourse in Sociohistorical Research*, Cambridge University Press, Cambridge.

Hamilton, E. (1940) *Mythology: Timeless Tales of Gods and Heroes*, Penguin, New York.

Harbison, R. (2006) 'Boudica: The Life of Britain's Legendary Warrior Queen', *Library Journal*, vol. 131, no. 11.

Hammami, R. (1990) 'Women, the Hijab, and Intifada', *Middle East Report*, vol. 20, no. 3/4.

Hansen, L. (2001) 'Gender, Nation, Rape: Bosnia and the Construction of Security', *International Feminist Journal of Politics*, vol. 3, no. 1.

Haraway, D. (1988) 'Situated Knowledges: The Science Question in Feminism and the Privilege of Partial Perspective', *Feminist Studies*, vol. 14, no. 3.

Hargreaves, S., and A. Cunningham (2004) 'The Politics of Terror', *Lancet* 363, 12 June.

Harman, D. (2003) 'A Woman on Trial for Rwanda's Massacre', *Christian Science Monitor*, 7 March, www.csmonitor.com/2003/0307/p09s01-woaf.html (accessed 1 January 2007).

Harnden, T. (2004) 'The Boy Bomber: "I Did It Because People Don't Like Me"', *Ottawa Citizen*, 26 March, http://web.lexis-nexis.com/universe (accessed 8 June 2006).

Harris, F. (2005) 'Lynndie England Convicted of Abusing Iraqi Prisoners', *Telegraph*, 27 September.

Hart, L. (1994) *Fatal Women: Lesbian Sexuality and the Mark of Aggression*, Princeton University Press, Princeton NJ.

Hartmann, H. (ed.) (2006) *Gendering Politics and Policy: Recent Developments in Europe, Latin America, and the United States*, Haworth Press, New York.

Harwood, A. (2004) 'Camp X-Rated: Lynddie's Shocking Sex Acts to Torment Iraqi Prisoners', *Daily Record*, 14 May.

Hedoes, S.J. (2004) 'Bush Calls Abuse of Prisoners Abhorrent', *Chicago Tribune*, 6 May.

Hegel, G.W. (1977) *The Phenomenology of Spirit*, Clarendon Press, Oxford.

Hendrix, S.N. (2000) 'In the Army: Women, Camp Followers, and the Gender Roles in the British Army in the French and Indian Wars, 1775–1765', in G.J. DeGroot and C. Bird-Peniston (eds), *A Soldier and a Woman: Sexual Integration*

in the Military, Pearson Education, Harlow.
Hermann, P. (2004) 'Lining Up to Die', *Baltimore Sun*, 31 January, http://web.lexis-nexis.com/universe (accessed 9 May 2006).
Hester, D.J. (2004) 'Intersexes and the End of Gender: Corporeal Ethics and Post-Gender Bodies', *Journal of Gender Studies*, vol. 13, no. 3.
Hey, V. (2006) 'The Politics of Performative Resignification', *British Journal of the Sociology of Education*, vol. 27, no. 4.
Hirschmann, N. (2004) *The Subject of Liberty: Towards a Feminist Theory of Freedom*, Princeton University Press, Princeton NJ.
Hirschmann, N. (1989) 'Freedom, Recognition, and Obligation: A Feminist Approach to Political Theory', *American Political Science Review*, vol. 83, no. 4.
Hoffman, B. (2006) *Inside Terrorism*, Columbia University Press, New York.
Hoffman, B. (2005) 'Does Our Counter-Terrorism Strategy Match the Threat?', testimony before the Committee on International Relations, Subcommittee on International Terrorism and Nonproliferation, US House of Representatives, 29 September.
Hoffman, D.E. (2004) 'Chechen Conflict Now Rages Beyond Expectations', *Washington Post*, 2 September, www.msnbc.msn.com/id/5890837/print/1/displaymode/1098/ (accessed 2 September 2004).
Hoffman, J. (2001) *Gender and Sovereignty: Feminism, the State, and International Relations*, Palgrave, New York.
Holt, M. (2003) 'Palestinian Women, Violence, and the Peace Process', *Development in Practice*, vol. 13, no. 2/3.
Hoogenson, G., and K. Stuvoy (2006) 'Gender, Resistance, and Human Security', *Security Dialogue*, vol. 37, no. 4.
Hoogenson, G., and S.V. Rottem (2004) 'Gender, Identity, and the Subject of Security', *Security Dialogue*, vol. 35, no. 3.
Hooper, C. (2001) *Manly States: Masculinities, International Relations, and Gender Politics*, Columbia University Press, New York.
House, E.R., and D. Southerland (1996) *A Very Violent Rebel*, University of Tennessee Press, Knoxville.
Hudson, H. (2005) 'Doing Security as though Humans Matter: A Feminist Perspective on Gender and the Politics of Human Security', *Security Dialogue*, vol. 36, no. 3.
Human Rights Watch/Africa (1996) *Shattered Lives: Sexual Violence During the Rwandan Genocide and Its Aftermath*, www.hrw.org/reports/1996/Rwanda.htm (accessed 1 January 2007).
Hussain, A. (2000) 'Joy Harjo and Her Poetics as Praxis', *Wicazo Sa Review*, Fall.
Huston, N. (1983) 'Tales of War and Tears of Women', in J. Steihm (ed.), *Women and Men's Wars*, Pergamon Press, Oxford.
Ignatieff, M. (1995) *Blood and Belonging: Journeys into the New Nationalisms*, Farrar, Straus & Giroux, New York.
Inglehart, R., and P. Norris (2003) *Rising Tide: Gender Equality and Cultural Change Around the World*, Cambridge University Press, Cambridge.
International Committee of the Red Cross. (2005) 'Women and War', www.icrc.org/eng/women/ (accessed 1 June 2006).

REFERENCES

Internet Weekly Report (2006) 'The Women of Al Qaeda', www.internetweekly. org/photo_cartoons/cartoon_women_of_al_qaeda.html (accessed 4 August 2006).

Isayev, R. (2004) 'The Chechen Woman and Her Role in the "New" Society', *Prague Watchdog*, 21 June, www.watchdog.cz/index.php?show=000000-000015-000006-000008&lang=1 (accessed 31 March 2006).

Isenberg, N. (1992) 'The Personal is Political: Gender, Feminism, and the Politics of Discourse Theory', *American Quarterly*, vol. 44, no. 3.

Itano, N. (2002) '3000 Women Await Trials for Genocide', *Women's ENews*, 20 December, www.womensenews.org/article.cfm/dyn/aid/1152.

Itar–Tass News Agency (2003) 'Two Would-be Women Suicide Bombers Killed in Chechnya', 24 July, www.hrvc.net/news6-03/25b-7-2003.htm (accessed 1 January 2007).

Jaber, H. (2003) 'Inside the World of the Palestinean Suicide Bomber', *Sunday Times*, 24 March.

Jacinto, L. (2002) 'Chechen 'Black Widows' Bring New Fears', *ABC News*, 29 October, www.abcnews.go.com/International/print?id=7819 (accessed 31 March 2006).

Jacobs, C. (2002) 'The 21st Century will be the Century of the Woman', *Moondance. org*, www.moondance.org/2002/fall02/sns/century.html (accessed 1 June 2006).

Jacobs, S., R. Jacobson and J. Marchbank (eds) (2000) *States of Conflict: Gender, Violence and Resistance*, Zed Books, London.

Jagger, M., and K. Richards (2005) 'Dangerous Beauty', *A Bigger Bang*, Virgin.

Jagodzinski, J. (2006) 'The Trauma of the Image: Prisoner "Abuse" in Abu Ghraib Prison', *Studies in Media and Information Literacy Education*, vol. 6, no. 1.

Jawaad, I.A. (1990) 'The Palestinian Woman's Movement in the Uprising', in M.C. Hudson (ed.), *The Palestinians: New Directions*, Center for Contemporary Arab Studies, Georgetown University: Washington D.C.

Jesch, J. (1991) *Women in the Viking Age*, Boydell Press, London.

Jones, A. (ed.) (2004) *Gender and Genocide*, Vanderbilt University Press, Nashville TN.

Jones, A. (2002) 'Gendercide and Genocide in Rwanda', *Journal of Genocide Studies* 4.

Jones, D.E. (1997) *Women Warriors: A History*, Brassey's, Washington DC.

Kabasakal, Z., and F. Arat (2004) 'Women for Ending Israeli Occupation in Palestine and for Building Peace', *International Feminist Journal of Politics*, vol. 6, no. 3.

Kabeer, N. (2003) *Gender Mainstreaming in Poverty Eradication and the Millennium Development Goals: A Handbook for Policymakers*, Commonwealth Secretariat, Ottawa.

Kahn, P. (2004) 'Rising Tide: Gender Equality and Cultural Change around the World', *Perspectives on Politics*, vol. 2, no. 2.

Kaldor, M. (2006) *New and Old Wars: Organized Violence in a Global Era*, Polity Press, Cambridge.

Kalman, M. (2004) 'Day of the Terrorist', *Daily Mail*, 1 September.

Kampfner, J. (2003) 'The Truth about Jessica', *Guardian*, 15 May.
Kanaana, S. (1993) 'The Role of Women in Intifada Legends', *Contemporary Legend* vol. 3, Aberystwyth.
Karpinski, J. (2006) Personal interview.
Karpinksi, J., and S. Strasser (2005) *One Woman's Army: The Commanding General of Abu Ghraib Tells Her Story*, Miramax Books, New York.
Katz, R.S. (2003) 'Genocide: The Ultimate Racial Profiling', *Journal of Law and Social Challenges*, vol. 5, no. 3.
Katz, Y. (2006) '68-Year-Old Woman Suicide Bomber Wounds Three Soldiers', *Jerusalem Post*, 24 November, http://web.lexis-nexis.com/universe (accessed 28 November 2006).
Kaufamn-Osborn, T. (2005) 'Gender Trouble at Abu Ghraib?', *Politics and Gender*, vol. 1, no. 4.
Keitner, C. (2002) 'Victim or Vamp? Images of Violent Women in the Criminal Justice System', *Columbia Journal of Law and Gender* 11.
Kelley, J. (2002) 'Al-Qaeda Fragmented, Smaller, But Still Deadly', *USAToday*, 9 September, www.usatoday.com/news/world/2002-09-09-1acover_x.htm (accessed 4 August 2006).
Kelly, L. (2003) 'Disabusing the Definition of Domestic Abuse: How Women Batter Men and the Role of the Feminist State', 30 Fla. St. U. L. Rev. 791.
Khalilov, R. (2003) 'Moral Justifications of Secession: The Case of Chechnya', *Central Asian Survey*, vol. 22 no. 4, December.
Khong, Y.F. (1992) *Analogies at War: Korea, Munich, Dien Bien Phu, and the Vietnam Decisions of 1965*, Princeton University Press, Princeton NJ.
Kipling, R. (1923) *Rudyard Kipling's Verse: Inclusive Edition, 1885–1918*, Doubleday, Garden City NY.
King, N., and M. McCaughey (2002) 'What's a Mean Woman Like You Doing in a Movie Like This', in *Reel Knockouts: Violent Women in the Movies*, University of Texas Press, Austin.
Knight, W.A. (2005) 'We Shouldn't Be Surprised by the Female Face of Terror', *Edmonton Journal*, 6 October, http://web.lexis-nexis.com/universe (accessed 8 June 2006).
Knowles, J. (2004) 'Crime and Punishment: Maxine Carr and the Evil Women', *The F Word: Contemporary UK Feminism*, January, at www.thefword.org/features/2004/06/crime_and_punisment_maxine_carr_and_other_evil_women (accessed 9 March 2007).
Kowalski, J.O. (2004) 'Role of Women Suicide Killers Studied', *Nottingham Evening Post*, 18 February.
Krajicek, D. (2004) 'Guts Blown Out', *CourtTV Crime Library*, www.crimelibrary.com.
Kramer, M. (2005) 'Guerrilla Warfare, Counterinsurgency and Terrorism in the North Caucasus: The Military Dimension of the Russian–Chechen Conflict', *Europe Asia Studies*, vol. 57, no. 2.
Kronsell, A. (2006) 'Methods for Studying Silences: Gender Analysis in Institutions of Hegemonic Masculinity', in B.A. Ackerly, M. Stern and J. True (eds), *Feminist Methodologies for International Relations*, Cambridge University Press, Cambridge.

Kumar, K. (2001) *Women and Civil War: Impact, Organization, and Action*, Lynne Rienner, Boulder CO.

Kurtz, H. (2001) 'Peter Jennings, in the News for What He Didn't Say', *Washington Post*, 24 September.

Kuthjaklvokovic, S., and J. Hagan (2006) 'The Politics of Punishment: The Siege of Sarajevo: Towards a Conflict Theory of Perceived International Justice', *Law and Society Review*, vol. 40, no. 2.

Laffey, M., and J. Weldes (1997) 'Beyond Belief: Ideas and Symbolic Technologies in the Study of International Relations', *European Journal of International Relations*, vol. 3, no. 2.

Lakoff, G. (1993) 'The Contemporary Theory of Metaphor', in A. Ortony (ed.), *Metaphor and Thought*, 2nd edn, Cambridge University Press, Cambridge.

Lakoff, G., and M. Johnson (1999) *Philosophy in the Flesh*, Basic Books, New York.

Lakoff, G., and M. Johnson (1980) *Metaphors We Live By*, University of Chicago Press, Chicago.

Landesman, P. (2002a) 'A Woman's Work', *New York Times* Magazine, 15 September.

Landesman, P. (2002b) 'The Minister of Rape', *Toronto Star*, 21 September.

Landsberg, M. (2002) 'Men Behind Most Atrocities, But Women Are Singled Out', *Toronto Star*, 21 September.

Landsberg, M. (2002) 'Misplaced Blame: With Many Men Behind the Rwanda Atrocities, Why Does the Media Single Out a Woman as a Unique Monster?', *Hamilton Spectator Magazine*, 28 September.

Lane, R.J., and J. Wurts (1998) *In Search of the Woman Warrior: Role Models for Modern Women*, Element, Boston MA.

Lavendera, E. (2005) 'House of Mirrors: Former Soldier Revisits Abu Ghraib Disgrace', CNN.com, 28 June, http://edition.cnn.com.2005/US/05/26/cruz.abu.ghraib/.

Lentini, P. (1996) 'Hegemonic Masculinities in Russia', in V. Rikhomirov (ed.), *Search of Identity: Five Years Since the Fall of the Soviet Union*, Centre for Russia and Euro-Asian Studies, Melbourne.

Levinson, A.G. (2004) 'The Role of Gender in Russia's Attitudes Towards the Second Chechen Campaign', *Sociological Research*, vol. 43, no. 2.

Life Application Bible (1991) Zondervan Publishing House, Grand Rapids MI.

Lindsey, R. (2002) 'From Atrocity to Data: Historiographies of Rape in the Former Yugoslavia and the Gendering of Genocide', *Patterns of Prejudice*, vol. 36, no. 4.

Lloyd, A. (1995) *Doubly Deviant, Doubly Damned: Society's Treatment of Violent Women*, Penguin Books, London.

MacDonald, E. (1992) *Shoot the Women First*, Random House, New York.

MacKinnon, C. (2001) *Sex Equality*, Foundation Press, New York.

MacKinnon, C. (1994) 'Rape, Genocide, and Women's Human Rights', *Harvard Women's Law Journal* 17.

MacKinnon, C. (1993) 'Crimes of War, Crimes of Peace', *UCLA Women's Law Journal* 4.

MacKnick, B.M. (1999) 'Military Women: Their Future Roles in Combat', *Strategic*

Research Report, Army War College, Carlisle PA.
McCreary, D.R. (1994) 'The Male Role and Avoiding Femininity', Sex Roles, vol. 3, no. 9–10.
McDonald, M. (2003) 'Chechnya's Eerie Rebels: Black Widows', The Gazette, 24 October.
McGraw, S. (2006) 'Leslie Nelson: Deadly Transsexual', CourtTV Crime Library, www.crimelibrary.com.
McKelvey, T. (2006) 'A Soldier's Tale', Marie Claire, http://magazines.ivillage.com/marieclaire/mind/issues/articles/0,,434739_703130,00.html (accessed 1 January 2007).
McKenzie, C., and N. Stolgar (eds) (2000) Relational Autonomy: Feminist Perspectives on Autonomy, Agency, and the Social Self, Oxford University Press, Oxford.
McLaughlin, D. (2003) 'Widows with a Death Wish Spearhead Terror War', Daily Telegraph, 7 July.
McNay, L. (2004) 'Agency and Experience: Gender as a Lived Relation', Sociological Review, vol. 52, no. 2.
Mainville, M. (2003) '"Black Widows" Terrorize Russia', Toronto Star, 13 July, www.cdi.org/Russia/264-10.cfm (accessed 31 March 2006).
Manners, T. (1995) Deadlier than the Male, Pan Books, London.
Marcus, J. (1978) 'Art and Anger', Feminist Studies, vol. 41, no. 1.
Margalit, A. (2003) 'The Suicide Bomber', New York Times Review of Books, vol. 50, no. 1.
Martin, S.T. (2003) 'Her Job: Lock Up Iraq's Bad Guys', St. Petersburg Times, 14 December, www.sptimes.com/2003/12/14/Worldandnation/Her_job_Lock_up_Iraq.shtml (accessed 1 January 2007).
Mason, C. (2005) 'The Hillbilly Defense: Culturally Mediating United States Terror at Home and Abroad', National Women's Studies Association Journal, vol. 17, no. 3.
Matthews, J. (2003) Women and War, University of Michigan Press, Ann Arbor.
Matthews, O. (2004) 'So Warped by Hate, They Will Kill Anyone to Take Revenge against Russia', Daily Mail, 4 September.
Maynard, M., and J. Purvis (eds) (1994) Researching Women's Lives From a Feminist Perspective, Taylor & Francis, London.
Messner, M.A. (1997) The Politics of Masculinities, Sage, London.
Melvern, L. (2004) Conspiracy to Murder: The Rwandan Genocide, Verso, London.
MEMRI (2005) 'Al-Jazeera Special About Hanadi Jaradat, Other Female Suicide Bombers, Their Families and the People Who Send Them to Die', http://memritv.org/Transcript.asp?P1=817 (accessed 17 November 2006).
Meyer, L.D. (1992) 'Creating GI Jane: The Regulation of Sexuality and Sexual Behavior in the Women's Army Corps during World War II', Feminist Studies, vol. 18, no. 3.
Miller, A.A. (2003) 'From the International Criminal Tribunal for Rwanda to the International Criminal Court: Expanding the Definition of Genocide to Include Rape', Pennsylvania State Law Review 108.
Miller, J. (2001) One of the Guys: Girls, Gangs and Gender, Oxford University Press, New York.

Milliken, J. (1999) 'The Study of Discourse in International Relations: A Critique of Research and Methods', *European Journal of International Relations* 5, June.

MIPT Terrorism Knowledge Base (2005) 'Al-Qaeda Organization in the Land of the Two Rivers Attacked Military Target', 28 September, www.tkb.org/Incident.jsp?inclD=25420 (accessed 21 November 2006).

Mischel, W. (1968) *Personality and Assessment*, Wiley, New York.

Mitchell, J.A. (2006) 'Soldier Girl? Not Every Tamil Teen Wants to be a Tiger', *The Humanist*, September/October.

Mohanty, C.T. (1991) *Third World Women and the Politics of Feminism*, Indiana University Press, Bloomington.

Moon, K. (1997) *Sex among Allies: Militarized Prostitution in U.S.–South Korea Relations*, Columbia University Press, New York.

Morf, G. (1970) *Terror in Quebec: Case Studies of the FLQ*, Clarke Irwin, Toronto.

Morgan, R. (1989) *The Demon Lover: The Roots of Terrorism*, Washington Square, New York.

Morrissey, B. (2003) *When Women Kill: Questions of Agency and Subjectivity*, Routledge, London.

Moser, C., and F.C. Clark (eds) (2001) *Victims, Perpetrators or Actors? Gender, Armed Conflict and Political Violence*, Zed Books, London.

MSNBC.com (2005) 'US Reservist Guilt of Abu Ghraib Abuses', 17 May.

Mudis, D.A. (2003) 'Current Developments and the Ad Hoc International Criminal Tribunals', *Journal of International Criminal Justice*.

Murphey, K. (2004) 'Chechen Women Being Seized to Preempt Bombings, Rights Groups Say', *Los Angeles Times*, 26 May, www.peacewomen.org/news/Chechnya/June04/bombings.html (accessed 31 March 2006).

Myers, S.L. (2004) 'Chechen "Black Widows": Women Entangled Terrorism in Russia', *New York Times*, 10 September.

Myers, S.L. (2003) 'Young, Female, and Carrying a Bomb', *International Herald Tribune*, 8 August.

National Coalition for the Protection of Children and Families. (2006) 'Abu Ghraib: Lessons in Sexual Morality', www.nationalcoalition.org/articles/ca050523.html (accessed 1 January 2007).

Neuburger, L., and T. Valentini (1996) *Women and Terrorism*, Macmillan, London.

New York Times (2004) May cover pages.

New York Times (1998) 'Former Air Force Cadet is Convicted of Murder', 25 July.

Niva, S. (1998) 'Tough and Tender: New World Order Masculinity and the Gulf War', in M. Zalewski and J. Parpart (eds), *The 'Man' Question in International Relations*, Westview Press, Boulder CO.

No Borders (2004) 'AI on Situation on Girls and Women in Chechnya', www.noborder.org/chechnya/display.php?id=75 (accessed 31 March 2006).

Obote-Odora, A. (2005) 'Rape and Sexual Violence in International Law: ICTR Contributions', *New England Journal of International and Comparative Law* 12.

Oliver, A.M. (2006) 'The Brides of Palestine', *Salon.com*, 20 July, www.salon.com/mrt/feature/2006/07/20/suicide_bombers/ (accessed 1 January 2007).

Olujic, M.B. (1998) 'The Embodiment of Terror: Gendered Violence in Peacetime and Wartime in Croatia and Bosnia-Herzegovina', *Medical Anthropology Quarterly*, vol. 12, no. 1.
Okin, S.M. (1998) 'Feminism, Women's Human Rights, and Cultural Differences', *Hypatia*, vol. 13, no. 2.
Onuf, N. (1989) *World of Our Making: Rules and Rule in Social Theory and International Politics*, University of South Carolina Press, Columbia.
Ovid (1958) *The Metamorphoses*, trans. Horace Gregory, Viking, New York.
Paechter, C. (2003) 'Masculinities and Femininities as Communities of Practice', *Women's Studies International Forum*.
Pape, R. (2005) *Dying to Win: The Strategic Logic of Suicide Terrorism*, Random House, New York.
Pape, R. (2001) 'The Wrong Battle Plan', *Washington Post*, 19 October.
Parfitt, T. (2004) 'Russian Soldiers Blamed for Civilian Rape in Chechnya', *Lancet* 363, 17 April.
Parfitt, T. (2003) 'Meet Black Fatima – She Programmes Women to Kill', *Sunday Telegraph*, 20 July.
Paukov, V., and A. Raskin (2003) 'Black Widows' Rock', *Vremya Novostay*, 7 July, http://web.lexis-nexis.com/universe (accessed 8 June 2006).
Paukov, V., and V. Svistunov (2003) '"Black Widows" Were Just Steps away from Kremlin', *Vremya Novostei*, 10 December, http://web.lexis-nexis.com/universe (accessed 31 March 2006).
Paul, P. (2005) *Pornified: How Pornography is Transforming Our Lives, Our Relationships, and Our Families*, Times Books, New York.
Peach, L.J. (1994) 'An Alternative to Pacifism? Feminism and Just-War Theory', *Hypatia*, vol. 9, no. 2.
Pearson, P. (1997) *When She Was Bad: Violent Women and the Myth of Innocence*, Viking, New York.
Peteet, J. (1991) *Gender in Crisis: Women and the Palestinian Resistance Movement*, Columbia University Press, New York.
Peterson, S. (2001) *Me Against My Brother: At War in Somalia, Sudan, and Rwanda*, Routledge, London.
Peterson, S.R. (1977) 'Coercion and Rape: The State as a Male Protection Racket', in M. Vetterling-Braggin, F.A. Elliston and J. English (eds), *Feminism and Philosophy*, Littlefield-Adams, Totowa NJ.
Peterson, V.S. (1999) 'Sexing Political Identities/Nationalism as Heterosexism', *International Feminist Journal of Politics*, vol. 1, no. 1.
Peterson, V.S., and A.S. Runyan (1999) *Global Gender Issues*, Westview Press, Boulder CO.
Peterson, V.S., and J. True (1998) 'New Times and New Conversations', in M. Zalewski and J. Parpart (eds), *The 'Man' Question in International Relations*, Westview Press, Boulder CO.
Pettman, J.J. (1996) *Worlding Women: A Feminist International Politics*, Routledge, London.
Phillips, A. (ed.) (1987) *Feminism and Equality*, New York University Press, New York.
Phillips, J. (2005) 'Women's Magazine Offers Tips to Terrorists', *Washington*

Times, 17 January, www.washtimes.com/world/20050117-122001-8417r.htm (accessed 4 August 2006).
Phillips, J. (2006) 'The Evolving Al-Qaeda Threat', *Heritage Lectures* 928, delivered 16 February, published 17 March.
Pinnick, K. (1997) 'When the Fighting is Over: The Soldiers' Mothers and the Afghan Madonnas', in M. Buckley (ed.), *Post-Soviet Women from the Baltic to Central Asia*, Cambridge University Press, Cambridge.
Points, M. (1991) 'Diaries of Iraqi Experiences', *Electronic Iraq*, http://electronicIraq.net/.
Post, J. (1998) 'Terrorist Psycho-logic: Terrorist Behavior as a Product of Psychological Forces', in W. Reich (ed.), *Origins of Terrorism: Psychologies, Ideologies, Theologies, States of Mind*, Woodrow Wilson Center Press, Washington DC.
Powell, A. (2005) 'Jury Selected, Trial Begins for Abu Ghraib Defendant', *Oxford Press*, 13 May.
Power, S. (2002) *A Problem from Hell: America in an Age of Genocide*, Harper-Perennial, New York.
Prague Watchdog (2004) 'Current Situation in Chechnya (updated February 2004)', 19 March, www.watchdog.cz/index.php?show=000000-000015-000002-000002&lang=1 (accessed 8 June 2006).
Pringle, R., and S. Watson (1992) 'Women's Interest and the Post-Structuralist State', in M. Barrett (ed.), *Destabilizing Theory*, Polity Press, Cambridge.
Prugl, E. (1999) *The Global Construction of Gender: Home-based Work in the Political Economy of the 20th Century*, Columbia University Press, New York.
Prunier, G. (1995) *The Rwanda Crisis 1959–1994: History of a Genocide*, Hurst, London.
Przyembel, A. (2001) 'Transfixed by an Image: Ilse Koch, the "Kommandeuse of Buchenwald"', *German History*, vol. 19, no. 3.
Puar, J. (2006) 'Mapping US Homonormatives', *Gender, Place, and Culture: A Journal of Feminist Geography*, vol. 13, no. 1.
Putley, J. (2003) 'Crime without Punishment: Russian Policy in Chechnya', *openDemocracy*, 28 July, www.opendemocracy.net/debates/article.jsp?id=2&debateId=118&articleId=13881-4 (accessed 31 March 2006).
Pyle, J.L., and K.B. Ward (2003) 'Recasting Our Understanding of Gender and Work during Global Restructuring', *International Sociology*, vol. 18, no. 3.
Radar Online (2005) 'Abu Ghraib goes to ABC', www.radaronline.com.
Ragavan, C., D. Pasternak and R. Sharpe (2003a) 'Femme Fatale? Al Qaeda's Mystery Woman', *US News and World Report*, 7 April.
Ragavan, C., D. Pasternak, R. Sharpe and A. Latif (2003b) 'All in the Family', *US News and World Report*, 21 April.
Rawstorne, T., and R. Benson (2002) '116 Hostages Were Killed by Nerve Gas', *Daily Mail*, 28 October.
Razavi, S., and C. Miller (1995) 'Gender Mainstreaming: A Study of Efforts by the United Nations Development Programme, the World Bank, and the International Labor Organization to Institutionalize Gender', Occasional Paper 4, August, United Nations Research Institute for Social Development, United Nations Development Program.

Reardon, B. (1985) *Sexism and the War System*, Teachers' College Press, New York.
Red Cross (2001) *Women Facing War: ICRC Study on the Impact of Armed Conflict on Women*, International Committee on the Red Cross, Geneva.
Rehn, E., and E.J. Sirleaf (2003) *Women, War, and Peace*, UNIFEM, New York.
Reich, W. (ed.) (1998) *Origins of Terrorism: Psychologies, Ideologies, Theologies, States of Mind*, Woodrow Wilson Center Press, Washington DC.
The Record (2005) 'Violence Escalates on West Bank; Palestinian Shooters Kill Israeli Motorist; Israel Detains Female Suicide Bomber', 21 June.
Richards, A.K. (1998) 'Woman as Medusa in Basic Instinct', *Psychoanalytic Inquiry*.
Richter-Montpetit, M. (2007) 'Empire, Desire, and Violence: A Queer Transnational Feminist Reading of the Prisoner "Abuse" in Abu Ghraib and the Question of Gender Equality', *International Feminist Journal of Politics*, vol. 9, no. 1.
Riddell, M. (2004) 'A New Monster-in-Chief', *The Observer–Sun*, 9 May.
Rissman, B. (2004) 'Gender as a Social Structure: Theory Wrestling with Activism', *Gender and Society*, vol. 18, no. 4.
Ritchie, J. (1991) *Myra Hindley: Inside the Mind of a Murderer*, Paladin, London.
Rosen, D.M. (2005) *Armies of the Young: Child Soldiers in War and Terrorism*, Rutgers University Press, Piscataway NJ.
Rosenberg, M. (2007) 'New Countries in the World', *About.com*, http://geography.about.com/cs/countries/a/newcountries.htm (accessed 9 March 2007).
Rowles, G. (2002) 'Feminist Atrocity', 24 October, www.fathers.ca/female_empowerment.htm (accessed 1 January 2007).
Rubec, S. (2003a) 'Troops on Lookout for Suicide Bomber', *Calgary Sun*, 25 October.
Rubec, S. (2003b) 'Veiled Assassin Stalks Canucks', *Ottawa Sun*, 25 October.
Rubin, E. (2006) 'If Not Peace, Then Justice', *New York Times* Magazine, 2 April.
Rubin, E. (2002) 'Gen X', *New Republic*, 15 April.
Rubinstein, W.D. (2004) *Genocide: A History*, Pearson/Longman, London.
Ruddick, S. (1989) *Maternal Thinking: Towards a Politics of Peace*, Houghton-Mifflin, New York.
Ruddick, S. (1983) 'Pacifying the Forces: Drafting Women in the Interest of Peace', *Signs: Journal of Women in Culture and Society*, vol. 8, no. 3.
Russell-Brown, S.L. (2003) 'Rape as an Act of Genocide', *Berkeley Journal of International Law* 21.
Russell, J. (2005) 'Terrorists, Bandits, Spooks and Thieves: Russian Demonization of the Chechens Before and Since 9/11', *Third World Quarterly*, vol. 26, no. 1.
Russell, J. (2002) 'Mujahedeen, Mafia, Madmen: Russian Perceptions of Chechens During the Wars in Chechnya, 1994–1996 and 1999 to Date', *Journal of Postcommunist Studies and Transition Politics*, vol. 18, no. 1, March.
Sageman, M. (2004) *Understanding Terror Networks*, University of Pennsylvania Press, Philadelphia.
Sakwa, R. (2004) *Putin: Russia's Choice*, Routledge, London.

REFERENCES

Saleh, B. (2005) 'Palestinian Suicide Attacks Revisited', *Peace Magazine*, April/June.

Saradzhyan, S. (2004) 'I Was an Outcast, Says Bomber', *Moscow Times*, 4 February, http://web.lexis-nexis.com/universe (accessed 8 June 2006).

Sauer, M., and H. Osman (2005) 'Female Suicide Bombers: A New Al Qaeda Tactic?', *ABC News*, 14 November, www.abcnews.go.com/WNT/Investigation/story?id=1312273 (accessed 4 August 2006).

Sayeh, M. (1986) 'Choosing the Revolution', in M. Gadant (ed.), *Women of the Mediterranean*, Zed Books, London.

Schecter, H., and D. Everitt (2006) *The A–Z Encyclopedia of Serial Killers*, Pocket, New York.

Scelfo, J. (2004) 'She Was Following Orders', *Newsweek*, 11 May.

Schiffman, J.R., and I. O'Toole (1997) *Gender Violence: Interdisciplinary Perspectives*, New York University Press, New York.

Schmid, A.P. (1983) *Political Terrorism: A Research Guide to the Concepts, Theories, Databases, and Literature*, Transaction Books, Somerset NJ.

Schneider, H. (2004) 'In Breaking Taboo, Photos Add Insult to Injury', *Washington Post*, 7 May.

Schweitzer, Y. (2006) 'Palestinian Female Suicide Bombers: Reality v. Myth', in Y. Schweitzer (ed.), *Female Suicide Bombers: Dying For Equality?*, Jaffee Center for Strategic Studies, Tel Aviv.

Schulz, J., and L. Schulz (1999) 'The Darkest Ages: Women under the Taliban', *Peace and Conflict* 5.

Schott, R.M. (1996) 'Gender and 'Postmodern War', *Hypatia*, vol. 11, no. 4.

Segal, M.W. (1995) 'Women's Military Roles Cross-Nationally: Past, Present, and Future', *Gender and Society*, vol. 9, no. 6.

Sekuk, S., D. McCreary and J. Mahalik (2004) 'Differential Reactions to Men's and Women's Gender Role Transgressions', *Journal of Men's Studies*, vol. 12, no. 1.

Shalhoub-Kevorkian, N. (2004) 'Racism, Militarism and Policing: Police Reactions to Violence against Palestinian Women in Israel', *Social Identities*, vol. 10, no. 2.

Shapiro, A. (2002) 'Unequal before the Law: Men, Women, and the Death Penalty', *American Journal of Gender, Social Policy, and Law* 8.

Sharoni, S. (1997) 'Gendering Conflict and Peace in Israel/Palestine and the North of Ireland', *Millennium*, vol. 27, no. 4.

Sharoni, S. (1995) *Gender and the Israel–Palestinian Conflict*, Syracuse University Press, Syracuse NY.

Shermatova, S., and A. Teit (2003) 'Masterminds Unknown', *Moscow News*, 16 July.

Silm, B. (2004) 'Al Khansa', ICPVTR Global Pathfinder Database.

Simons, M. (2001) 'Belgian Jury Convicts 4 of 1994 War Crimes in Rwanda', *New York Times*, 9 June.

Sjoberg, L. (2007) 'Agency, Militarized Femininity, and Enemy Others', *International Feminist Journal of Politics*, vol. 9, no. 1.

Sjoberg, L. (2006) *Gender, Justice, and the Wars in Iraq*, Lexington Books, Lanham MD.

Skapouilli, E. (2004) 'Gender Codes at Odds and the Linguistic Destruction of a Hybrid Identity', *Journal of Language, Identity, and Education*, vol. 3, no. 4.
Smith, C.S. (2005) 'Raised as Catholic in Belgium, She Died as a Muslim Bomber', *New York Times*, 6 December, www.nytimes.com/2005/12/06/international/europe/06brussels.html?ex=1168491600&en=c9b61ab7ea879dea&ei=5070 (accessed 6 December 2005).
Smith, R.J., and J. White (2005) 'Army Closed Many Abuse Cases Early', *Washington Post*, 25 January.
Snider, L. (2003) 'Constituting the Punishable Woman: Atavistic Man Incarcerates Postmodern Woman', *British Journal of Criminology*, Spring.
Speckhard, A., and K. Akhmedova (2006) 'Black Widows: The Chechen Female Suicide Terrorists', in Y. Sheiwtzer (ed.), *Female Suicide Bombers: Dying for Equality?*, Jaffee Center for Strategic Studies, Tel Aviv.
Sperling, C. (2006) 'Mother of All Atrocities: Pauline Nyiramusuhuko's Role in the Rwandan Genocide', *Fordham Urban Law Journal* 33.
Spinner, J. (2005) 'Female Suicide Bomber Attacks U.S. Military Post', *Washington Post*, 29 September.
Spinner, J. (2004) 'Soldier: Unit's Role Was to Break Down Prisoners', *Washington Post*, 8 May.
Spivak, G.C. (1998) *In Other Worlds: Essays in Cultural Politics*, Routledge, New York.
Stapleton, K., and J. Wilson (2004) 'Gender, Nationality, and Identity', *European Journal of Women's Studies*, vol. 11, no. 1.
The Statesman (India) (2004) 'Old Motive, New Method', 3 September, http://web.lexis-nexis.com/universe (accessed 8 June 2006).
Steans, J. (1998) *Gender and International Relations: An Introduction*, Rutgers University Press, New Brunswick NJ.
Stephen, C. (2003) 'Moscow Concert Suicide Bombers Linked to Chechen "Black Widows"', *Irish Times*, 9 July, http://web.lexis-nexis.com/universe (accessed 8 June 2006).
Stern, S. (2007) *With the Weatherman: The Personal Journey of a Revolutionary Woman*, Rutgers University Press, Rutgers NJ.
Stern, S. (1975) *With the Weathermen*, Doubleday, Garden City NY.
Stiehm, J. (1983) *Women and Men's Wars*, Pergamon Press, Oxford.
Stiehm, J. (1982) 'The Protected, the Protector, and the Defender', *Women's Studies International Forum*, vol. 4, no. 3/4.
Stiglmayer, A., and M. Faber (1994) *Mass Rape: The War in Bosnia–Herzegovina*, University of Nebraska Press, Lincoln.
Stoller, S., and C. Nielsen (2005) 'Asymmetrical Genders: Phenomenological Reflections on Sexual Difference', *Hypatia*, vol. 20, no. 2.
Stone, C. (1996) 'Gender Values and Identity: Carol Gilligan's Work on Women's Moral Development', in T. Cosslet, A. Easton and P. Summerfield (eds), *Women, Power and Resistance: An Introduction to Women's Studies*, Open University Press, Buckingham.
Straus, S. (2001) 'Contested Meanings and Conflicting Imperatives: A Conceptual Analysis of Genocide', *Journal of Genocide Research*, vol. 3, no. 3.
Strauss, J. (2004) 'Russians Stage Purge of Chechen Widows: Secret Police See

Them as Potential Suicide Bombers', *Daily Telegraph*, 8 April.

Strickland, R., and N. Duvvury (2003) *Gender Equity and Peacebuilding: From Rhetoric to Reality – Finding the Way*, International Center for Research on Women, Washington DC.

Sudanwatch.org (2006) 'Janjaweed Women Complicit in Genocide, Says Amnesty Report', 10 January, www.sudanwatch.blogspot.com/2006/01/janjaweed-women-complicit-in-rape-says.html (accessed 1 January 2007).

Suljalic, E. (2003) 'Kisses as Bosnian War Kicked Off', *Institute for War and Peace Reporting*, www.iwpr.net/?p=tri&s=f&o=163907&apc_state=henitri2003 (accessed 1 January 2007).

Summers, A. (1975) *Damned Whores and God's Police: The Colonization of Women in Australia*, Penguin, New York.

Sunday Mail (2002) 'Sleeping Gas and Storm Troops End Theatre Stand-Off', 27 October.

Sylvester, C. (2002) *Feminist International Relations: An Unfinished Journey*, Cambridge University Press, Cambridge.

Sylvester, C. (1999) 'In-between and In Evasion of So Much: Third World Literatures, International Relations, and Postcolonial Analysis', *Postcolonial Studies*, vol. 2, no. 3.

Sylvester, C. (1994) *Feminist Theory and International Relations in a Postmodern Era*, Cambridge University Press, Cambridge.

Sylvester, C. (1990) *Feminists and Realists on Autonomy and Obligation in International Relations*, University of Southern California, Center for International Studies, Los Angeles.

Taguba, General A. (2004) 'Article 5–16 Investigation of the 800th Military Police Brigade', unofficial release of classified report, www.npr.org/iraq/2004/prison_abuse_report.pdf.

Talbot, R. (2001) 'Myths in Representations of Women Terrorists', *Eire-Ireland: Journal of Irish Studies* 25.

Tannen, D. (1993) *Framing in Discourse*, Oxford University Press, Oxford.

Taylor, C. (2000) '"And Don't Forget to Clean the Fridge": Women in the Secret Sphere of Terrorism', in G. DeGroot and C. Bird-Peniston (eds), *A Soldier and a Woman: Sexual Integration in the Military*, Pearson Education, Harlow.

Telegraf (1996) 'Interview with Biljana Plavsic', *Nedeljni Telegraf* (Belgrade), 16 November.

Tetreault, M.A. (2006) 'The Sexual Politics of Abu Ghraib: Hegemony, Spectacle, and the Global War on Terror', *NWSA Journal*, vol. 18, no. 3.

Thomas, E., D. Klaidman, M. Isikoff, B. Dehghanpisheh, S. Johnson, A. Murr, M. Hosenball, T. Lipper, E. Flynn and A. Karshmer (2004) 'Enemies amongst Us', *Newsweek*, 5 July.

Tickner, J.A., and L. Sjoberg (2006) 'Feminism', in T. Dunne, M. Kurki and S. Smith (eds), *Feminism*, Oxford University Press, Oxford.

Tickner, J.A. (2001) *Gendering World Politics*, Columbia University Press, New York.

Tickner, J.A. (1992) *Gender in International Relations: Feminist Perspectives on Achieving Global Security*, Columbia University Press, New York.

Tickner, J.A. (1991) 'Hans Morgenthau's Principles of Political Realism: A

Feminist Reformulation', in R. Grant and K. Newland (eds), *Gender and International Relations*, Indiana University Press, Bloomington and Indianapolis.

Toles Parkin, T. (2004) 'Explosive Baggage: Female Palestinian Suicide Bombers and the Rhetoric of Emotion', *Women and Language*, vol. 27, no. 2.

Top Security Project No. 2 Part IV – Summary and Analysis (1976) 'The Female Terrorist and Her Impact on Policing', MIPT Terrorism Knowledge Base (2006) www.tkb.org/.

Tran, T. (2004) 'Abu Ghraib Abuser Sentenced', *Washington Times*, 22 October.

True, J. (2003) 'Gender Mainstreaming in Global Public Policy', *International Feminist Journal of Politics*, vol. 35, no. 3.

True, J. (1996) 'Feminism', in S. Burchill and A. Linklater (eds), *Theories of International Relations*, Macmillan, London.

20/20 (2005) 'Harman Tells Her Story', ABCNews.com, 20 January, http://abcnews.go.com/2020/News/story?id=429459&page=1 (accessed 11 January 2007).

Usher, G. (2002) 'Six Killed by Jenin Camp Bomber', *Guardian*, 13 April.

Valiyev, A. (2005) 'The Rise of Salafi Islam in Azerbaijan', *Terrorism Monitor*, vol. 3, no. 13, 1 July.

Vallance, B. (2000) 'Russia's Mothers: Voices of Change', *Minerva: Quarterly Report of Women in the Military*, vol. 18, no. 3/4.

Vasagar, J., and E. MacAskill (2004) 'Janjaweed Women Complicit in Rape', *Guardian*, 20 July.

Verhovek, S.H. (1996) 'A Tale of Love and Murder in a Small Town', *New York Times*, 10 September.

Victor, B. (2003) *An Army of Roses: Inside the World of Palestinian Women Suicide Bombers*, Rodale Press, New York.

Victoroff, J. (2005) 'The Mind of the Terrorist', *Journal of Conflict Resolution*, vol. 49, no. 1, February.

Vinogradova, L. (2003) 'Deadly Secret of the Black Widows', *The Times*, 2 October.

Voss, S. (2004) '"Black Widows" Threaten the Lives of Russian Children', *Deutsche Presse-Agentur*, 2 September, http://web.lexis-nexis.com/universe (accessed 8 June 2006).

Wagner, C. (2000) *RuBlands Kriege in Tschetschenien: Politsche Transformation und militarische Gewalt*, LIT, Munster.

Walker, C., and R. Beeston (2002) 'Israel on Alert for More Female Suicide Attacks', *The Times*, 29 January.

Walker, R.B.J. (1990) 'Sovereignty, Identity, Community: Reflections on the Horizons of Contemporary Political Practice'. in R.B.J. Walker and Saul H. Mendlovitz (eds), *Contending Sovereignties: Redefining Political Community*.

Walsh, N.P. (2005) 'Sisters in Arms', *Guardian*, 1 September.

Walsh, N.P. (2004) 'Women Moved by Family Not Ideology', *Guardian*, 1 September.

Walsh, N.P. (2003) 'Putin in Warning on Bombers', *Guardian*, 8 July, www.guardian.co.uk/russia/article/0,2763,993814,00.html (accessed 1 January 2007).

Walt, S. (2000) 'Rigor or Rigor Mortis? Rational Choice and Security Studies',

in M.E. Brown (ed.), *Rational Choice and Security Studies: Stephen Walt and His Critics*, MIT Press, Cambridge MA.
Walton, A. (2001) 'Of Feminism and Foxholes', *CNN Interactive*, www.cnn.com/Specials/2001/gulfwar/legacy/women.
Waltz, K. (1959) *Man, the State, and War*, Columbia University Press, New York.
Ward, O. (2004) 'The Changing Face of Terror', *Toronto Star*, 10 October.
Washington Post (2006) 'Female Bomber Blows Herself Up in Gaza', 6 November, www.washingtonpost.com/wp-dyn/content/article/2006/11/23/AR2006112300307.html (accessed 17 November 2006).
Weber, M. (2003) 'Extermination' Camp Propaganda Myths', in E. Gauss (ed.), *Dissecting the Holocaust*, Theses and Dissertation Press, Berlin.
Weber, C. (1999) *Faking It: U.S. Hegemony in a 'Post-Phallic' Era*, University of Minnesota Press, Minneapolis.
Weber, C. (1998) 'Performative States', *Millennium: Journal of International Studies*, vol. 21, no. 1.
Weber, C. (1995) 'Good Girls, Little Girls and Bad Girls: Male Paranoia in Robert Keohane's Critique of Feminist International Relations', *Millennium: Journal of International Studies*, vol. 23, no. 2.
Welsh, S. (2003) 'Abu Ghraib Court Marshall: Spc. Megan Ambuhl, USA', *Law Watch*, www.cdi.org/news/law/abu-ghraib/ambuhl.cfm (accessed 1 January 2007).
Weinberg, L.B., and W. Eubank (1994) 'Cultural Differences in the Behavior of Terrorists', *Terrorism and Political Violence*, Spring.
Weinburg, L., and W. Eubank (1985) 'Italian Women Terrorists', *Terrorism: An International Journal* 9.
Weindling, P. (2006) 'The Nuremberg Medical Trial: The Holocaust and the Origin of the Nuremberg Medical Code', *English Historical Review* 123.
Weir, F. (2003) 'Chechen Women Join Terror's Ranks', *Christian Science Monitor*, 12 June.
Wendt, A. (1999) *Social Theory of International Politics*, Cambridge University Press, Cambridge.
Wheeler, J. (2004) 'Take It Like a Man', *Washington Times*, 21 May.
Whitaker, B. (1972) *The Fourth World: Victim of Group Oppression: Eight Reports from the Field Work of the Minority Rights Group*, Shocken, New York.
White, J. (2006) 'Former Abu Ghraib Guard Calls Top Brass Culpable for Abuse', *Washington Post*, 23 January.
Wight, S., and A. Myers (1996) 'Introduction', in A. Myers and S. Wight (eds), *No Angels: Women Who Commit Violence*, HarperCollins, London.
Wikipedia (2006) 'Leela (Doctor Who)', http://en.wikipedia.org/wiki/Leela_%28Doctor_Who%29 (accessed 11 August 2006).
Wikipedia (2007) 'The Battle of Al Qadisiyyah', http://en.wikipedia.org/wiki/Battle_of_al-Q%C4%81disiyyah (accessed 3 September 2007).
Wilk, S.R. (2000) *Medusa: Solving the Mystery of the Gorgon*, Oxford University Press, New York.
Williams, D., and I. Thomas (2002) 'Held by the Black Widows', *Daily Mail* (Queensland), 26 October.

Wolf, N. (2004) 'Equal Wrongs', *New York Magazine*, 24 May, http://metro.com/nymetro/news/politics/columns/n_10405/ (accessed 1 January 2007).
Women in the Military: Deployment in the Persian Gulf War (1992) GAO/NSIAD, August.
Wood, P. (2001) 'The Pursuit of "Terrorists" in Chechnya: Blood on Whose Hands?', *Human Rights Review*, April–June.
Wood, S. (2004) 'A Woman Scorned for the "Least Condemned" War Crime: Precedent and Problems with Prosecuting Rape as a Serious War Crime in the International Criminal Tribubal for Rwanda', *Columbia Journal of Gender and the Law* 12.
Xinhua General News Service (2006) 'Update: Palestinian Woman Blew Herself Up in Gaza, Wounding 4 Israeli Soldiers', 23 November, http://web.lexisnexis.com/universe (accessed 28 November 2006).
Youdell, D. (2006) 'Sex–Gender–Sexuality: How Sex, Gender, and Sexuality Constellations are Constituted in Secondary Schools', *Gender and Education*, vol. 17, no. 3.
Young, I.M. (2003) 'The Logic of Masculinist Protection: Reflections on the Current Security State', *Signs: Journal of Women in Culture and Society*, vol. 129, no. 1.
Young-Eisndrath, P., and F. Wiedemann (1987) *Female Authority: Empowering Women through Psychotherapy*, Guilford Press, New York.
Youngs, G. (2000) 'Breaking Patriarchal Bonds: Demythologizing the Public/Private', in M. Marchand and A. Sisson-Runyan (eds), *Gender and Global Restructuring: Sightings, Sites, and Resistances*, Routledge, London and New York.
Yudkin, M. (1983) 'Reflections on Woolf's "Three Guineas"', in J. Stiehm (ed.), *Women and Men's Wars*, Pergamon Press, Oxford.
Yuval-Davis, N. (1997) *Gender and Nation*, Sage, London and Thousand Oaks CA.
Zakaria, F. (2003) 'Suicide Bombers Can Be Stopped', *Newsweek*, 25 August.
Zalewski, M. (1996) '"All These Theories Yet the Bodies Keep Piling Up": Theory, Theorists, Theorising', in S. Smith, K. Booth and M. Zalewski (eds), *International Theory: Positivism and Beyond*, Cambridge University Press, Cambridge.
Zalewski, M. (1995) 'Well, What is the Feminist Perspective on Bosnia?', *International Affairs*, vol. 71, no. 2.
Zarrella, J. (2002) 'Wuornos' Last Words: I'll Be Back', CNN, 15 October, http://archives.cnn.com/2002/LAW/10/09/Wuornos.execution/index.html (accessed 10 October 2006).
Zaucha, A. (2003) *Moskwa Nord-Ost*, Bosz, Olszanica.
Zedalis, D.D. (2004) *Female Suicide Bombers*, Strategic Studies Institute, Carlisle PA.
Zernile, K. (2003) 'For Three Lovelorn GIs, A Soap Opera Triangle at Abu Ghraib', *International Herald Tribune*, 11 May.

INDEX

Abu Ghraib, 23, 58–60, 63–7, 69–74, 76–83, 86–7, 205–8, 226 n2, 231 n12, 232 n3, 233 n10
Afghanistan, 114, 203, 205, 237 n16
al-Aqsa Martyrs Brigade, 119, 121, 138, 236 n7
Al Jazeera, 123
Al Khansa, 124, 126–7, 139, 211
al-Qaeda, 24, 35, 237 n16
  and Chechnya, 93, 96,
  in Iraq, 128
  organizational issues, 127, 237 n16
  and Palestinian resistance organizations, 115
  recruitment of women, 114, 124–6, 131, 138–9, 211
  and the Taliban, 113
  women bombers, 128
Albright, Madeleine, 154
Amazons, 42–4, 69, 231 n10
Ambuhl, Megan, 23, 67, 72–3, 75, 83, 232 n8
Arab National Movement, 115
Arendt, Hannah, 195

Basayev, Shamil, 98, 103
Battle of Al Qadisiyyah, 237
Baudrillard, Jean, 29, 230 n1
Beard, Celeste, 48

Beijing Platform for Action, 2
Bell, Derrick, 51
Bildt, Carl, 154
'Black Fatima', 103
'black widows', 23–4, 35–36, 88–9, 93, 94, 100, 186
  defined, 88
  in the media, 101–3
  political device, 110–11, 125, 210
Bloom, Mia, 136–8, 186, 188
Boraine, Alex, 154
Borden, Lizzie, 15, 229 n13
Boudica, 38–9, 148, 230 n7, 230–31 n8
Brady, Ian, 49
Bryant, Kelly, 71
Byman, Daniel, 199, 200, 203, 204, 215, 216, 220, 242 n1

Charlesworth, Hilary, 52, 135, 174–5
Chechnya, 24, 88
  Adat, 92, 99, 101
  and al-Qaeda, 93, 96
  Bespredel, 91, 109
  human rights, 89, 91–3, 108–9
  kontraktniki, 92
  Moscow hostage crisis, 98, 234 n6, 235 n13
  Palestinianization, 97–8, 103, 111, 234 n1

post-Cold War, 89–90
 personal impacts of the crisis,
    208–9
 and Russia, 36, 90, 94–6, 210–11
 terrorism, 98, 234, 235 n17
 and Vladimir Putin, 96
 and women's rights, 183
 zachistki, 92, 101, 109
child soldiers, 236 n7
Churchill, Winston, 199
Cockburn, Cynthia, 36, 135–6
Connell, R.W., 206, 213, 228 n9, 229
    n14
Cox, Robert, 29

discourse, 28, 52, 53; *see also* narrative
 agency, 22–4
 apparent neutrality, 174
 in the Chechen conflict, 94–5, 210
 frames, 56
 of gender, 6–7, 9, 19, 136, 176,
    211–12, 213, 222–3, 226 n5, 233
    n10, 239 n27
 of genocide, 143
 heteronormative, 80
 manifest and latent, 224
 as politics, 51, 53, 139
 and reality, 29, 230 n1
 and relational autonomy, 17, 194
 of security, 4, 28, 36, 76, 202
 sexualized, 46, 214
 subordination, 55–6, 139
 of terrorism, 227 n7
Dohrn, Bernardine, 45
Doss, Nannie, 47
Dworkin, Andrea, 74

Ehrenreich, Barbara, 20, 148, 224
Elshtain, Jean Bethke, 3–4, 33, 194
England, Lynndie, 23, 66, 67–70, 72, 73,
    74, 75, 81–3, 216, 217
Enloe, Cynthia, 174, 199, 200–202, 209,
    216, 226 n4, 235 n1
Fateh Tanzim, 236 n9
female terrorism, 17, 38, 136
 monster narrative in, 105
 mother narrative in, 33
 whore narrative in, 46, 106, 133,
    231 n11
feminism, 3, 12, 200, 223, 239 n3
 as discursive destabilization, 53
 and essentialism, 19

and gender-blindness, 52
motherhood in, 36
and power, 195, 200, 217, 242 n3
and theory, 19, 20–21, 52, 197, 230
    n2
and violence, 18, 148, 168, 172
Freud, Sigmund, 178–80
Frowick, Robert, 154
frustration-aggression theory, 182–3

gender, 5
 deviance, 7
 femininities, 6, 7, 9, 11, 12, 13, 19,
    21, 22, 23, 30, 32, 33, 36, 44, 46,
    50, 51, 53, 54, 55, 59, 60, 63, 64,
    65, 68, 70, 76, 80, 84, 86–7, 91,
    109, 110, 132, 135, 140, 147, 149,
    152, 172–3, 180, 183, 188, 191,
    197, 207–9, 212, 216, 221–3, 229
    n14, 234 n17, 235 n1, 239 n28
 masculinities, 2, 3, 6, 7, 10, 12, 16,
    17, 19, 24, 25, 42, 49, 52, 54, 79,
    85, 90, 108, 110, 138, 139, 149,
    156, 171, 172–3, 174–6, 178, 180,
    183–4, 185, 186, 187, 188, 194,
    196, 197, 202, 204, 206–7, 209,
    212, 213, 218, 219, 222, 223, 227
    n6, 228 n9, 229 n14, 231 n12
 and power, 5, 8, 11, 17, 26, 45,
    51–2, 66, 107, 136, 147, 157, 163,
    175, 185, 192–5, 198, 200, 207,
    209, 213, 215, 217–18, 220, 229
    n14, 238 n12
 and sex, 5–6
 subordination, 2, 3, 5, 6, 9, 10,
    11, 12, 17, 20, 26, 53, 55,
    56, 66, 80, 94, 113, 115, 172,
    183–4, 204–5, 209, 212, 213, 214,
    220–24, 229 n14, 238 n21
gender mainstreaming, 2
genocide, 142–4
Geneva Convention, 71, 164
gorgons, 37–8, 40
Graner, Charles, 67–9, 73, 75, 81, 83,
    206, 231 n1
Gubar, Susan, 30, 36

Habyarimana, Agathe, 158, 160, 161
Habyarimana, Juvenal, 158, 161
Hamas, 115, 118–19, 133, 138, 237 n11
Hamilton, Edith, 30–31
Harman, Sabrina, 1, 23, 65, 66, 67,

INDEX 273

70–71, 81–2, 83, 231 n1
hegemonic masculinity, 38, 174–5, 206, 209, 228 n9, 229 n14
Helen of Troy, 203
Hindley, Myra, 49, 69
Hirschmann, Nancy, 16–17, 190–96
Hitler, Adolf, 61, 199, 217
Holocaust, the, 159, 160
Hooper, Charlotte, 171, 177
human security, 202
Hussein, Saddam, 64, 217, 235 n12, 238 n18

Interahamwe, 162, 168, 170, 239 n6, 240 n7
International Criminal Tribunal for the Former Yugoslavia, 151, 153–4, 157
International Criminal Tribunal for Rwanda (ICTR), 144, 159, 163, 164
Isenberg, Nancy, 56
Islam
 battle of Al Qadisiyyah, 237 n18
 and the Chechen conflict, 93, 96, 102
 early history, 114
 Islamism, 114–15
 masculinities, 219
 in the Palestinian conflict, 113–14, 124, 131
 Salafists, 234 n4
 and women, 114–15

Janjaweed, 145
Jezebel, 41–2

Kambanda, Jean, 161
Karpinski, Janis, 23, 66, 67, 69, 75–84, 85, 114, 232 n3, 232 n9, 233, n10
Khaled, Leila, 132
Kipling, Rudyard, 31
Kronsell, Annica, 174–5

Lenin, Vladimir, 199
Liberation Tigers of Tamil Elam (LTTE), 136
Limbaugh, Rush, 74
Lorenz, Konrad, 179–80
Lynch, Jessica, 85–6, 234 n17

MacKinnon, Catherine, 74, 143–4, 191
Mao Zedong, 199
Medea, 30–32, 35, 128, 130, 230 n3

Medusa, 38, 82, 148
metaphor
 functions, 55, 171
 categories, 28
 in the Chechen conflict, 210
 and control of women, 49, 134, 173
 narratives as, 27
militarization
 Chechen, 90
 of masculinity, 24, 76, 108, 110, 209
 and nationalist struggle, 139
 of women, 7, 9, 23, 45–6, 49, 59, 63, 77, 84–7, 212, 233 n10
Miller, Maj. Gen. Geoffrey, 72
Milosevic, Slobodan, 149, 153, 156
monsterization, 37
monster narrative, 12–13, 36–41, 52–6
 and Abu Ghraib, 68, 82
 and agency, 50, 190
 and al-Qaeda, 132
 of Biljana Plavsic, 156
 and the Chechens, 100, 102, 205, 235 n10
 and the female terrorist, 38, 98
 and genocide, 156, 170
 of Lynndie England, 68, 82
 of Pauline Nyiramasuhuko, 170
 and murder, 39–40
 and narcissism, 186
 of Nazi German women, 61–2
 and Palestinians, 132
 and pathology, 37, 137, 190
 roots in Freud, 180
 and women's violence, 188
Moon, Katharine, 201, 205, 215
mother narrative, 8, 12–13, 30–36, 52–6
 and Abu Ghraib, 81, 82
 and al-Qaeda, 35, 126, 130–32
 of Biljana Plavsic, 155–6
 and the Chechens, 35, 91, 100, 103
 and genocide, 155, 165
 of Janis Karpinski, 82
 of Lynndie England, 81
 and the media, 35
 and nationalism, 36
 nurturing, 33–4, 102
 and Palestinians, 32–3, 120–21, 123, 128, 130–32
 of Pauline Nyiramasuhuko, 165–70
 and Russians, 210
 and Sabrina Harman, 81
 and treatment of women, 109

vengeful, 33–5, 100, 102
and women's violence, 69–70, 188
Mujahidaat, 114

narcissism theory, 185–7
narrative, 27–8, 50–57, 223–5, 230 n1
  of Beautiful Souls, 3–4
  dominant narratives, 27, 51, 53, 63
  gendered, 29, 30, 33, 36, 50, 54, 55,
    181, 204, 215, 222, 238–9 n 27
  interrogating, 21–22
  and power, 53, 230 n1
  as practice, 56, 198
  and psychoanalytic theory, 181
  and the rational-actor model, 177
  war narratives, 28
  and women's violence, 11–12, 22,
    33, 50–57, 198, 204, 215, 222,
    223–5, 228 n10, 229 n12
  see also under mother; monster;
    whore
Nelson, Leslie, 48
new wars, 89
Northern Ireland, 7–8
Ntaryamira, Cyprien, 158
Ntahobari, Maurice, 165
Nyiramasuhuko, Pauline, 25, 141, 146,
  147, 149, 159, 160–72, 213, 214, 240
  n7, 240 n8, 240 n9

Ovid, 31

Palestinians
  family, compensation for
    martyrdom, 235 n12
  family, importance of, 116
  female suicide bombers, 117,
    119–20; *see also shahida*
  intifada(s), 113, 116, 131
  mobilization, 116, 138, 230 n4
  Palestinian Authority, 113
  and women, 116
Palestinian Islamic Jihad, 115, 121, 128,
  237 n10
Palestine Liberation Organization, 115,
  236 n9
Palestinian Resistance Movement,
  115–23
Pape, Robert, 134–6, 241 n3, n7
Peterson, Spike, 11, 53, 65, 217, 238 n21
Plavsic, Biljana, 25, 141, 147, 149,
  151–5, 155–8, 168, 172, 186, 204,
  213, 214, 218
Playboy, 133
Pollack, Kenneth, 199, 200, 203, 204,
  215, 216, 220, 242 n11
Popular Front for the Liberation of
  Palestine, 115, 116
psychoanalytic theory, 178–80

radical Islam
  Chechnya, 93, 96
  and Palestine, 113, 115, 128, 131
rational-choice theory, 176–8
Raznjatovic, Zalkjo (Arkan), 151, 152,
  156–7
relational autonomy, 13, 16–18, 189–97,
  217
  and choice, 193–5
  and consent, 192–3
  and hybridity, 195–6
  and individual violence, 21, 190,
    196–8, 215
  and the narratives, 190
  and non-voluntary obligation, 16,
    191–2
relative deprivation theory, 183–5
Republika Srpska, 150, 151, 155, 157
rhetoric, Russian, 94–7
Rice, Condoleeza, 54
Rolling Stones, 68
Roosevelt, Franklin, 199
Runyan, Ann Sisson, 11, 65, 217
Rwanda, 25, 143, 144, 148, 158–60, 161,
  162, 163, 164, 165, 169, 173, 214,
  240 n7, 240 n9

Saad Al Faqih, 127, 137, 139
Salafism, 96, 234 n4
Saleh, Basel, 135
self-martyrdom
  and al-Qaeda, 127–9
  and Iraq, 112–13, 236 n3, 238 n19
  and Palestinian culture, 112–13,
    117–18
self-martyrs
  female, 112, 127
  Myrium Goris, 128
  Sajida Mubarak Atrous, 128
sex categories, 5–6
shahida, 112, 119, 129, 138–9, 237 n15
  Andelib Suleiman Takafka, 133
  Arien Ahmed, 138
  Ayat Akras, 121

INDEX

Ayat Allah Kawil, 133
Dareen Abu Aysheh, 121, 131
Hanadi Jaradat, 123, 130
Hiba Daraghmah, 121
  rationale, 122–3
Reem al-Riyashi, 121
Wafa Idris, 118, 120, 131, 134, 204, 218
shakhidki, 88–9, 92–4, 97
  actions, 98, 101
  and Islam, 102
  Mareta Dudayeva, 105
  Raisa Ganyev, 106, 235 n13
  recruitment, 98–99, 110
  slavery, 105–6
  Zarema Muzikhoyeva, 99, 106–7, 235 n15
  zombification, 104
Sheik Tantawi, 132
Sheik Yassin, 118–19
Siddiqui, Aafia, 125
silence, 12, 52, 91, 174–5
Sillanpaa, Sanna, 39
social learning theory, 180–82
Stalin, Josef, 199
Stiehm, Judith, 172
structural violence, 202
Sudan, 145–6
suicide bombers
  and the media, 129–31, 133
  and women, 235
  see also shahida, shakhidki, self-martyrs
suicide terrorism, 1, 135–40, 186, 211–12, 238
  and women's agency, 4, 24, 32, 35, 49, 90, 138–40, 188, 204, 219, 222
Sylvester, Christine, 53–4, 193

Taguba Report, 76, 78
Tarlton, Tracey, 48
Tickner, J. Ann, 54, 177–8, 240 n2
True, Jacqui, 204

Um Osama, 126, 131
United Nations Security Council Resolution 1325, 2

Victor, Barbara, 121–2, 133, 136–7, 186
Volzer, Harry, 73

Wahhabite *see* Islam
Weather Underground, 34, 45
Wendt, Alexander, 203
whore narrative, 12–13, 41–9, 52–6
  and Abu Ghraib, 75, 80, 83–4
  and the Amazon, 43
  and al-Qaeda, 132–4
  and Bernadine Dohrn, 45
  and Biljana Plavsic, 156, 157
  and Chechens, 103–7, 219, 235
  erotic dysfunction, 47–9
  erotomania, 46–47
  and genocide, 147, 156, 157, 170–71, 214
  and Greek mythology, 42–3
  and Ilse Koch, 61–2
  and Janis Karpinski, 83–4
  and lesbianism, 48
  and Lynndie England, 81, 83
  and men's control, 49
  and military history, 43–5, 49
  and Myra Hindley, 49
  and the Palestinians, 132–4, 235 n15
  and Pauline Nyiramasuhuko, 170–71
  and Sabrina Harman, 83
  and women's violence, 188, 190
Wiesel, Elie, 154
Wikipedia, 132
women
  and Abu Ghraib, 58–9, 64–73, 205–8
  agency, 12, 17, 20–21, 177, 197, 203
  and al-Qaeda, 124–8, 131
  biology, 50
  in Chechnya, 49, 88–91, 208–11
  in criminology, 15
  in Freud, 179–80
  and frustration, 183
  and genocide, 144–8, 171–3, 213–15
  in gendered institutions, 10
  grouped with children, 3
  invisibility, 12, 89, 175, 181
  and knowledge, 174, 194
  and the Middle East, 114–15, 211–12
  and narcissism, 188
  in the Nazi military force, 61–2
  and political representation, 8
  and the protection racket, 4, 201, 203
  and rights, 2, 9–10, 183, 191, 220
  stereotypes of, 3, 5–10, 14, 20, 30,

50, 75, 80, 100, 177, 201, 223;
see also under mother, monster,
whore
targets, 92–3
in the United States military, 9, 59,
63–4

as victims, 4, 18
and violence, 1, 11, 20, 29, 49, 57,
175–6, 197, 201, 215–20
Women's Royal Army Corps, 7
Woolf, Virginia, 201
Wuornos, Aileen, 40